STUDIES IN CHADIC MORPHOLOGY AND SYNTAX

AFRIQUE ET LANGAGE
Collection dirigée par France Cloarec-Heiss

La collection **Afrique et Langage** a pour ambition de permettre aux langues d'Afrique subsaharienne d'être à la fois mieux connues et mieux prises en compte dans les débats théoriques les plus actuels qu'ils soient d'orientation linguistique, culturelle ou cognitive. Elle se propose d'accueillir des ouvrages qui contribueront à faire connaître le patrimoine linguistique et culturel de ce continent tout autant que des synthèses théoriques. Y trouveront donc naturellement leur place des monographies (grammaires et dictionnaires), des ouvrages concernant le développement linguistique (standardisation, terminologie), des analyses et éditions de textes littéraires ou de tradition orale, des études ethnolinguistiques présentant des systèmes conceptuels originaux et leurs implications cognitives tout autant que des travaux ayant trait à l'histoire et à la genèse des langues.

Déjà paru dans la collection:
1. Bernard Caron (éd), 2000, *Topicalisation et focalisation dans les langues africaines*, 323 p.
2. Robert Nicolaï (éd), 2001, *Leçons d'Afrique. Filiations, ruptures et reconstitution de langues. Un hommage à Gabriel Manessy*, 581 p.
3. Guillaume Segerer, 2002, *La langue Bijogo de Bubaque (Guinée Bissau)*, 310 p.

COLLECTION
AFRIQUE ET LANGAGE
4

Studies in Chadic Morphology and Syntax

Zygmunt FRAJZYNGIER

Ouvrage publié avec le concours de l'Université du Colorado

PEETERS
Louvain-Paris
2002

D. 2002/0602/124

ISBN 90-429-1203-0 (Peeters Louvain)
ISBN 2-87723-675-7 (Peeters France)

© Peeters Press, Louvain-Paris

Couverture: conception STANDARD - Graphiste.

ACKNOWLEDGMENTS

The work on this volume and on the studies included was supported by the National Endowment for the Humanities, Grants Nr. R0-0259-80-2095 and RT 21151-90, Center for Applied Humanities, University of Colorado, and by the National Science Foundation Grant Nr. BNS-84 18923. I had the opportunity and privilege to discuss the issues treated in this volume with friends working in the area of Chadic linguistics. Many colleagues have also generously shared with me their knowledge of various Chadic languages. I would like to express my gratitude to: Daniel Barreteau, Jean-Pierre Caprile, Karen Ebert, Cheryl Fluckiger, Marta Giger, Beat Haller, Sylvia Hedinger, Carleton Hodge, Carl Hoffmann, Elizabeth Jarvis, Herrmann Jungraithmayr, Ruth Lienhard, Roxana Ma Newman, Paul Newman, Michka Sachnine, Russell G. Schuh, Theda Schumann, Margaret Skinner, Neil Skinner, Henry Tourneux, and Ekkehard Wolff. For interpretations and errors to be found in the volume I alone am responsible.

I would like to thank Dr. Bruce Ekstrand, Vice Chancellor for Academic Affairs, University of Colorado, for his support, which made the preparation of this volume possible. I am also grateful to Maria Thomas-Ruzic and Maria Safran, for the editorial work on various papers in the present volume. The publication of this volume was made possible by grants from the University of Colorado Committee on University Scholarly Publications.

INTRODUCTION

Chadic group, at some one hundred and forty languages, constitutes the largest and also the most diversified branch of the Afroasiatic family. Other groups of this family are Semitic, Cushitic, Berber, and Egyptian. Chadic languages are spoken in Cameroon, Chad, Nigeria, and Niger.

The present volume contains a selection of the papers on Chadic comparative syntax and morphology that I have published over the past fifteen years. Some of these papers emerged as reactions to the discussion of topics that were ongoing at that time; others present topics never before discussed in the Chadicist literature. Most of the papers have been revised for this volume. Revisions range from matters concerning the analysis or conclusions to purely stylistic. The format of all the papers has been made consistent and there is a cumulative list of references, all of which have been updated. The index of topics and personal names has been included.

In the first paper, "The Underlying Form of the Verb in Proto-Chadic," I propose that the underlying form of the verb was made up of the consonants and only one vowel. The remaining vowels are either epenthetic or, more important, grammatical markers. This is especially true for the last vowel of the polyconsonantal verbs. The paper on "West Chadic Verb Classes" provides additional support for the hypothesis about the grammatical role of verb final vowels in Chadic. The function of the verb final vowel in the P.C. remains to be discovered.

The paper "Plural in Chadic" is an attempt to deal with the fact that in some Chadic languages -- from all three branches -- there is no category of nominal plural. There are also languages in which the nominal plural derives from demonstratives, pronouns, and anaphoras hence representing a relatively recent grammaticalization of the category. Within the verbal system, however, most of the languages have systematic means of plural verb formation. In addition, the markers of nominal plural are morphologically and phonologically similar to the markers of the verbal plural. I do not find that it is possible to reconstruct a nominal plural marking for Proto-Chadic. Moreover, I postulate that plural marking through reduplication and/or gemination, or through the use of vowel /a/, has been borrowed into the nominal system from the verbal system.

In the paper "On the Proto-Chadic Syntactic Pattern" I discuss some of the ergative characteristics of a reconstructible system. In particular, it appears that Proto-Chadic did not have intransitivizing devices but did have transitivizing devices. The plural encoding had an ergative pattern viz. the number of an intransitive subject or transitive object was encoded, but not the number of a transitive agent. The hypothesis about ergative characteristics is additionally supported in the paper "Ergative and Nominative-Accusative Features in Mandara."

The issue of the marking syntactic relations in Proto-Chadic was raised for the first time in the Chadic literature in the paper "Marking Syntactic Relations in Proto-Chadic." I postulate there that the main devices to mark syntactic relations in P.C. was word order, and moreover, that P.C. had VSO word order rather than SVO, as represented by the majority of contemporary Chadic languages. For an alternative analysis of some of the issues first raised in this paper, cf. Williams 1989. The paper "On Intransitive Copy Pronouns" describes the function of this class of morphemes, also found in non-Chadic languages of the area. It is specifically claimed that these morphemes do not have an intransitivizing function but rather inceptive or destativizing function.

"'Causative' and 'benefactive' in Chadic" deals with the problem of markers that have been variously described as 'causative', 'benefactive', 'efferential', etc. I postulate that all of these represent one morpheme whose basic function was to indicate the presence in the clause of one more argument beyond the unmarked frame for a given verb.

In "Encoding the locative in Chadic" I postulate that PC had only one locative preposition, and its function was to indicate the role of the argument. Spatial relationship and directionality were encoded with the help of serial verb constructions and nouns derived from body parts and geographical direction.

Many Chadic languages have verbal extensions. In "Ventive and centrifugal in Chadic" I discuss two of those extensions, postulating that they derive from verbs 'to come' and 'to go'. The stage preceding the formation of verbal extensions was that of serial verb constructions.

There were two devices used in formation of interrogative sentences in Proto-Chadic. One was the clause final interrogative marker, derived from a copula, and the other were tonal changes. The specific interrogative markers (wh- question words) are identical with indefinite pronouns for human and non-human referents. There is no evidence of actual or virtual wh-movement in Chadic.

Some Chadic languages have a rich system of reference utilized in embedded clauses when the main clause has a verbum dicendi. The system encodes not only coreference and disjoint reference with the subject of the main clause but also coreference or disjoint reference with the addressee of the main clause. There is, however, no evidence that the system existed in Proto-Chadic.

With respect to copulas there was an interesting process in some Chadic languages whereby a verb 'to be at a place' became a locative preposition, which in turn became an equational copula. The paper "From Preposition to Copula" provides evidence for this grammaticalization process as well as possible motivations.

The last paper of the volume discusses the implications of the results of the reconstruction of various elements of Chadic syntax for the theory and methodology of syntactic reconstruction.

PROVENANCE OF THE PAPERS

The underlying form of the verb in Proto-Chadic. (1983. The Chad Languages in the Hamitosemitic Nigritic Border Area, ed. by H.-H. Jungraithmayr, 123-143.) Reprinted with the kind permission of the Publisher.

Another look at West-Chadic Verb Classes. (1982. Africana Marburgensia 15.1.25-43.) Reprinted with the kind permission of the Editors of Africana Marburgensia.

The plural in Chadic. (1977. Papers in Chadic Linguistics, ed. by P. Newman and R. Ma Newman. Leiden: Afrika-Studiecentrum 1977, 37-56.) Reprinted with the kind permission of the Editors.

On the Proto-Chadic Syntactic Pattern. (1984. Current Progress in Afro-Asiatic Linguistics: Papers of the International Hamito-Semitic Congress, ed. by John Bynon, Amsterdam: Benjamins, 139-160.) Reprinted with the kind permission of John Benjamins, B.V.

Ergative and Nominative Accusative Features in Mandara. (1984. Journal of African Languages and Linguistics 6.35-45.) Reprinted with the kind permission of the publisher, Foris Publications.

Marking Syntactic Relations in Proto-Chadic. (1983. Studies in Chadic and Afro-Asiatic Linguistics, ed. by E. Wolff and H.Meyer-Bahlburg, Hamburg: Buske, 115-138.) Reprinted with the kind permission of the Publisher.

On the Intransitive Copy Pronouns in Chadic. (1977. Studies in African Linguistics, Supplement 7.73-84.) Reprinted with the kind permission of the editor.

'Causative' and 'benefactive' in Chadic. (1985. Afrika und Übersee 68.23-42.) Reprinted with the kind permission of the Editors of Afrika und Übersee.

Encoding locative in Chadic. (1987. Journal of West African Languages 17.1.81-97.) Reprinted with the kind permission of the Editor of the Journal of West African Languages.

Ventive and centrifugal in Chadic. (1987. Afrika und Übersee 70.1.31-47.) Reprinted with the kind permission of the Editors of Afrika und Übersee.

Interrogative sentences in Chadic. (1985. Journal of West African Languages 15.1.57-72.) Reprinted with the kind permission of the Editor of the Journal of West African Languages.

Logophoric systems in Chadic. (1985. Journal of African Languages and Linguistics 7.23-37.) Reprinted with the kind permission of the publisher, Foris Publications.

From preposition to copula. (Proceedings of the Twelfth Annual Meeting of the Berkeley Linguistics Society, Vassiliki Nikiforidou, Mary VanClay, Mary Niepokuj, and Deborah Feder, ed. 371-386. 1986). Reprinted with the kind permission of the BLS.

Theory and method of syntactic reconstruction: Implications of Chadic for diachronic syntax. (1987. Linguistische Berichte, vol. 109, 184-202.) Reprinted with the kind permission of the Editors of Linguistische Berichte.

THE UNDERLYING FORM OF VERBS IN PROTO-CHADIC

1. Introduction

1.1. The problem

Newman 1975 postulates the existence in Proto-Chadic of verbal classes in both monosyllabic and polysyllabic verbs. In the monosyllabic verbs he claims the existence of three classes with the endings a, ə, and i/u and in polysyllabic verbs ('polyverbs') of the classes a and ə. In addition the verb classes are determined by tone, HI-HI, LO-LO and LO-HI. The final vowel in Newman's reconstruction is a 'lexically intrinsic vowel' (Newman 1975:81): 'All verbs contained a final vowel as an integral, lexically determined component. This vowel was as much a part of the specification of that lexeme as the consonants and the internal vowels.'

In lieu of the evidence for this hypothesis Newman provides examples of the occurrence of the final vowels as postulated in the hypothesis in eight languages, four from the Plateau-Sahel branch (now West Chadic in Newman 1977) and four from Biu-Mandara. The verbal forms are not described as to their place in the paradigms in particular languages so that one is not really sure that all the forms are comparable. If it is the case that a vowel ending in one of the languages constitutes a morpheme there is no way to determine it from Newman's paper. In the translations provided all the examples from the eight languages are translated by the English infinitive but surely they are not all infinitives in all of the languages. Moreover, we do not know the proportions of the examples conforming with the hypothesis relative to those that do not, and more importantly the illustrations do not show the fact that the number of verbs belonging to the 'a' class is very small when compared with the 'ə' class.

Newman's hypothesis has been accepted by some scholars, e.g. Schuh 1977 and 1978. It has also been a subject of discussion. Instead of the vowel ə [as high vowel class] postulated for Proto-Chadic Schuh 1977 has proposed -u in West Chadic. Frajzyngier (1982b) has postulated that there is no evidence for u in West Chadic and instead has proposed *-i* as the final vowel for high vowel verbs. There is also a possibility that *i* should be the high vowel in other Chadic languages instead of Newman's *ə*.

Nobody, however, has actually tested Newman's main claim, viz. that the final vowel is an integral part of a verb, as much the property of the verb as its other vowels and its consonants. The purpose of this paper is to do just this. Anticipating the analyses to follow I would like to propose that the traditional analyses of Chadic languages in which the final vowel was not considered an integral part of the verb were actually correct. While these analyses were not up to present standards, which require an explicit justification for every claim, I do not think that it would be right to fault them for this, rather one can be amazed at how correct those largely intuitive statements were in separating the final vowel from the rest of the verb. The present paper will present the evidence to show that the final high vowel is not an integral part of the verb and that therefore it must have constituted a grammatical formative. It would follow from this that the final low vowel could also be considered a grammatical formative but the evidence for this will not be of such a nature as to completely exclude other possibilities, such as the lexical hypothesis. The evidence alluded to above will concern only polysyllabic verbs. For monosyllabic verbs there is a strong possibility that the final vowel was a part of the underlying representation.

1.2. The choice of data

There is a difficulty involved in the choice of data for this paper. Ideally this discussion should be based on the same data as in Newman 1975; unfortunately, some of the data used by Newman are simply unavailable to me, such as the data for Kotoko taken from fieldnotes. The same goes to a certain degree for Bolanci, for Newman has used his own fieldnotes in addition to Lukas 1970-1972. Even when the same data were available, they were not always useful. Thus for West Chadic languages, the data from Kanakuru and Bolanci contained the evidence needed for the traditional separation of the verb final vowel, while data from Tera, Ga'anda, and Margi did not, or at least I could not find such evidence. Instead I have supported the traditional hypothesis with data from Mubi and Migama, Bachama, and Musgu. The total number of languages discussed in the present paper will be six: from West Chadic: Pero and Kanakuru; from Biu-Mandara: Musgu and Bachama; and from East Chadic: Mubi and Migama. For Pero I rely on my own fieldnotes; for other languages I draw on published data already discussed in the literature.

The value of this evidence should not however be dismissed just because the number of languages is small. First of all, the number is only one language fewer that in the Newman's 1975 paper. Second, it represents three branches of Chadic rather than two (as was the case) in Newman 1975. Now if the similarities are found in languages from three branches out of the postulated four, one should consider these similarities to be retentions from the proto-language rather than common innovations. Thus, while the number of languages analyzed is relatively small in comparison with the total number of Chadic languages, their distribution within the Chadic family is more significant than their number. Moreover, the nature of these similarities is such that it precludes innovations as the reason for similarity.

2. Formulation of the hypothesis

The formulation that will follow has, to my knowledge, never been stated before in the present terms nor is it a compilation of some unexplicit assumptions to be found in various analyses of Chadic languages. Rather it is a result of analyses of the verbal systems in several Chadic languages. Some of the statements in the hypothesis however have been formulated before by other people and these will be duly noted. The hypothesis consists of the following points:

    1. There was a basic division in Chadic between the monoconsonantal and polyconsonantal verbs. This point is similar to Newman's division between monosyllabic and polysyllabic verbs. It will be shown, however, that it is the number of consonants rather than the number of syllables that determines the form of the verb.

    2. The underlying form of the verb, i.e., the form necessary to derive all other forms of the verb, consisted of all the consonants of the verb and the first vowel. This will be proved for the polyconsonantal verbs but only suggested for monoconsonantal verbs.

    3. The vowel ending found in the contemporary languages constitutes a grammatical formative, in many languages non-productive, and thus the function of the formative cannot be determined on the basis of synchronic analyses in these languages. This last point is the non-explicit assumption in many Chadic grammars.

    The evidence for the above will begin with the evidence for point 3, followed by the evidence for point 2, and the conclusions from the two will provide sufficient justification for point 1.

The general line of the evidence will be the following. If it is true that the final vowel constitutes an integral part of the verb, as the other vowels and the consonants do, then there should be no constraints on the form of this vowel; moreover there should be no difference in the behavior of this vowel and that of other vowels in the verb. Also as is the case for other vowels in the verb, the final vowel should have no bearing on the form of other segments in the verb. It will be shown that this is not the case, for the final vowel does indeed behave in a manner different from other vowels. It is for instance often lowered as the result of application of phonological rules dependent on the preceding vowels or the weight of preceding syllables. It also often causes raising or lowering of the preceding vowels, a fact not known to occur with non-final vowels in Chadic languages.

If the Newman's hypothesis is true, there should be no difference between verbs and nouns in the language with respect to the final vowel, i.e. the final vowel should be equally unpredictable in both classes of morphemes. Therefore for the six languages under consideration I will examine the behavior of final vowels in verbs and nouns. In particular I will examine the constraints on the form of the final vowel, and the existence of phonological rules involving a final vowel, rules that affect the verbal stem.

I will first deal with the mono-consonantal verbs in order to discuss the second vowel in these verbs. The order of presentation within each group will follow Newman's classification of 1977.

3.   Mono- and biconsonantal verbs
West Chadic
Kanakuru (Bole-Tangale group)

Polysyllabic verbs in Kanakuru in the 'perfective' form end in either -*i* or -*e*.
1975 considers the two endings to be reflexes of the -*ə* class and the -*a* class respectively, but Frajzyngier 1976 shows that the two are phonologically conditioned variants of the same underlying vowel /i/. This vowel is lowered to [e] when the first syllable of the verb is heavy or when the verb is trisyllabic. The rule operates even when the first syllable of the verb is light but its derivational history indicates that it is heavy. The evidence for the rule is to be found in Frajzyngier 1976, the following are a few selected examples to illustrate its operation.

First syllable heavy:	béelè	'choose'
	màané	'return
	làmbé	'court or seek a woman'
	kìrké	'contradict'
	júurè	'efface previous flavor'
	gándè	'put down'
Trisyllabic:	tìtiré	'draw or cut lines on'
	shùmburé	'to quiet'
	jùpulć	'tumble down'
First syllable light:	àní	'sharpen
	múrì	'die'
	(but plural, through gemination, mútè)	
	púi	'go out'
	pàní	'to transplant'

Monosyllabic verbs in Kanakuru end in -i or -e, e.g. gài 'to prevent', túi 'to eat', yíe 'to do', dèe 'finish', lùe 'put aside', kói 'to catch', nái 'call' etc. All of the verbs are quoted in the perfective form. An interesting fact about these verbs is that some of them derive synchronically or diachronically from a biconsonantal form with the second consonant deleted. The evidence for this is provided by the plural form when the second consonant is actually pronounced because of the gemination which is a part of the plural verb formation, e.g. búi 'give', pl. búpè. The second consonant is obviously p which becomes w in intervocalic position and then is deleted. Since it has has been shown that the final /i/ in biconsonantal stems is not a part of the underlying structure there is no reason to assume that -i at the end of the mono consonantal verbs is anything different; therefore I will take the -i ending for these verbs to represent the same grammatical formative as in poly-conso-nantal verbs. The underlying vowels of the mono-consonantal verbs would be therefore the penultimate vowels such as -a-, -u-, -i-, -e-, and -o-, almost all the vowels postulated for Kanakuru by Newman. Thus the mono-consonantal verbs in Kanakuru represent not two but five classes if a classification is to be based on the final vowel. Since all the vowels are represented in the mono-consonantal verbs, the classification according to the final vowels serves no purpose since it does not reveal anything interesting about the verbal system. Furthermore, this classification cannot in any way support the reconstruction of the Proto-Chadic verbal system as containing two or three classes of verbs.

In the nominal system of Kanakuru the constraints on the height of the final vowel do not exist. Thus one finds a high vowel at the end of the first syllable heavy nouns, e.g. *dánkì* 'bed', *dénnì* 'porcupine', *dímbì*, 'skin, body, *gómbì* 'type of melon', *kóori* 'black cobra snake', and finally, one finds a high vowel at the end of trisyllabic nouns, e.g. *bilbili* 'a swallow', *túubíní* 'right side'.

As can be seen, the behavior of the final vowels in verbs and nouns is quite different. If one considers the final vowel to be an integral part of the noun, and there is no suggestion so far that it is not so, then obviously one cannot consider the final vowel of the verb to be an integral part of the verb, for it is dependent on some other factors in the structure of the verb. If it cannot be considered a part of the underlying structure then it must be considered a formative. The only question that remains is what is or was the function of this formative. The answer to this question lies in the distribution of the forms ending in *i/e* as opposed to the distribution of the forms ending in different vowels. It appears that the only different vowel ending in Kanakuru is *-u*, the marker of the imperative form. There are also other suffixes in Kanakuru, such as verbal extensions, and they also should be taken into consideration in determining the function of *-i*. But it is rather obvious that *-i* was a marker of a major division in Kanakuru verbs, for the forms ending in this vowel occur in several tenses. In particular it is found in the 'perfective' and 'subjunctive' (optative), both affirmative and negative.[1] Instead of a front vowel in the imperative form we have a back vowel. Thus the imperative forms in Kanakuru have the *-u* ending. There is no *-a* ending in bi-consonantal verbs in Kanakuru, and therefore there are no grounds for investigating its possible function in this language.

Pero

Monosyllabic verbs in perfective form end in [i], [e], and at least one verb ends in [a]. In the imperative verbs end as follows (for perfective it is stem before suffix *-ko*):

Perfective		Imperative		Gloss
-i	cí	-u	cú	'eat'
-e	cé	-o	có	'drink'
	lé	-a	lá	'give birth'
-a	cáa	-a	cáa	'descend'

There is evidence which will not be repeated here (cf. Frajzyngier 1989) that the imperative form of the verb is not an underlying form but a derived one. Occurrence of the vowel -a in the derived form rules out the possibility of its being an underlying vowel and therefore a reflex of an alleged Proto-Chadic -a class. There is still a possibility that some of the verbs with the -e ending in perfective represent the -a verbs, those that have -a in the imperative being the prime candidates for this role. Even so, however, we would come up with at least three (if one does not count the exception cáa) and not two verb classes.

As is often found in Chadic languages the number of vowel endings in monosyllabic verbs exceeds the number of endings in polysyllabic verbs. The explanation of this fact is more natural if one accepts the notion that the verbal endings in polysyllabic verbs represent grammatical formatives.

In monosyllabic verbs, if only the consonant were to be considered underlying, it would result in the maximum number of verbs to be equal to the number of consonantal phonemes in the language. Addition of a vowel as an underlying segment increases the number of potential monosyllabic verbs (number of vowels time number of consonants). For the bi- and triconsonantal verbs the number of possibilities is much greater and there is no danger of too many homophones, even without the final vowel. Although not all the possibilities for the underlying consonant are actually utilized in Chadic languages, we do come across monosyllabic verbs with an identical underlying consonant, the most frequent example being the pair for the verbs 'to eat' and 'to drink' which in many languages differ only in their vowel and not in the consonant (although in Proto-Chadic they might have had different underlying consonants).

In Pero in addition to the above two there is also the verb cáa 'to descend'. Another such pair is lu 'to put', and lá 'to give birth'. All the verbs are quoted in imperative.

I expect that in all Chadic languages all the possibilities for the final vowel will be utilized in monosyllabic verbs, provided the tense/aspect paradigm allows it.

Since the basic dichotomy in the aspectual paradigm of Pero is between the front vowels for the 'perfective' form and the back vowels for the 'imperative' form we would not expect any other vowels in the perfective apart from i and e. Therefore, all the vowels allowed by the constraints on the grammatical form of the verb occur at the end of monosyllabic verbs in Pero. Unlike the vowel of monosyllabic verbs, consonants cannot be predicted from any other information, they are completely arbitrary, constrained only by the distributional properties of consonants (see Frajzyngier 1978). While in monosyllabic verbs the perfective form has to be non-back and the imperative form has to be back, there is still a problem of predicting which verb ending in mid-vowel in the perfective will have the -*a* ending and which will have the -*o* ending in the imperative. This fact indicates that the perfective forms of the verb derive from three different classes whose differences were neutralized by some changes. I postulate that there was a suffix -*i* added to the monosyllabic verbs to give the perfective form. The reconstructed verb forms and the results of addition of a suffix are as follows:

       1. Ci + i ---> Ci
       2. Ce + i ---> Ce
       3. Ca + i ---> Ce

Rules 1 and 3 are independently supported by synchronic rules in Pero. Rule 2, however, is not, for the product of [e] + [i] is consistently [ey]. But this rule is historically possible through the reduction of final -*i* as the perfective marker.

An alternative analysis of the facts in Pero in a diachronic perspective is to postulate as the underlying forms the vowels of the imperative form, i.e. /u/, /o/, and /a/ and postulate the same suffix -*i*.

       Cu + i ---> Ci
       Co + i ---> Ce
       Ca + i ---> Ce

Although this second set of underlying forms displays more differentiation than in the derived forms, synchronically they are not adequate, for the product of [u] + [i] is not [i] but rather [uwi] and the product of [o] + [i] is sometimes [e] and sometimes [oe]. Whether or not one chooses this derivation over the first one, there are still three classes of verbs. In both solutions we have to postulate a suffix in the perfective form which can be best reconstructed as -*i*. There is also no reason why one could not combine the two series of derivation, and instead of three possible endings postulate five, allowing all vowels to occur in verb final position. There is however no evidence whatsoever to support such an analysis.

Whichever series of derivation one chooses, there is an important difference between nouns and verbs in Pero. While in nouns all vowels occur in word final position, in verbs only three vowels are possible. These vowels, however, may well be the lexical ones for mono-consonantal verbs.

Polysyllabic verbs

A detailed analysis of vowel alternations in polysyllabic verbs can be found in Frajzyngier 1980. The following is only an illustrated summary of rules that operate in the verbal system and are pertinent to our discussion.

In the perfective form of polysyllabic verbs in Pero the final vowel is epenthetic, depending on the following vowel and, in certain specified conditions, the preceding vowel. Therefore, for these verbs the perfective form is not particularly revealing.

The imperative form of the verb can end in either -a or one of the round vowels, -u or -o. The round vowels are variants of the same underlying /u/ and the height of the vowel depends on the structure of the verb in a way similar to Kanakuru. Thus /u/ becomes [o] when:

1. The first syllable of the verb is heavy; e.g. kúmmò 'put on ground', cíppò 'cut', cécrò 'talk', cúurò 'fry'; cf. páwù 'pray', dígù 'build', etc.

2. When the verb has three syllables; e.g. démbúlò 'lick', and the following plural verbs derived from the singular verbs: bábbúnò 'search', bìttùrò 'hold many things', cúnù 'skin', cúccúnò 'skin many (animals)'.

3. When the first syllable of the verb contains a mid vowel, e.g. tóbò 'tie up', lófò 'beat with a stick', mérò 'turn'.

There is also a number of bisyllabic verbs which have -a as the final vowel. All of these verbs have a high vowel in the first syllable which is never heavy, e.g. kúmá 'listen', cínà 'sleep', pínà 'wash (intr.)', píyà 'beat (drum)'.

Although the perfective form of these verbs does not contain a vowel at the end, other than epenthetic, by analogy with the monosyllabic verbs one can reconstruct the vowels of perfective as /i/, /e/ and possibly /a/ since at least one monosyllabic verb in perfective ends in this vowel.

The above constraints on the height of the non-low vowel in Pero do not operate in the nominal system of the language. Thus we have a high vowel when the first syllable of the noun is heavy, e.g. kpándì 'food', kíndì 'poor', kírgù 'sky', gúurù 'sickle'.

We have also a high vowel ending when the first vowel of the noun is mid, e.g. *dóojì* 'tomorrow', *fóorì* 'sun', *wórì* 'female name', *kópɓì* 'hole', etc.

There are no constraints concerning the occurrence of -*a* in the word final position, e.g. when the first vowel of the noun is mid. *kémà* 'fat', when the noun is trisyllabic: *kínnímà* 'idol', when the first syllable of the noun is heavy, e.g.: *gáppà* 'rice'.

The above considerations demonstrated that there is a difference between the word final vowel in nouns and verbs. Since there appear to be no constraints on the word final vowel in nouns one has to assume it to be a part of the underlying, lexical representation for this class of morphemes. The word final vowel in verbs is entirely different and has to be considered a formative, and the interesting question is, what kind of a formative is it? The obvious answer that it is a suffix is not a satisfactory one because other suffixes in the language behave in a different way from verbal endings. Thus the consecutive suffix to a verb in sentence final position -*i* raises the preceding vowels if they are not already high and does not undergo any changes itself. The same goes for the definite suffix to nouns. Not wanting to postulate yet another category of formatives in the language, I propose that we deal here with suffixes that once were productive in the language but are no longer so. In this way we can explain verbal classes in Pero as containing the old affixes, which in the synchronic analysis can no longer be considered suffixes. An interesting conclusion regarding the relative chronology of phonological rules is that the raising rule must have emerged in the language after the affixes became fused with the verbs and were no more perceived as such by its speakers. This conclusion should by no means be taken as applying to the whole field of Chadic, for we find raising rules in many languages and they have to be considered as characteristic for the whole family, if not reconstructible for the proto-language, then at least as an areal characteristic.

There are two questions that still remain to be answered for Pero and indeed for the whole family of Chadic. The first question is why do we have two affixes, high and non-high, and second, what are or were the functions of these affixes? If the answer to the second question would show historically different functions for -*u* and-*a* (in imperative), we would have an answer to the first question as well. Unfortunately, synchronically there does not appear to be any difference between the verbs ending in -*a* and those ending in -*u*, save perhaps for the fact that the verbs ending in -*a* are intransitive except for the verb *píyà* 'to beat a drum'. Verbs ending in -*u* are both transitive and intransitive. The only contrast that one can actually study is the one between the forms ending in -*i* or -*e* and those ending in -*u* and -*a*. Since polysyllabic verbs occur without the final ending when derivational suffixes are added, it is the monosyllabic verbs that are the most revealing for this purpose. The front vowel ending is used in the perfective and the imperfective ventive form. The back vowel ending is used in imperative, future and the remaining tenses. While the common characteristics of the tenses built on the 'front vowel stem' are difficult to determine, one can find a common characteristic of the 'back vowel stems'. All of the tenses built on the latter indicate that the action has not started yet, and that it has yet to happen.

No acceptable explanation can be offered now for the existence of two markers of the non-perfective form of the verb. It is likely that the verbs that now have the marker -a possess a certain semantic characteristic that required this marker sometime in the history of the language; however the number of these verbs is too small to allow us to detect this characteristic.

It appears that whatever the function of the two affixes was, they did not have to be in opposition within the same paradigm, such as perfective -- non-perfective, etc. Rather it appears that the low vowel suffix was required by conditions not related to the high vowel suffix.

Biu Mandara: Musgu and Bachama

In Musgu the difference between an underlying final vowel and a grammatical formative is well marked. Suffixes to the verb trigger a number of changes in the preceding vowels. One of them, attested in a number of Chadic languages (see Frajzyngier 1981), is a raising rule, which can be formulated as follows: A non-long vowel is raised when followed by a consonant and a suffix consisting of a high vowel, i.e.:

$$V \longrightarrow [+\text{high}] \quad / \quad C\underline{\quad\quad}C + V$$
$$[-\text{long}] \qquad\qquad\qquad\qquad\qquad [+\text{high}]$$

hos-   +   i   ---> husi
throw down Pl.

kol-   +   i   ---> kuli
praise

soɗ-   +   i   --->   suɗi
whip

There also appears to be a fronting rule by which a back vowel becomes front when followed by a high front vowel suffix, e.g.:

bund-   +   i   --->   bindi
become

mul-   +   i   --->   mili (all examples from Meyer-Bahlburg 1972):
take

There are, however, not enough examples to formulate exactly the conditions for this rule, which does not apply to forms to which the raising rule has applied.

The above rules do not obtain when the underlying vowels are involved. The appropriate examples of non-application of the rule cannot be drawn from the set of verbs since, as will be shown later, no verb has more than one underlying vowel. What remains, therefore, is the set of nouns. Here we encounter another difficulty, viz. there is no ready-made list of nouns, and material has to be extracted from the existing sources; also, a great portion of nouns in Musgu end in a consonant. Nevertheless one can find the following examples of the mid-high sequence which is not allowed when the high vowel belongs to a different morpheme:

motitini	'gull'
fenkiya	'cup'
kókúl-áy	'Aasgeier'
sligeni	'camel'[2]

Even more interesting is the absence of a fronting rule when the second vowel in a sequence is an underlying high front vowel, e.g.:

hùrdí	'scorpion'
áwsì	'rat' (cf. fákà pl. fíkí 'stand')[3]

Note that the phonological changes as a result of the addition of a suffix are by no means a property of verbs only. Similar changes take place when a suffix is added to nouns, e.g.:

dalam   +   i   --->   delemi
house   Dimin.   'room'

kalan   +   i   --->   kilini
well, stream   'small stream'

Although in both cases a raising rule has operated, the products of this rule are different and there are not enough examples to determine the conditions for the operation of the rule or rules.

Although the preceding data from Musgu are very fragmentary and may be analyzed in a different way in a description of Musgu phonology, it seems clear that addition of a grammatical morpheme may cause phonological changes in the preceding segments. The final underlying vowel, however, does not cause such changes. Therefore the data from Musgu support our hypothesis for Chadic that if a segment causes any changes in the preceding segments it is not a part of the underlying representation but rather a grammatical formative, in our case a suffix.

Regarding the function of the suffixes -*i* and -*a* in Musgu, one can conclude for the time being that it has nothing to do with the identically represented formatives in other Chadic languages: -*a* in Musgu is a marker of singular, while -*i* is the marker of plural, both of them depending on the number of the subject of the sentence. These functions are not the ones that one finds in Kanakuru, Tera, Ga'anda or other languages discussed in Newman 1975 or in the present paper.

Bachama

The data from Bachama are brought in for two reasons. First they indicated that in this language as in Chadic languages the differentiation in the vowel endings of monoconsonantal verbs is much greater than in polyconsonantal verbs. Second, they indicate that there is no reason to establish two verbal classes on the basis of vowel endings.

Rather, for monosyllabic verbs one has to postulate more than two classes, while for poly-consonantal there is no ground for any division among verbs on the basis of this criterion.

The importance of the first reason rests on the following argument. If there were to exist classes of verbs based on the final vowel, their number should be similar in both monoconsonantal and polyconsonantal verbs. If there are drastic differences, then we are not dealing with classes based on two or three final vowels. Monoconsonantal verbs in the past tense can end in: -*a*, as in *pà* 'meet', *nzà* 'sit down'; -*o*, as in *mbó* 'finish', *kò* 'hunt'; -*i*, as in *ni* 'look for', *pi* 'breath'; and finally, -*e*, as in *ne* 'build', *be-* 'hide'. An interesting fact about the mono-consonantal verbs to be found in Carnochan 1970 is the absence of the -*u* and -*e* endings. It is not possible to judge from the data in the source examined whether this absence is accidental or not, and therefore I will not venture any attempt at explanation of the fact. Polysyllabic verbs end in -*o* or -*e*, the latter vowel occurs only in three examples, viz. *dawe* 'cut down', *hiiwe* 'pray' and *viruwe* 'turn around'. There are also two examples of verbs ending in -*a*, viz. *mada* 'get up' and *mbilicita* 'swarm around'. Except for these last examples, the poly-consonantal verbs represent a grammatical formative, possibly even the past tense marker added most probably to the stem ending in a conso-nant, while the vowel ending in the mono-consonantal verbs, even if it represents a gram-matical formative, is a result of some changes that occurred when this formative was added to the verb final vowel. These changes could also be responsible for the lack of the verb final -*u* and -*e* in both mono- and poly-consonantal verbs.

The data from Bachama support the general conclusion of the present paper that for monoconsonantal verbs one has to postulate the final vowel as the integral part of the verb while for polyconsonantal verbs it is enough to postulate the consonant structure plus the first vowel as the only underlying segments, the final vowel being supplied from grammat-ical information.

East Chadic: Migama

The following analysis is based on data in Jungraithmayr 1975. For an alternative analysis see Wolff 1977, who despite his claim (p.164) does not support Newman's hypothesis of two vowel classes.

As in other languages, the main line of argumentation is that the final vowel of the verb causes certain phonological changes in the preceding segments, or that it itself is somehow

dependent on the preceding segments. Although not everything that follows is directly rel-
evant to the discussion of verbal classes, it is, however, necessary for the better understanding of the argument.

Since every verb in the perfective form in Migama ends in the vowel -e, I will take this
vowel to be one of the markers of the perfective aspect. It cannot be considered an integral
part of the verb as other segments for the simple reason that no other segments are uniformly identical for all the verbs in the language as quoted in Jungralthmayr 1975.

We will take the form of the verb minus the perfective -e to constitute the root of the
verb or, in other words, to constitute its underlying representation containing all that is necessary and only the necessary information to derive both the perfective and the imperfective
form of the verb. The plural form of the verb is also derived from the underlying representation through the gemination of the second consonant.

The imperfective stem is derived through the suffix -aa and either an infix -kk- or
reduplication of the second consonant. Which of the additional markers is actually used
depends on the structure of the root and does not affect the problem under discussion.
Addition of the suffix -aa has, however, an effect on the preceding vowels, viz. it lowers
the preceding vowels by one degree, e.g.:

> bir-   +   a   --->   beraa
> give   Imperf.

> tin-   +   a   --->   tenaa
> bury

More examples will be given in the discussion of triconsonantal verbs. The imperfective ending -a cannot be considered as an integral part of the verb for two reasons: First, it
occurs with all verbs in this form and therefore it cannot be a part of the representation of
every verb. Second, unlike the underlying segments, it affects other segments in the word,
in this case vowels, by lowering them. We have seen, then, that neither -e, the marker of
perfective, nor -aa, the marker of imperfective, is a reflex of the postulated final vowels of
Proto-Chadic. It does not appear that -a in Migama is cognate with the -a appearing in
other languages as the marker of different functions. It is, however, interesting that in Pero
some verbs have the -a ending in the non-perfective form.

Mubi

The following presentation of Mubi has as its purpose the addition of more data to show that the final word representing a grammatical morpheme, either affects the preceding segments or is affected by the preceding segments.

The presentation is based on data in Jungraithmayr 1978 and on analyses in Newman 1977c and Frajzyngier 1981. For biconsonantal verbs in Mubi it is postulated that the underlying form consists of the two consonants and the first vowel of the perfective stem. There is no vowel ending in the perfective.

The analysis of the infinitive is presented in order to show the operation of the raising and lowering rules and also to show that the final vowel is affected by the preceding segments.

The underlying form of the infinitive marker is the suffix /i/ added to biconsonantal roots with non-low vowels. When this suffix is added to other roots, i.e. triconsonantal roots or bi-consonantal roots with low vowel, it is lowered to [e]. We have therefore conditions similar to the ones described in Frajzyngier 1976 for Kanakuru and Pero.

Addition of these vowels to the root has a further effect in that the underlying vowels are raised when a high vowel suffix is added and lowered when a non-high suffix is added. The formalization of these rules can be found in Frajzyngier 1981. Selected examples only are shown here. The lowering rules will be illustrated in the discussion of triconsonantal verbs, so the following examples of the raising rule apply to biconsonantal verbs only. Note that the vowel which is raised is also lengthened:

Underlying	Suffix	Raising & Lengthening	Gloss
deg	deg-i	diigi	'carry on head'
ged	ged-i	giidi	'descend'
zob	zob-i	zuubi	'be dark'
bag	bag-i	_____	'roast'
cam	cam-e	_____	'eat'

4. Triconsonantal verbs

In the previous section it has been shown that one cannot postulate the final vowel of the biconsonantal verbs to be a part of their underlying representation. Therefore the bisyllabic verb has actually been reduced and now it is formed by the first three segments, viz. CVC-. If one accepts the notion that the last vowel of the biconsonantal stem represents a reflex of a grammatical morpheme, then it should also represent the same morpheme in triconsonantal verbs. The evidence in the present section will be of a slightly different nature from that in the previous sections. I will present the derivation of the triconsonantal verbs in several Chadic languages in which it will be shown that the second vowel can be predicted. I do realize that this kind of evidence is not completely satisfactory and that the hypothesis may be proved wrong if a language is found in which the second vowel of the triconsonantal verb cannot be predicted. I will also show that the underlying representation of triconsonantal verbs can contain only the information about the consonantal structure of these verbs and the first vowel. Data for the present section are derived from: Pero (West Chadic), Musgu (Biu-Mandara), Mubi and Migama (East Chadic).

Pero

A full description of the vowel alternations in the verbal system of Pero can be found in Frajzyngier 1980. It is shown there that the second vowel in triconsonantal verbs is always epenthetic, inserted whenever the morpheme structure or syllable structure conditions require it. It is always high and the value of the feature round depends on several factors. The chief among them is the last vowel which when present determines the value of the feature round. Thus if the following vowel is round the epenthetic vowel will also be round, e.g.:

> ɗémb-l +   o   --->   ɗemb-lo   Epenthesis
> lick   Imper.   ɗémbúlò

If the following vowel is non-round the epenthetic vowel is also non-round, e.g.:

d'émb-l	+	ji	--->	d'imb-l-ji	Epenthesis
					d'ímbíĺíjì

An additional argument against the claim that the final vowels are an integral part of the verb, is provided by the fact that this allegedly underlying vowel is added after the other suffixes, in this case the plural and the tense/aspect suffixes, e.g.:

ill	'get up'	+	t	+	o	--->	íllútò
			PL		Imper		
íll-		+	t	+	ji	--->	íllítíjì
					Cont		

Musgu

Meyer-Bahlburg 1972:111, discussing the structure of the root in Musgu, postulates several types of triconsonantal verbs. One of them is the type that consists of the consonants and the first vowel only, viz. CVCC, e.g.: *salb-* 'to ask', *sumn-* 'to sit', etc. The other type is postulated with a second vowel, viz. CVCVC-. If the hypothesis presented in this paper is correct, the second vowel in these verbs should be completely predictable. This, however, is not the case, at least not for all the verbs. For some verbs the second vowel is identical with the first, e.g.: *miliŋ-*(P) 'erstarren (be numbed)', *sadal-* 'to crawl', *subur-* 'be watchful', *gadam* 'to graze cattle'. There are, however, two verbs that do not conform to the rule, viz. *bud'eh* (P) 'to fall' and *cikad'* 'to sift'. Whether the differences in the last two vowels are phonologically conditioned or not would have to be answered by a description of Musgu phonology.[4]

Migama

In Migama the second vowel of trisyllabic verbs is also epenthetic and it is always identical to the preceding vowel in all its features. The epenthesis takes place in the imperfective forms, which, as has been described previously, have a suffix -*a* and an infix -*kk*- or gemination of the second consonant. Recall also that the underlying vowel of the verb is lowered because of the suffix -a. The following is the proposed derivation of the bi-consonantal and triconsonantal imperfective forms for Migama verbs found in Jungraithmayr 1975, all of which require an epenthesis:

Root	Affixes	Lowering	Epenthesis	Gloss
gíɗ	gíɗ kk a	gɛ́ɗ-kk-á	gɛ́ɗɛ́kká	'sell/buy'
'ún	'ún-kk-á	'ón-kk-á	'ónókká	'to feel, to touch'
kútm	kútm-m-a	kótm-m-á	kótómmá	'wrap up'
túrgw	túrgw-w-á	tórggw-w-á	tórgówwá	'raise'
'ípr	'ípr-rá	'épr-r-á	'épérrá	'untie'

Note that in the last verb we have evidence that the glottal stop in Migama has a phonemic status since in the derivation of the imperfective stem there is gemination of the last consonant, a phenomenon limited to triconsonantal verbs. The bi-consonantal verbs with a short first vowel add the infix -kk- in the first two examples above.

Insertion of the vowel as it occurs in the above verbs can be captured by the following formula:

$$\emptyset \quad \longrightarrow \quad \begin{matrix} V \\ \alpha \text{ high} \\ \beta \text{ round} \end{matrix} \quad / \quad C \quad \begin{matrix} V \\ \alpha \text{ high} \\ \beta \text{ round} \end{matrix} \quad C\_\_\_\_ C \quad C$$

Derivation of the perfective form of triconsonantal verbs differs considerably from the derivation of the perfective form of the bi-consonantal verbs. Although there is the same suffix -e added to the verb, there is also an infix, characteristic of the perfective form only, which one must consider to be another marker of the perfective form, occurring only with triconsonantal verbs. This marker is always a high vowel. It is non-round except when the first vowel is round and high or the consonant following it is round. When either of the last two conditions is met the infix is round also. The following formula is proposed to account for the alternations of the perfective marker /i/:

$$i \quad \longrightarrow \quad u \, / \, C \quad U \quad C\_\_\_\_ C$$
$$/ \, C \quad V \quad C\_\_\_\_ W$$

Formulation in terms of features is more revealing since it shows both the cause and effect of the change, and it shows that the rule is natural.

$$
\begin{array}{ll}
\text{V} & \text{---> [+round]} \quad / \quad \text{C} \quad \text{V} \quad \text{C} \quad \text{C} \\
\text{[+high]} & \qquad\qquad\qquad\qquad\qquad +\text{high} \\
& \qquad\qquad\qquad\qquad\qquad +\text{round} \\
& \qquad\qquad\qquad \text{CVC}\underline{\qquad}\text{C[+round]}
\end{array}
$$

The following are examples of derivation of perfective forms for some of the triconsonantal verbs.

Root	Infix	Suffix	Gloss
kútm	kútùm	kútùmé	'wrap up'
túrgw	túrgùw	túrgùwé	'raise'
'ápr	'ápìr	'ápìré	'to choose'
'ípr	'ípìr	'ípìré	'untie'
hookl	hookil		'shout'

No exceptions to the rule for forming the perfective have been found in Jungraithmayr 1975.

Thus it has been shown that there is in Migama an infix -*i*- which in addition to the suffix -*e* is a marker of the perfective form. None of the vocalic endings in Migama have been found to be an integral part of the verb. Although -*i*- as the marker of perfective is found to occur only with trisyllabic verbs, it is worth noting that in some other languages discussed so far it also marked perfective, albeit as a suffix and not an infix.

It was also shown that for Migama one needs to know only the consonant structure of the verb and the first vowel in order to derive the perfective and the imperfective form of the verb for both bi-consonantal and triconsonantal verbs.

Mubi

As in the case of bi-consonantal verbs the following analysis is based on data in Jungraithmayr 1978 as analyzed in Frajzyngier 1981. As for Migama and other languages discussed in the present paper the underlying form for the three consonantal verbs consists of the three consonants and the first vowel as it appears in the perfective form of the verb. In order to show that the second vowel of triconsonantal verbs is predictable, I will show first the proposed derivation of perfective and imperfective forms in which the second vowel is a part of grammatical formative, and then, the infinitive in which it is inserted by a phonological rule.

Perfective

For bi-consonantal verbs the perfective is identical with the underlying form of the verb. For triconsonantal verbs the marker of the perfective is a high vowel inserted between the second and third consonant, and the value of the feature round is determined by the value of this feature in the preceding vowel, e.g.:

Root	Infix	Gloss
derm	derim	'to rest'
filg	filik	'change, alter' (final devoicing applied)
gudl	gudul	'bend'

One can postulate the underlying form of the perfective marker for triconsonantal verbs to be /i/ and a rule that will change /i/ to [u] when preceded by [u].

Imperfective

The imperfective form of triconsonantal verbs in Mubi is derived in a manner different from the derivation of bi-consonantal verbs. The following schema shows the rules involved in the derivation of the imperfective form for triconsonantal verbs only:

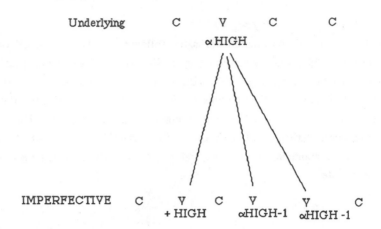

The schema indicates that the underlying vowel is raised in the imperfective form and moreover that a vowel derived from the underlying vowel of the verb is inserted between the second and third consonant. The inserted vowel is long and moreover it is one degree lower than the underlying vowel. Compare the following derivation of the imperfective form for some of the triconsonantal verbs culled from Jungraithmayr 1978:

Underlying	Raising	Insertion/Lowering/Lengthening	Gloss
gerg	girg	giraag [giraak]	'share'
derm	dirm	diraam	'rest
heyd	hiyd	hiyaad [hiyaat]	'sleep'
kurd	-----	kurood [kuroot]	'scratch'
gudl	-----	gudool	'bend'

No exceptions to the operation of the above rules have been found in the data presented in Jungraithmayr 1978.

Infinitive

The underlying form of the infinitive marker in Mubi is the suffix /i/. It occurs as [i] after bi-consonantal verbs with non-low vowel. After all other verbs it is lowered to [e]. Addition of this suffix has an effect on the preceding vowels in that they are raised when a high suffix is added and lowered when the non-high suffix is added. The second vowel of the triconsonantal verb in the infinitive form is epenthetic and identical for all of its features with the preceding vowel. The following are some of the examples giving the derivation of infinitive form for triconsonantal verbs:

Underlying	Suffix	Lowering	V-Insertion	Gloss
gerg	gerg-e	garg-e	garage	'divide, share'
filg	filg-e	felg-e	felege	'change, alter'
lugy	lugy-e	logy-e	logoye, logoy	'shake'
			$(V \rightarrow \emptyset \; / \; [+\text{sonorant}]\_\_ \; \#)$	
kurd	kurd-e	kord-e	korode	'scratch'

No exceptions to these rules have been found in Jungraithmayr 1978.

Conclusions for Mubi

It has been shown that the second vowel of triconsonantal verbs is fully predictable for every grammatical form. For the perfective and imperfective forms the second vowel is provided by grammatical information, i.e. it is a part of the marker for the perfective and imperfective forms, and for the infinitive it is an epenthetic vowel inserted when the syllable structure conditions, or better, when the constraints on allowed consonant clusters, require it.

5. Conclusions

I have attempted in this paper to provide a reconstruction of the underlying form of verb in Proto-Chadic. The data for this reconstruction have been drawn from the West Chadic branch (Pero, Kanakuru), Biu-Mandara (Bachama, Musgu) and East Chadic (Mubi and Migama). Although the total number of languages is not large in comparison with the total number of known Chadic languages, the occurrence of the same phenomena in the three branches constitutes a strong argument against common innovation as the explanation for the similarity of the phenomena involved. A common retention from Proto-Chadic seems to be a more likely explanation of the similarity between the three branches of Chadic. It has been postulated and shown that for the six languages investigated the underlying form of the verb consists of its consonants and one vowel. In order to prove that this it was necessary to prove that the final vowel in biconsonantal and triconsonantal verbs constitutes a reflex of a grammatical formative (not productive in many languages), and also that one of the non-final vowels of the triconsonantal verbs is predictable either through phonological rules or grammatical rules for formation of various aspects or tenses.

No detailed study has been done for the monosyllabic or monoconsonantal verbs. It is assumed that full specification of the monosyllabic verb includes a final vowel, for we have a few monosyllabic verbs in Chadic languages that differ solely in the height of the vowel. Most probably, however, not all the vowels could occur with monosyllabic verbs for there is a strong indication that the contrast round/non-round was utilized for grammatical purposes, as it is now in many languages for the indication of aspectual or tense forms. The underlying forms of the verbs in Proto-Chadic could therefore be proposed to have the following forms: C(V), CVC, CVCC, or CCVC.

I have also posed a question concerning the function of the final vowel in verbs. In traditional analyses of Chadic languages, analyses which were never explicit, no function was proposed for the final vowel, which was treated as a grammatical formative. On the basis of data presented here it appears that /i/ might have been a grammatical formative indicating a major category, including perhaps aspect or tense. A precise answer to this question must await a detailed study of the functions of what is commonly being referred to as perfective and imperfective aspects in Chadic. The paper also provides evidence to support the largely intuitive traditional analyses in Chadic languages which separate the final vowel as a formative different from the verbal root.

Another question which has been left unanswered is what were the reasons for the presence in some but not all Chadic languages of two formatives, one /i/ and the other a low vowel /a/ or sometimes /e/.

As a by-product of this paper an alternative analysis for verbal forms of Migama has been presented which derives all the forms from one underlying verbal form. Also, a new analysis of monosyllabic verbs in Kanakuru was proposed.

The conclusion reached in the present paper applies to the verbal system only and should by no means be treated as a way to analyze all the lexical items in Chadic in the same manner.

Footnotes

*Work on this paper was partially supported by a grant from the Council on Research and Creative Work, University of Colorado. Attendance at the Symposium was made possible through the help of the Deutsche Forschungsgemeinschaft. Sincere thanks to both institutions for their help. I am grateful to the following persons with whom I have discussed the present paper: Paul Newman, Roxana Ma Newman, Herrmann Jungraithmayr, and Daniel Barreteau. Special thanks are due to Henry Tourneux who read through the Musgu part of the paper, made comments on it and provided explanations for some of the facts.

[1] Schuh 1977 proposes that there is no perfective ending in Kanakuru and that rather, whenever there is a final -i we are dealing with the subjunctive ending. For a discussion of this claim, see Frajzyngier (1982b).

[2] Henry Tourneux in a private communication has pointed out that in the dialect he studied the above forms could not occur, that they would have to have high vowel. The conclusion is that both verbal and nominal forms display the same rules concerning the raising of the preceding vowels. In his analysis Tourneux 1978a and b. postulates that all vowels of both nominal and verbal stems are predictable. There is still, however, a difference between the manner in which the first and the other vowels are predictable . In order to predict the first vowel one has to know the phonological characteristic of the consonants involved. Therefore, the hypothesis proposed in the present paper is supported by a different phonological analysis as well.

3 The verb *faka* is not attested by Henry Tourneux.

4 From a discussion with Henry Tourneux, it would appear that the vowel of the last two verbs should have the same value for the feature high and also for the feature front.

ANOTHER LOOK AT WEST CHADIC VERB CLASSES

Abstract

The paper examines the validity of the claim made in Schuh 1977 that the final vowel of the verb in West Chadic was -u. The evidence provided for this claim is found to be insufficient. Instead it is proposed that the final vowel in the perfective form (taken by Schuh to be basic) of West Chadic was -i rather than -u. This proposal is supported by analyses of data from Bole, Kanakuru, Pero, and the Bauchi languages described in Schuh 1978.

1. Introduction

Newman (1975) has proposed that the Proto-Chadic verb in its underlying form included a final vowel. Such proto-forms are thus radically different from their equivalents in individual extant Chadic languages, which are almost always analyzed as having basic verbal forms without a final vowel. Newman has also postulated that there were only two verb-final vowels, viz. /a/ and /ə/. Although many of the examples which he uses to illustrate his hypothesis are in the perfective form, e.g. those from Tera, Kanakuru, and Bolanci, Newman never states explicitly which verbal forms should exhibit the postulated endings. It appears, however, that the perfective is assumed to be such a form.

Schuh (1977) explicitly postulates the perfective to be the underlying form because of the maximum differentiation he claims it exhibits in West Chadic languages. However, instead of Newman's pair /a/ and /ə/ he postulates that proto-West Chadic verbs had -a and -u as the endings of the underlying form.

In the present paper I will show that the evidence is not strong enough to maintain -u as the ending of the underlying form and that instead there is a strong possibility that the underlying vowel of the perfective, if any, was front rather than back.[1] Moreover it will be shown that the distinction between the two vowel classes does not have to be exhibited by the perfective form but instead can be manifested in the derived forms of the verbs.

The rest of the paper will be divided into two parts: first a review of the evidence provided by Schuh (1977) for the underlying -*u*, followed by my rejection of this evidence; secondly, an alternative proposal concerning the vowel endings of verbs in West Chadic.

2. Review of the evidence for underlying -*u*

The evidence that Schuh provides for his hypothesis consists of the following:

a.   Comparisons of the perfective form of verbs in the Bole and also in the Bade groups of West Chadic.

b.   An explanation of the perfective form in Kanakuru (which belongs to the Bole group), where a front rather than a back vowel occurs in the perfective,thus contradicting the hypothesis proposed by Schuh.

In the following review I will follow the above order to facilitate a comparison with Schuh's paper and to ensure that no evidence has been missed.

2.1. The perfective form of the Bole group

The chart below, which constitutes the main evidence for the reconstruction of -*u* and -*a* in the Bole group, is taken directly from Schuh (1977:149), except for the numbers indicating rows which I have added for ease of reference:

	Bolanci	Karekare	Kirfi	
1. Cii/uu	tíi-	túu-	tíi-	'eat'
2. Caa	sáa-	sáa-	shée-	'drink'
3. SCu/Ø	wódú-	yád-	'ár-	'bite
	sól-	ɗák-	búrú	'build'
4. SCaa	kùmáa-	kàláa-	(kwálú-)	'hear'
5. SCu	dònɗú	dànɗú	dòonú	'sew'
	mbàalú	mbùlmú-	bàmbú-	'bury'

In the first row there is only one entry that has the vowel -*u*, viz. *túu* in Karekare. This language does not have any other entries with -*u* except for those in the last two rows. In the third row there is only one entry, *wódú* in Bolanci, and in the fourth there is also only one entry, *búrú* in Kirfi. This last word, however, is not cognate with its counterparts in Bolanci or Karekare. As the data stand now for the first row one would rather reconstruct the final vowel as -*i* rather than -*u*, for the simple reason that one would expect a change in one language rather than changes in two languages producing independently identical results. The data as presented in rows three and four may be seen as an indication that the vowel -*u* was the ending in the Proto-language, but in the absence of phonological descriptions of these languages, this certainly is not conclusive evidence for the hypothesis. The strongest evidence for Schuh's hypothesis is presented in the last two rows, where all the languages have the final vowel -*u*. As Schuh has noted, all these verbs have a first syllable heavy, and he explains the fact that the vowel has not been deleted in any language (unlike in the previous rows) by pointing to the impossible consonant clusters that would have resulted had the deletion occurred.

It appears, however, that the last two rows represent the weakest evidence for the hypothesis concerning final -*u*. Let us assume for the time being that (as proposed in Lukas 1970/71) the basic form in Bolanci and other languages has no final vowel, i.e. it has the form, for the last two rows, CVVC- or CVCC-. For the last group of verbs the basic forms would be:

Bolanci	Karekare	Kirfi	Gloss
dònɗ-	dànɗ-	dòon-	'sew'
mbàal-	mbùlm-	bàmb-	'bury'

Addition of the perfective suffix which Schuh reconstructs as *ko* would require in all the cases some phonological changes in order to prevent a disallowed syllabic structure from occurring. In Bole as in many other West Chadic languages phonetic structures of the form CVV/CCC are not allowed, and none is to be found in the published material on Bolanci and Karekare (cf. Lukas 1970/71 and 1971). The most obvious, and actually attested phonological process by which a possible violation of the syllable structure constraint is avoided is the insertion of a vowel. It has been shown in several Chadic languages (e.g. Kanakuru, Newman 1974; Pero, Frajzyngier 1980) that the inserted vowel is always high. In addition, it has been shown that the value of the feature [back] of the inserted high vowel is determined by the following or preceding vowel. Were a similar rule to operate in Bolanci and Karekare, the epenthetic vowel before a perfective suffix would have to be [u], since the suffix contains a back vowel.

It therefore seems that the fact that all verbs with heavy first syllables have the vowel /u/ in their perfective forms can be interpreted differently from ways that Schuh has proposed. One of the interpretations would be that the first syllable heavy verbs do not end in a vowel when the suffix is attached to them, i.e. that even if there is an underlying verb final vowel it is deleted before the addition of any suffixes, as a result of a morphological and not a phonological rule. Subsequently a phonological rule of vowel insertion introduces a vowel between the last consonant of the stem and the consonant of the suffix. This is what actually happens in Pero, another West Chadic language. The following is one form such a rule might have:

Vowel insertion rule 1

$$\emptyset \dashrightarrow V \qquad\qquad / \quad SC\rule{2cm}{0.4pt}C \qquad V$$
$$\text{[+high, }\alpha\text{ back]} \qquad\qquad\qquad\qquad\qquad \text{[}\alpha\text{ back]}$$

This is not postulated as an actual rule occurring in Bole, Karekare, and Kirfi but rather as a rule to account for the examples from these languages as quoted in the chart in Schuh (1977:149). The same facts that Schuh has used as evidence for the underlying /u/ can be used with the same degree of likelihood as evidence for the vowel insertion rule. While the verbs with first syllable light show considerable variation in both the quality of the last vowel and in the presence of the last vowel, verbs with the first syllable heavy have uniformly the vowel [u] before the perfective suffix. This uniformity may be caused not by the retention of the underlying form from Proto-West Chadic, but rather by the operation of this rule, attested in a number of Chadic languages, whose scope is not limited to the verbal paradigm only.[2]

The strongest kind of evidence that one would wish to show for this rule would be an alternation of epenthetic vowel, such that instead of the [u] we would have another vowel, e.g. [i] when the rightmost environment of the rule is a front vowel. Unfortunately the morphological make-up of the verbal piece in Bolanci and most probably in Karekare does not provide such an environment. Although there is an alternation between /u/ and /i/, the latter is not a phonologically conditioned variant but rather an independent morpheme suffixed before a pronominal object.

In lieu of this unavailable evidence we may consider the formation of the perfective form for verbs of denominal origin in Bolanci. Lukas (1971:3) gives the following examples of the formation of the intensive extension through the lengthening of the last consonant from the nouns *rutá* 'work' and *ruwe* 'leisurely walk' (Spaziergang).

'n-rutt-ú-woo-yíi	'I have worked'
'n-ruw-ú-woo-yíi	'I went through'

If it were only the matter of lengthening of the consonant we would expect the forms: * '*n-rutt-á-woo-yíi* and * '*n-ruw-é-woo-yíi*, i.e. one would expect the vowel of the nominal form to be retained. However, instead of the expected /a/ and /e/ we have the vowel *u*. This vowel cannot be taken as an evidence for the retention of the underlying form of the verb, since we know that the underlying forms, the two nouns listed above, do not have the final -*u* but rather /a/ and /e/. Therefore, on the basis of this evidence the most that one could claim is that -*u* has been grammaticalized to be a marker of the pre-perfective form. But Schuh does not propose this solution and I do not see any merit in it, therefore it will be left without further discussion. The vowel -*u* in the above verbs can however be taken as evidence for the rule of vowel insertion described above.

There is one more piece of evidence against underlying /u/. As Lukas (1971:4) describes the formation of the causative extension in Bolanci, it consists of the suffixation of -*t*. Verbs with the first syllable light have this suffix attached without any phonological changes, e.g. *ɗán-* 'to be saved', *ɗan-t* 'save', *ɓol-* 'be broken', *ɓol-t* 'break', *ɗyor-* 'to stand, to get up', *ɗyor-t* 'to stop something'. Verbs with the first syllable heavy have, however, a different form, e.g. *tamb-* 'to be lost, to get lost', *tambit* 'to lead astray',

daarit 'to cure'. Lukas (1971:3) correctly labels the vowel [i] in the above forms as a
Hilfsvokal, i.e., as an epenthetic vowel. If the above verbs had an underlying /u/ in verb
final position, the causative form of these verbs would have been: **tambut* and **daarut*
respectively. Since we have /i/, there are two possibilities for its analysis: one is to
follow Lukas' suggestion and to postulate a rule of vowel insertion because of the
different environment, and the other is to postulate that the underlying final vowel of the
verb is /i/. But in no case can we postulate on the basis of the available evidence that the
underlying final vowel is /u/. The rule of vowel insertion to account for the last two
examples and for others that Lukas did not quote could have a form similar to the
following:

Vowel insertion rule 2

$$\emptyset \longrightarrow V \qquad / \qquad CV \qquad V/C \qquad C\underline{\hspace{1cm}}C$$
$$[\text{+high, } \alpha \text{ round}] \qquad\qquad [\alpha \text{ round}]$$

The vowel agrees in the value of the feature [round], with the preceding vowel, since
there is no vowel in the environment to the right. The two rules can be collapsed since
the motivation for both is the same, viz. to prevent the disallowed syllable structure from
occurring.

On the basis of the preceding discussion for the Bole group we can conclude the following: There is considerable evidence that the underlying final vowel for monosyllabic
verbs was /i/. It has been also shown that /u/ could not have been the underlying final
vowel for verbs with the first syllable heavy. For the analysis of the last group of verbs
one can postulate that the underlying form does not contain a final vowel. Thus the shape
of the underlying form for the monosyllabic and disyllabic verbs will differ in that the latter will be postulated without a final vowel. There is also the possibility that all
disyllabic verbs had the final vowel /i/. If this is assumed then one also has to postulate a
rule of vowel assimilation by which /i/ --> [u] in order to account for the [u] in the pre-
perfective form. Such a change would presumably be caused by the back vowel of the
perfective suffix. This rule of assimilation would have to be confirmed independently on
other data in Bolanci.

2.2. The perfective form of the Bade group

The evidence presented by Schuh for underlying /u/ in the Bade group is even less convincing than that for the Bole group. The perfective marker in Bade and Ngizim, closely related languages of this group, is the suffix -*w*. Some of the verbs in the perfective end in -*aw* (the '-*a*' class of verbs) and the others end in -*u*. It is this class of verbs that according to Schuh shows the reflexes of his Proto-West Chadic -*u*. Yet, as he himself points out (Schuh 1977:151) the final [u] in these verbs is a product of contact between the stem final high vowel and the perfective suffix -*w*. Therefore the final vowel of the perfective form in Bade and Ngizim is the product of a synchronic phonological rule, and not a retention from the earlier stages of the language; hence it cannot be taken as evidence for the reconstruction of the Proto-West Chadic verb ending.

One could argue, as Schuh does implicitly but not explicitly, that it is the stem final vowel that should be taken into consideration. But there is no way to establish the shape of this vowel in the perfective in Bade and Ngizim, since for high vowels the position before the word-final -*w* is the position of neutralization. It appears that there is a rule in Ngizim by which:

$$i \longrightarrow u \ / \ \_\_ \ w \ \#.$$

The rule states that /i/ will become [u] when followed by [w] in word final position. Schuh (1972:9) states: 'Essentially, *u* is conditioned by a [+round] consonantal environment (preceding or following *w* or labialized velar).' Whether this statement is the confirmation of the above rule I am not sure. But a perusal of Schuh (1972 and 1978) did not turn up any instances of [i] followed by [w] although it did turn up instances of /i/ preceded by /w/. It appears therefore that the rule of assimilation is correct. Because of the neutralization of the feature [back] before the word final [w] the value of the perfective form for the reconstruction of the underlying verb final vowel in Bade and Ngizim is nil. At best one can claim that it was either /u/ or /i/. For disyllabic verbs there is not even good evidence that there is a final vowel in the underlying form, except for -*a* class verbs. Consider the verbs ending in -*u* in the following chart from Schuh (1977:151), representing the verbs in the perfective aspect as they appear before a pause:

	Bade (Gashua)	Ngizim	Duwai	Gloss
Cu	jú	jú	jùwó	'go'
	(táw)	(táw)	tùwó	'eat'
	---	(máw)	mùwó	'take'
Ca	sáw	sáw	sàwó	'drink'
	---	---	màwó	'return'
SCu	bə̀nú	bə̀nú	bə̀nó	'cook'
	kə̀lú	kə̀rú	kə̀ró	'steal'
	màsú	màsú	(màasó)	'buy'
SCa	(də̀rú)	də̀ráw	də̀ràwó	'wait for'
	kə̀ɗáw	ɗə̀káw	kə̀ɗá-	'surpass'
	nàwáw	nàwáw	nùwàwó	'ripen'

If we were to assume that the underlying form of the disyllabic verb has no final vowel, i.e. its structure is CVC-, then the addition of the perfective suffix -*w* would produce a disallowed syllable structure in word final position; this would require a vowel insertion. As has already been shown, the inserted vowel in Chadic is always high, and by the same rules of assimilation the high vowel plus -*w* would result in final [u].

Since at least three explanations are possible for the final [u] in the Bade group, this vowel, when occurring in word final position, cannot be taken as evidence for a Proto-West Chadic **u*.[3]

2.3. The perfective form in Kanakuru

In the analysis of verb classes in the Bole group Schuh has encountered a difficulty in Kanakuru, where a verb in the perfective form ends in -*i* or -*e*, and therefore cannot serve as evidence for the reconstructed Proto-West Chadic classes -*u* and -*a*. In Frajzyngier 1976 it was shown that -*e* is a phonologically conditioned variant of -*i*, a product of the rule:

$$i \longrightarrow e \: / \: SC\underline{\hspace{1cm}}\#$$

a rule which has since been found to have numerous counterparts in other Chadic languages, e.g. Bole (Schuh 1977), Pero (Frajzyngier 1976), and Mubi (Frajzyngier 1981). While Newman (1975) claims that the verbs ending in -*i* show reflexes of the Proto-Chadic -*ə* class, Schuh (1977), despite Frajzyngier (1976), claims that some of the verbs ending in -*e* are reflexes of the Proto-West Chadic (and hence presumably Proto-Chadic) -*a* class. Since Schuh does not say which verbs those are, nor provide any evidence to support his claim, there is no point to discuss this claim any further. No vowel of the perfective ending has been shown to be a reflex of the West Chadic -*a* ending.

Concerning the -*i* ending of the perfective in Kanakuru, Schuh claims that it actually represents the marker of the subjunctive form which has been added to the lexical stem. Schuh appears to be acknowledged the difficulty with this interpretation when he states: 'The historical path by which Kanakuru began utilizing the subjunctive stem as its lexical stem remains to be discovered' (Schuh 1977:158).

The only evidence that Schuh provides in support of this hypothesis is the following comparison between Bole and Kanakuru.

	Bolanci		Kanakuru
	Perfective	Subjunctive	
'refuse'	kúɗú-	kùɗí	kùrí
'spit'	túfú-	tùfí	rùɓí
'sweep'	dàmáa-	dàmé	dàmé
'cook	ɗìnkú-	dìnké	dìngé
'sow'	kàppú-	kàppé-	kàpé

'It is immediately apparent from these data that the final vowels of the Kanakuru lexical forms correspond not to the Bolanci lexical (perfective) forms, but to the Bolanci subjunctive' (Schuh 1977:157).

Although indeed the Kanakuru forms are similar to the Bolanci subjunctive forms, that does not constitute proof that the two have the same source. That is, the fact that the final [i] in both cases represents the subjunctive forms, does not constitute proof that the two have the same source, i.e. that the final [i] in both cases represents the subjunctive morpheme. Any high front vowel in verb final position in Kanakuru will result in the phonetic form as in the chart above; moreover, there is comparative evidence (to be discussed in the third part of the present paper) that the verb final -*i* in Kanakuru is not due to the subjunctive morpheme.

Instead of the hypothesis proposed by Schuh, one which involves a quasi-conspiracy in Kanakuru resulting in total reversal of the semantics of the verbal system, there is a much simpler explanation which does not involve any drastic change in the system and which in fact will show the system in Kanakuru to be very similar to the one in Bolanci and other languages of the Bole group. For the time being this discussion will be concerned only with perfective since this is the only aspect used as evidence by Schuh.

The major difference between the perfective forms of Kanakuru and those of other Bole languages lies in the fact that in Kanakuru there is no suffix *-*ko*/*-*wo*. Since this suffix occurs in other languages, it was most probably deleted in Kanakuru after the split of Proto-West Chadic. The possible reasons for such a deletion are irrelevant to our discussion; suffice it to say that it would not be an unusual process, since the deletion of word final segments is well attested in linguistic literature. It is certainly a much simpler process to postulate than the semantic reversal of the verbal system. It is worth pointing out, however, that the less likely hypothesis, viz. that the Kanakuru perfective never had a suffix to begin with, does not affect the explanation proposed below.

Since there is no perfective suffix which is postulated to have a round vowel, there is no environment in Kanakuru to affect the final vowel other than the weight of the first syllable as described in Frajzyngier 1976. That is to say, unlike Bolanci, Karekare, Kirfi, and Pero, Kanakuru has no phonological environment which can cause the final vowel of the verb to become round. Moreover, since there is no suffix in the perfective, there is no reason to delete the final vowel, a frequent process in Chadic languages affecting polysyllabic verbs, a rule which most probably was at least a historical rule in Bolanci.

It appears therefore that Kanakuru, rather than representing in its perfective form a product of the reversal of the verbal system, actually is the only language that can give us a definite answer concerning the quality of the final vowel in the perfective form of the disyllabic verbs.

Interestingly, the final front vowel in the perfective in Kanakuru agrees with the final vowel of the monosyllabic verbs in the perfective in Bolanci and other languages of the Bole group. The problems raised by the identity of the subjunctive and perfective forms in Kanakuru are discussed in the following section of the paper.

3. Verb Classes in Pero

3.1. Significance of the data

The purpose of this section is to provide additional data to the discussion of the verbal classes in West Chadic to indicate that the basic dichotomy between low and high vowels may be preserved in aspects other than the perfective, and also to provide what is probably the decisive argument against the hypothesis of the system reversal in Kanakuru. Ultimately the analysis presented here should point out the considerable similarity in the perfective forms among the languages of the Bole group. Furthermore, it will add comparative evidence for a front vowel in the perfective of the non-*a* class verbs in the Bole group. The material presented below should by no means be considered as the presentation of the complete verbal system in Pero, since it is specifically limited to addressing only the problems pertinent to the discussion of verb classes.

3.2. The two verb classes

Schuh (1977:148) implies that the vowels on which the two classes of verbs are based are manifested in perfective (or basic) forms in West Chadic languages. In Pero however, this distinction is manifested in the non-perfective, derived form of the verb. Compare the following stems of the verb: the imperative, i.e. one of the derived forms, and the perfective, which in Pero seems to be the closest to the underlying form. The 'perfective' stem is the form of the verb occurring before the perfective suffix -*kò*, the ventive non-perfective -*tu*, and a few others suffixes.

Perfective	Imperfective	Gloss
yí-	yú	'do'
cí-	cú	'eat'
cé-	có	'drink'
rí-	rú	'enter'
yé-	yó	'call'
ké-	ká	'cut'
lé-	lá	'give birth'
dí-	díyà	'become'

cá-	cá	'go down, descend'
bír-	bírù	'strike'
áɗ-	áɗú	'eat'
cál-	cálù	'wander from place to place'
áɗɗó-	aɗɗò	'eat (something hard)'
áppú	áppò	'divide'
cépó-	cépò	'trace'
cín-	cínà	'sleep'
kájó-	kájá	'move'

In the above chart (and indeed in my data) there is only one verb that ends in -*a* in the perfective form. Otherwise the -*a* ending is a characteristic feature of some verbs in the non-perfective form. One cannot predict which verbs will end in -*a* in the non-perfective form and which verbs will end in -*u* or -*o*. Knowing, however, the forms of the verb in the imperative, one can, to a certain degree only, predict the form of the verb in the perfective. The limitation on predictability results from the fact that there is no way one can predict the vowel -*a* for the verb cà 'to descend'. The final vowels of the polysyllabic verbs in the perfective form are epenthetic, i.e. they are predictable for all of their features (for the rules concerning the epenthetic vowels see Frajzyngier 1980). The following regularities, described in Frajzyngier 1977 and 1980 can be noted: monosyllabic verbs ending in -*u* in the imperative have -*i* in the perfective, those ending in -*o* in the imperative have -*u* in the perfective. Polysyllabic verbs ending in -*u* in the imperative have the first syllable light and the verbs ending in -*o* have the first syllable heavy, or the vowel of the stem is -*e* or -*o*.

As it stands, the non-perfective form of the verb in Pero represents more differentiation than does the perfective form; moreover, it is almost always possible to predict the perfective form from the non-perfective form. Nevertheless, it is the perfective rather than the non-perfective which is the basic form of the Pero verb. The reason for this claim is the following: there are two basic stems in Pero from which all other forms are derived, the singular and the plural. The plural form of the verb is derived from the perfective rather than the imperfective form. Compare the following examples of the derivation of the plural stem:

Singular	Plural (Imperative)	Gloss
cé	céyyo	'drink'
cí	cíyyo	'eat'
ké	kéyyo	'cut'
lé	léyo	'give birth'
cá	cáyyo	'descend'

The plural forms of the verbs behave like all other polysyllabic verbs in the derivation of the perfective and the non-perfective forms, i.e. the final vowels of these verbs are predictable.

Since it has been shown on the basis of monosyllabic verbs and plural verb formation that the basic form of the verb in Pero is the perfective, and that the non-perfective form displays the most differentiation one has to postulate the existence of verb classes in terms of their derivational properties rather than in terms of the underlying vowels. Accordingly class -a may be manifested in one or the other conjugational form but one cannot write phonological rules by which the appropriate final vowel is assigned to the verb.

Such a model would normally be rather disturbing, since it may imply that a part of the verbal system is not rule governed, until one remembers that the verbs belonging to the -a class are very few not only in Pero but in most other Chadic languages. The complete list in my Pero data contains the following verbs, quoted in the imperative: cá 'go down', lá 'give birth', bá 'fetch (water)', ká 'cut', má 'return', cínà 'sleep', díyà 'become', kájá 'move'. Certainly remembering that these verbs have a different form from the rest of the verbs in certain parts of the paradigm does not constitute an impossible load on the memory of a speaker. The imperative form in Pero, after the exclusion of -a class verbs, is similar to the imperative form of the verb in Kanakuru. The perfective form of the verb in Pero is similar to the perfective forms of the verb in Kanakuru, at least for monosyllabic verbs. Schuh explains the perfective in Kanakuru as resulting from the addition of the subjunctive suffix, which he provisionally reconstructs as -*i. We can show now that this explanation is erroneous.

3.3. The consecutive in Pero

The form which Schuh (1977) labels subjunctive does not bear semantic or syntactic similarity to the generally accepted range of the term subjunctive in linguistic literature. I will label this term consecutive in Pero. As in Bolanci, it is marked by *-i.* I have no data concerning the syntactic distribution of this morpheme in Bolanci, but in Pero it is attached to the verb only in sentence final position. If the verb is not sentence final, e.g. if it is followed by an object, the form of the verb is the same as the imperative. In sentence final position disyllabic verbs add the suffix *-i* to the root, i.e. the form without the final vowel. Monosyllabic verbs have as their consecutive form their 'perfective' form, i.e. they do not have the suffix *-i* attached. If the stem of the verb contains a front mid-vowel it is raised in the environment of a following high vowel. Such raising rules are independently attested in Pero (see Frajzyngier 1980).

Compare now the consecutive form of the verb with forms in the 'perfective' and in imperative.

Perfective	Imperative	Consecutive	Gloss
wár-	[wáaro]	[wáarì]	'go'
dán-	[dánù]	[dánì]	'wait'
tók-	[tóɣò]	[tóɣì]	'kill'
kém-	[kémò]	[kímì]	'satisfy'
pér-	[péro]	[pírì]	'go out'
cék-	[céɣò]	[cígì]	'be lost'

The forms in the column labeled 'perfective' are quoted in their pre-suffixal form. But we can attempt a synchronic reconstruction of these forms based partially on the behavior of the monosyllabic verbs and on the form of the imperative of the polysyllabic verbs. Applying the regularities noted previously we will obtain the following endings for the polysyllabic verbs:

Perfective	Non-perfective
-i	-u
-o	-o

Applying now these correspondences to the polysyllabic verbs in the chart above we would obtain the following reconstructed forms:

*wáate   *dáni   *tókè   *kémè   *pérè *cékè

If one looks at the first three verbs there is already some indication that the consecutive form is not the same as the reconstructed perfective form since the two forms differ in the quality of the final vowel for verbs whose first syllable is heavy and for -e and -o verbs. But when one looks at the last three examples it is not only the final vowel that is different, but also the medial vowels, and in the case of the consecutive forms the medial vowels are raised as the result of the consecutive suffix -i. Therefore one cannot claim that the perfective and consecutive in Pero are the same form. The final vowel of the perfective form as it is attested for the monosyllabic verbs and as it would have been reconstructed for the polysyllabic verbs is not therefore a product of addition of the consecutive suffix -i. Since it has been shown that the perfective in Pero is similar to the perfective in Kanakuru, one may conclude that also in Kanakuru the front vowel of the perfective form is not due to the addition of the consecutive suffix. One cannot determine whether it is part of the underlying form of the verb; but one may conclude, at least for the evidence provided by the perfective forms of the verb or by any other forms quoted in Schuh 1977 that u was not the underlying final vowel of the verb.

4. Conclusions

We have now shown that, contrary to the claims in Schuh 1977, one cannot postulate the vowel -u to be the underlying vowel of any class of verbs in the West Chadic group of languages. It has been also shown that the final vowel of the perfective, which Schuh considers to be underlying for the non-low class of verbs, should be reconstructed as -i or -e depending on the syllabic make-up of the verb. It has been shown that the -a ending of the other class may be manifested in the non-perfective forms of the verb and neutralized in the perfective forms.

Monosyllabic verbs in Pero and in other languages of the Bole group behave in a different way from the polysyllabic verbs, in that they never delete the final vowel in the process of suffixation. Therefore for the monosyllabic verbs one needs the information concerning all the segments of the verb in order to derive all of its conjugational forms. For the remaining verbs the only thing that one needs to know is whether the verb is an *-a* class verb or not. If the verb is a non *-a* class then all of the endings are predictable, perfective and non-perfective alike.

As a by-product of this analysis it has been shown that the perfective form of Kanakuru represents most probably the proto-West Chadic verbal endings in the perfective form.

Footnotes

[1] The present paper will not address the problem of whether or not the final vowel is indeed the underlying. This problem is addressed in Frajzyngier 1983.

[2] Vowel insertion rules in one form or another have been noted for Kanakuru (Newman 1974), Bade (Schuh 1978), Bolanci (Lukas 1971, not stated explicitly), Pero (Frajzyngier 1980), Mubi and Migama (Frajzyngier 1981).

[3] It is not possible on the basis of the data presented in Schuh (1977) to choose from among these explanations of the synchronic origin of the underlying vowel of the verb.

THE PLURAL IN CHADIC

1. Introduction

The aim of this paper is to describe the relationship between nominal and verbal plural formations and to consider certain hypotheses concerning the nominal plural in Proto-Chadic
(PC).

One of the characteristic features in a number of Chadic languages is the identity of
markers of nominal plural with the markers that indicate the frequentative, intensive form of
the verb and at the same time, often, plurality of object. In this paper, these forms of the
verb will be called plural verbs. The number of languages in which the markers of nominal
and verbal plurality are similar and the number of morphemes involved make any argument
against accidental identity superfluous.

There are essentially three possible explanations for the similarity between the verbal
and nominal plural markers. The first two involve internal borrowing, from paradigm A to
paradigm B or vice versa, in this case, from verbal plural to nominal plural or from nominal
plural to verbal plural. Such borrowing is plausible since the forms that are borrowed have
the same semantic function, i.e. as markers of plurality. The third possibility is that there is
a form, e.g. marker of plurality, which is not attached to any paradigm in particular and
which is, as it were, used by any paradigm whenever certain semantic conditions require it.
Historically this could be interpreted as the existence of a plural morpheme before the
noun/verb distinction emerged in a given language. I will not consider this hypothesis in
the present paper, concentrating rather on the first two hypotheses. One of the hypothesis
will be rejected and the implications for the reconstruction of the PC nominal plural markers
will be discussed.

The most widespread device for the formation of nominal plural is gemination of a consonant and/or reduplication of part of a stem. It will be shown that at a certain stage in the
history of Chadic this was a device used only for the formation of verbal plural, and that it
was subsequently borrowed to mark the nominal plural as well. The same hypothesis will

be tested for another frequent marker of nominal plural, *a*, which along with gemination, was postulated by Diakonoff (1965) to be a Proto-Afroasiatic device. These two hypotheses, if accepted, would rule out the possibility that either of the devices was a nominal plural marker in PC.

The third plural marker, less widespread than the previously mentioned two, involves a morpheme of the form -*Vn*, i.e. a vowel followed by a nasal stop. It occurs almost exclusively as a nominal marker. A hypothesis concerning the origin of this affix is advanced and argued, and the possibility of *Vn* being a PC nominal plural marker is rejected.

In order to present and defend the hypothesis, the data on nominal and verbal plurals from the languages for which I have data are presented, first from Pero and then from Kanakuru. Pero does not have a nominal plural marker at all, but instead has a rich system of verbal plural markers. Next data from Kanakuru, a closely related language, serve as evidence for the claimed direction of borrowing of gemination from verbal plural to nominal plural. Third, analysis of the nominal and verbal plural formations in other Chadic languages shows that the nominal plurals in those languages are a relatively recent innovation. Finally, we turn to the discussion of the possible origin of -*Vn* and some related affixes as markers of nominal plural.

2.   Pero

The following analysis of plural formation in Pero is pertinent for two reasons. First, it is the first presentation of the data. Second, the data from Pero show the connection between gemination and reduplication of a syllable, discussed briefly later in the paper.

Pero verbs are disyllabic (the largest group), trisyllabic, and monosyllabic. Theoretically, every verb should be able to have a plural form. In practice, this is not always the case, and there are some verbs for which speakers were not able to provide a plural form.

Trisyllabic verbs form the plural by gemination of the consonant of the second syllable. This can be formalized by the following rule:

$$(C_1) \; VC_2VC_3V \; \text{---} > (C_1) \; VC_2C_2VC_3V_{[plural]}$$

Singular1	Plural		Gloss
úgújò	úggújò	[úkkújò]	'throw on ground'
lígúnò	líggúnò	[líkkúnò]	'answer'

Monosyllabic verbs form the plural by adding a suffix -yy- to the verbal stem:

cá	cá-yy-ù	'go down'
cé	cé-yy-ò	'drink'
cí	cí-yy-ò	'eat'

Disyllabic verbs with a sonorant at the onset of the second syllable form the plural by the following rule:

$$C_1V_1SV_3 \longrightarrow C_1V_1C_1C_1V_2SV_3[\text{plural}] \quad (S = \text{sonorant})$$

V_2 in the plural form is epenthetic. After a high front stem vowel the epenthetic vowel is -i-; elsewhere it is -u-.[2]

Singular		Plural	Gloss
ménò		mémmúnò	'like'
cínà		cíccínà	'sleep'
bínà	[pínà]	bíbbínà	'wash'
tánù		táttúnù	'run'

The above group of verbs is particularly important in the present investigation since it shows that reduplication of syllable and gemination of consonant are essentially variants of the same device in Pero. The use of reduplication rather than gemination of a consonant is phonologically conditioned. It is the presence of a sonorant at the onset of the second syllable that apparently requires reduplication.

Disyllabic verbs with a sonorant at the onset of the second syllable where the first syllable has either a long vowel or a sonorant form the plural by the following rule:

$$CV_1\{V_1, S\}SV_3 \longrightarrow \qquad CV_1\$V_2SV_3 \text{ [plural]} \quad (\$ = \text{syllable boundary})$$

bírrò	bí$írò	[pí?írò]³	'make fire'
túllò	tú$úlò	[tú?úlò]	'scatter'
géelò	gé$ólò		'incline the head'
káarò	ká$órò		'check, examine (medically)'
táamò	tá$úmò		'wait'
cúrrò	cú$úrò	[cú?úrò]	'fry'
bánnò	bá$únò	[bá?únò]	'look'

   Disyllabic verbs which have the structure CVCCV, i.e. those that have the first syllable closed, add either a suffix -t- which becomes [r] in intervocalic position (t ---> r /V___V) or a suffix -j-. It is still possible to reconstruct the rule which governs the choice of -t- or -j-. Verbs that have an alveolar consonant as the stem-final add the suffix -t-; all the other verbs in this group add the suffix -j-.

Singular	Plural	Gloss
-t-		
fúndò	fúndú-t-ò [fúndúrò]	'cook'
cóttò	cóttú-t-ò [cóttúrò]	'wring water out of cloth'
báddò	báddú-t-ò [báddúrò]	'finish'
díllò	díllú-t-ò [díllúrò]	'fetch small amount of water'
-j-		
ámbò	ámbú-j-ò	'climb'
yémmò	yémmú-j-ò	'carve in wood'
céɓɓò	céɓɓú-j-ò	'plant'
múmmò	múmmú-j-ò	'close'
bénjò	bénjú-j-ò	'saw'

   There are only a few examples which do not allow the postulation of the above rule as still operating in Pero. All of them have the singular form CVCV rather CVCCV. Two of these examples involve a final velar consonant and the plural suffix -t- rather than the expected -j-.

cékò [céɣò]	cékkú-t-ò	'lose'
cúgà	cúkkú-t-ò	'fall down'

The remaining exceptions all involve the suffix -j-.

cámù		cámmú-j-ò		'twist a rope'
ífù	[ívù]	íffú-j-ò		'catch'
cákù	[cáɣù]	cákkú-j-ò		'rub'
béjò		bójjújò	[péccújò]	'thatch'
májù		májjújò		'ask'

The plural class $C_1VC_2C_2VC_2V$ has as its source singular verbs of the structure C_1VVC_2V:

wáatò	[wáarò]	wáttúrò	[wáttúrò]	'come'
dáafò			[dáffúvò]	'apply cream'
cúkkò	[cúugò]		[cúkkúgò]	'spread water'
díekò	[díeɣò]	díkkúkò	[díkkúgò]	'fetch water'
fóojò		fójjújò	[fóccújò]	'push'

The last major class of plurals includes verbs of the structure $(C_1)VC_2C_2V$, i.e. with the second consonant reduplicated. The main sources for this class of plurals are verbs of the (C)VCV structure and verbs which have the first vowel long:

ádù		áɗɗò	'eat something hard'
lófò	[lóvò]	lóffò	'beat'
kóofò		kóffò	'pass'
déefò		déffò	'discuss'
páatò	[páarò]	páttò	'pour'
túuɓò		túɓɓò	'take from container'
lóokò	[lóoɣò]	lókkò	'hang'

This rule of plural formation is of course the same as the rule for trisyllabic verbs, and could be formalized in the following way:

$$C_1VC_2V \longrightarrow C_1VC_2C_2V(C_3V)[\text{plural}]$$

2.1. Summary of plural formation in Pero

Singular	Plural
$(C_1)VC_2VC_3V$	$(C_1)VC_2C_2VC_3V$
CV	CV-yy-V
$C_1V_1SV_3$	$C_1V_1C_1C_1V_2SV_3$
	$V_2 = i$ if $V_1 = i$
	$V_2 = u$ elsewhere
$CV_1(V_1S)SV_3$	$CV_1\$V_2SV_3$
	(For value of V_2 see footnote 3)
$C_1VC_2C_3V$	$C_1VC_2C_3V(t/j)V$
	t/C_3 alveolar
	j/C_3 non-alveolar
C_1VVC_2V	$C_1VC_2C_2VC_2V$
$(C_1)V(V)C_2V$	$(C_1)VC_2C_2V$

2.2. Conclusion from the Pero data

Despite the considerable variation and complexity in the formation of the verbal plural, there is still a rather large degree of regularity and most of the forms are predictable from the singular form of the verb. It seems that the reduplication of the second consonant is relatively earlier than suffixation of *-t-* or *-j-*. This conclusion is based on the following observations. A number of verbs have plural forms which have already specialized meanings, usually narrower when compared with the meaning of the normal plural form:

bétò	'cut into two'	béttò	'cut into pieces'
áfù	'open'	áffò	'split'
ádù	'eat (e.g., peanuts)'	áddò	'eat something hard (meat)'
cúbù	'show'	cúbbò	'teach'

Some of these verbs have a secondary pluralization by means of suffixes, conveying the most general semantic notion implied by the plural verb:

áffò	áffújò	'split, divide'
áɗɗò	áɗɗútò	'eat many times, many things'
cúbbò	cúbbújò	'show, teach many things'

It is important to note that Pero has no infix or suffix a in the plural forms of the verb. This affix occurs rather frequently in other Chadic languages.

The gemination and reduplication are not due to recent innovation in Pero. This conclusion is supported by the fact that the suffixes -t- and -j- are used only when the gemination cannot apply because the stem already has the structure CVCCV, with the word-medial consonants identical or not.

3. Kanakuru

Kanakuru has a nominal plural realized in essentially three different ways which are not predictable on phonological or semantic grounds (Newman 1974:82). One is the suffix -ngin with what appear to be its variants -ṅjín/-ṅjén; the second is the suffix -iyán/-uyán with its variants ín, án, yen, and en. The third means of forming the nominal plural is through gemination (Frajzyngier 1976; Newman 1974 analyzes it as hardening) of the second consonant and an addition of one of the above suffixes.

Kanakuru has a verbal plural as well, formed by gemination of the second consonant of the verb (Frajzyngier 1976), thus partially resembling the third means of forming the nominal plural. The difference consists in the suffixes, which are present in the nominal plural but absent in the verbal plural.

It appears that gemination is an older device than suffixation in the formation of nominal plurals in Kanakuru. The argument for this conclusion is the following. There is a small number of verbs which have a plural as well as a singular form. There is also a much larger group of verbs in Kanakuru which are plural in form, i.e. they have geminated second consonant, but no recorded corresponding singular forms. This may of course be attributed to the incompleteness of our data, although the number of such verbs makes this an unlikely explanation. The other possible reason for the lack of the singular counterparts is that they were lost and are not used anymore. If this is the case, it would indicate that the gemination of the second consonant is a relatively old device in the formation of verbal plural, although it is no longer productive. The small set of nouns which form their plural in the same way in which the verbs do may therefore manifest the oldest device of forming the nominal plural in Kanakuru, since this set is closed as well.

The following is an explanation for the development of the plural markers in Kanakuru. After gemination ceased to operate as a device for marking the plural, the various suffixes on nouns emerged as result of compensatory change. The old verbal plurals were not perceived anymore as plural forms and, therefore, there existed two forms containing essentially the same semantic characteristics. One of those forms disappeared from usage.

It is possible that the whole process was the opposite from the one described above. One could argue, for instance, that the nominal suffixes marking plural developed first, and then gemination as the morphological device ceased to operate because it was duplicating the function of the nominal suffixes. But this direction of development is contradicted by examining a number of languages, e.g. Hausa, where there is a large number of nominal plural markers and, at the same time, reduplication of part of the verb is a productive device for the derivation of frequentative forms.

4. Other Chadic languages

In the presentation of the plural formation in other Chadic languages, I will use the classification in Newman (1977b) in which four branches are distinguished: West, Biu-Mandara, East, and Masa. The analysis below is based on data for some of the languages from three branches of the Chadic family. Whenever I did not have data, this fact is indicated by '?'. Most of the data are quoted as presented in the sources I have been using, in most cases without any attempt at reanalysis. The list of languages is by no means exhaustive.[4]

EAST

	Nominal		Verbal
	Suffix	Infix	
SUBBRANCH A			
Dangla	------------	-a-	?
Jonkor	-to	------	vocalic changes, e.g., o ---> a.
Jegu	-an, -e, -i, -o, -ik, -nau.		?

	Tonal changes.	
	Singular suffixes	
	-o, -e.	
Mubi	Vocalic changes.	
	Gemination	
Migama	?	Gemination

SUBBRANCH B

Kera   -n.

The forms in Jegu and in Kera show similarity, viz. the suffixes -an and -n. The forms in Dangla and Jonkor are different from each other and from Jegu and Kera. The markers involving -n and -k will be dealt with later in this paper. The infix -a- could be a retention of a very old morpheme (see Greenberg 1955) which will be discussed later as well. Unfortunately I did not have sufficient data concerning the verbal plural in this branch, but from Lukas (1975) it appears that the intensive form of the verb in Jonkor involves the change from o ---> a in the prefix.

BIU-MANDARA

	Nominal	Verbal
SUBBRANCH A		
Ga'anda	-cə	Reduplication of first consonant and insertion of -a-. Rule (from R. Newman 1971:35: $C_1VC_2(V)$[int] ---> $C_1əC_1aC_2(V)$
Tera	-ku	None.
Margi	'yar, -i (traces).	Plural via reduplication.
Kapsiki	Plural marked with very few nouns denoting humans and animals. Suffixes: -li (-eli), -śi, -lemu, -ati. Reduplication of part	Reduplication of part of stem.

	of stem.	
Bachama	Vocalic suffixes.	Internal vowel change. Infix *-a-*.
Gisiga	*-ay*, postposition *hay*.	Plural form of verb marked by suffixes *-am* or *-ak* indicates plurality of subject.

SUBBRANCH B

Musgu	*-ai* (*-oi*), *-akai*, *-ad*.	Verb is number-sensitive, it is in plural form when subject is plural.
Kotoko	Gemination of final consonant. Suffixes: *-e, -en, ni-i*. Internal vowel change.	
Logone	Gemination of final consonant. Internal vowel change to *-a*, suffix *-en, -e*.	Information not available about verbal plural for most languages of this subgroup
Buduma	Suffixes: *-ai, -ei, -e*. Other devices as in Kotoko.	

In subbranch A of Biu-Mandara there is no obvious form which one could postulate to be common to all languages of this subbranch. The verbs in subbranch A form plurals through reduplication or through the vocalic change to *a*, e.g. as in Ga'anda, Bachama. This fact will be an important argument later in this paper for the direction of internal borrowing of forms in Chadic languages. Apparently, Tera has lost the plural forms of the verb, since it is the only language in the subbranch that does not have a mechanism for the derivation of verbal plurals.

In subbranch B, in Kotoko (Gulfei dialect) and Logone there is an *en* suffix. Gemination occurs as a device in at least three languages. In addition, there is an *-a* suffix in this subbranch. As far as the nominal plural formation is concerned, these two subbranches do not have much in common except for the Gisiga suffix *-ay*, which is similar to the plural markers in subbranch B. In Gisiga and in Musgu the verb encodes the number of the subject.

WEST

	Nominal		Verbal
	Suffix	Infix	
SUBBRANCH A			
Daffo	*-ay, -ash, -e.*	*-a(a)-.*	Infix *-a-.*
Sha	*-a, -aa, -ash, -e.*		Suffix *-an.*
			Reduplication.
	Tonal changes.		
Kulere	*-egy.* Reduplication		Infix *-a-.*
Bokkos	*-ha, -ash.*	*-a-* with reduplication.	?
Fyer	*an, ash, -ash, e,*		
	-ee, -i. Reduplication.	*-a-, -aa-.*	Infixes *-i-, -a-, -aa-.*
			Suffixes *-aŋ, -an.*
Hausa	*-unaa, -ukaa, -uwaa,*		Reduplication of first
	-C'aa, -ai, -uu, -ii, -aa,		three phonemes or of
	-akuu, -akii, -annii,		second syllable.
	-aC'ii. Infix *-a-.* Re-		
	duplication of a conso-		
	nant is involved in a		
	number of suffixes.		
Angas	*-mwa.*		Plurals not numerous.
Sura	Postposition *-mo.*		Reduplication of stem.
			Change of tone.
			Shortening of vowel.
			Infix *-a-.* Suffixes: *-ap, -el, -k.* Infix *-l-.*

Chip	Postposition -*mu*.		Suffix -*p*. Infix -*a*-.
			Suffixes: -*ak*, -*an*.
			Tonal changes.
Bole	?		Reduplication of initial
			syllable, gemination of
			last consonant of the
			stem.
Kanakuru	-*ngin*, -*njin*/-*njen*,		Reduplication.
	iyan/*uyan*, -*in*, -*an*,		
	-*yen*, -*en*. Reduplication		
	of consonant of stem.		
Pero	No plural		Reduplication.

SUBBRANCH B

Bade	Final vowel change:	-*aa*-	?
	a --> aa, ə, oo --> a,		
	e, -*ən*, -*at*, -*let*, -*ə*, -*yit*,		
	-*agə*, -*oot*, -*ageet*, -*cin*, -*tin*.		
	Reduplication		

It seems impossible to reconstruct a common plural marker for the West branch. Within the Ron languages, one can determine a common plural marker; this is also true for Angas, Sura, and Chip. However, the plural marker of Angas, Sura, and Chip is a recent innovation, identical with third person plural pronoun (for an early analysis cf. Greenberg 1955:202). The most widespread markers of plural in the West branch are the infix (sometimes suffix) /a/ and reduplication, which has been noted for almost all of the languages except for Angas, Sura, and Chip.

The verbal plural has been noted in all West languages, except for Bade, but there my data might be incomplete since the source for this language was an article dealing explicitly with the nominal system. In most of the languages, the verbal plural is marked either by reduplication or by the affix /a/. Sura and Chip have a few additional affixes not shared by other languages in the table. Those affixes seem to be innovations. It is worth noting that neither Pero nor Kanakuru have /a/ as a plural marker.

5. Analysis of the three branches

5.1. Nominal plural

The most frequent devices used to mark plural in the three branches of Chadic are /a/ and reduplication or gemination. Within each branch there is an abundance of plural markers which are not cognate within the branch, e.g. Margi -'yar, Tera -ku. Many of the languages have a variety of plural morphemes whose occurrence is often unpredictable on any grounds. This leads to a conclusion that except for /a/ and reduplication, the rest of the plural markers in Chadic languages are the result of a process or processes which must have occurred after Proto-Chadic split into the three or more branches. Moreover, quite often these plural markers did not emerge until the particular branches split into the modern languages. Evidence for this relative chronology is provided by the diversity of the plural markers within each branch of Chadic.

5.1.1. The plural morpheme /a/

This marker occurs in all of the branches of Chadic, most often as an infix, but it may be a suffix as well. The languages for which it was not recorded, such as Pero and Kanakuru, either did not have it or lost it.

5.1.2. Reduplication

This process occurs in all of the branches of the Chadic family, but not in all languages. In subbranch A of Biu-Mandara it occurs only in Kapsiki. In the West branch it does not occur in the Sura-Angas-Chip group. In the East branch it occurs only in Mubi.

5.2. Verbal plural

This category occurs in all languages for which I have data. The meaning of this form always includes an indication of intensity of action, repetition of an action and, in all but two languages, it implies plurality of the object. Musgu and Gisiga are important exceptions, in that verbs in these languages agree in number with the subject and have the plural form if the subject is plural. It is important to remember that for the rest of the Chadic languages the plural form of the verb is not usually a function of verb-object agreement, although this has been noted as well, e.g. in Kanakuru (Newman 1974:72). In Margi (Hoffmann 1963:57), if the verb has a plural form the noun does not have to have the plural suffix. Thus the verbal markers in verb and noun in Margi are, as it were, complementary.

The most common devices for formation of the verbal plural are reduplication of a syllable or gemination of a consonant in the verb. Since this device occurs in all of the branches of Chadic and in almost all the languages, one can assume that it is a retention from the Proto-Chadic verbal system. The rules for formation differ from language to language, and those differences have to be attributed to innovations in particular languages.

The morpheme /a/ occurs as the plural marker of verbs in the Biu-Mandara branch (Ga'anda and Bachama) and in the West branch (Ron languages, Sura, Chip). In the East branch it has been noted in Jonkor. On the evidence of the Biu-Mandara and West branches alone, one could conclude that /a/ was a morpheme marking plural in the verbal system of Proto-Chadic. The suffixes which occur in Sura and Chip, viz. -p and -k must be innovations that emerged in these languages after they had split from the other languages of the West branch.

The hypothesis that gemination/reduplication and affix /a/ were originally markers of the verbal plural is most strongly supported by the fact that in the majority of languages there is a verbal plural having one of the above forms even though there is no nominal plural, or else the nominal plural has a different form from the verbal plural. It has been shown, therefore, that Proto-Chadic had the verbal plural, which still exists in all the branches of the group, marked by reduplication or an affix /a/. Some Chadic languages have taken this device and used it in the formation of nominal plurals. That is why we find nominal plurals by reduplication or by an affix /a/ in some languages only. The data from Kanakuru suggest that the plural by reduplication is older than the other forms of the plural.

5.3. Suffix -Vn

Another candidate for a Proto-Chadic plural marker is a suffix which contains at least an alveolar nasal, and usually has the form -Vn. The hypothesis that it was a Proto-Chadic nominal plural marker will be reviewed and rejected in what follows.

In the East branch the -Vn marker occurs in Kera. It also occurs in Jegu as one of the many suffixes that mark nominal plural. Dangla and Jonkor do not have such a suffix. If one were to accept -Vn as a Proto-Chadic plural marker, one would have to assume that Dangla and Jonkor lost it and, moreover, that Jonkor developed a new suffix -to.

In subbranch A of Biu-Mandara there are no suffixes of the form -Vn with the possible exception of Margi. Carl Hoffmann (p.c.) pointed out that r in the Margi plural marker 'yar derives from an alveolar nasal, and is therefore a reflex of the Proto-Chadic plural marker. As noted in the Biu-Mandara chart, Margi has some traces of the plural suffix -i, the only other plural marker apart from 'yar. Some of the words that take it are:

Singular		Plural	Gloss
mdə	'person, man'	mjì	'people'
sál		shílí	'man, husband'
ŋkwà		ŋkwà'ì	'girl, daughter'

As Hoffmann writes (1963:59), all these plural forms may take, in addition, the plural suffix 'yar when used with demonstratives, e.g.:

mjì'yàr kə	'these people' (besides mjì kə)
shílí'yàr kə	'these men', etc.

The semantic nature of the words which still take the suffix -i rules out its having been borrowed. Besides, -i occurs as a plural marker in a number of other Biu-Mandara languages, e.g. Kotoko and Buduma. It appears therefore that the suffix 'yar is not the oldest plural marker in Margi. This conclusion is additionally supported by the spread of this suffix in the language.

In subbranch B of Biu-Mandara, a -Vn suffix occurs in Kotoko and Logone, two closely related languages.

Among the closely related Ron languages, only Fyer has a - *Vn* suffix *-an*, e.g. *yuur-u* 'eye', pl. *yiran* /y-i-r-an/ (Jungraithmayr 1970). In this word there is already a plural marker *-i-*. In the description of Fyer, there is one more word, *humu* 'ear', pl. *humuaŋ / humwaŋ*, which contains a suffix with a nasal, but it is a velar nasal.

The suffixes *-aŋ* and *-an* occur more frequently as markers of the verbal plural in Fyer. Another Ron language, Sha, also has *-an* as the marker of the verbal plural, but does not have it as the marker of the nominal plural. The two instances containing the - *Vŋ* and - *Vn* morphemes in Fyer could be explained by postulating that, as in several other instances mentioned earlier in this paper, those plural markers have been internally borrowed from the verbal system. It seems that the fact that the two cases are different, together with the other arguments presented above, rules out the possibility that the Fyer morphemes are reflexes of the Proto-Chadic nominal plural marker.

While Hausa has at least two suffixes that may be claimed to have developed from the Proto - *Vn* suffix, another subgroup of the West, consisting of Sura, Angas, and Chip, does not have a - *Vn* suffix.

In the Bole cluster, Kanakuru has a - *Vn* suffix among several other suffixes which contain a - *Vn* as part of the morpheme. There is, however, evidence that the various - *Vn* suffixes in Kanakuru are relatively later devices when compared with gemination of the second consonant of the stem. There is a group of nouns which, in addition to suffixes, have the second consonant geminated; The following examples, based on the data in Newman (1974:84), are presented according to the analysis in Frajzyngier (1976):

dúu	(<dúhú)	dúkkúyán	'boar'
lípè	[líwè]	líppén	'calabash'
yáapè	[yáawè]	yáappìyán	'chicken'
tàkà	[táà]	tákkín	'shoe'

These data indicate that a suffix containing - *Vn* has been added to the geminated noun, probably when gemination was not perceived any more as a pluralizing device. Pero, a language from the same cluster, does not have any nominal plural markers.

Bade, a language from Subbranch B of the West branch, has an infix *-ən*, among eight other affixes, reduplication, and vowel change to mark the nominal plural.

The peculiar distribution of the - *Vn* suffixes in Chadic languages may have two possible explanations:

(a) A certain suffix containing a nasal consonant functioned as a plural marker in Proto-Chadic. This marker was subsequently dropped by the majority of languages. The reasons for such a massive reduction of this suffix in languages from various groups are not known. This hypothesis has its major weakness in our inability to explain why the suffix was lost.

(b) The other possibility is to postulate that in various languages, a -*Vn* suffix developed independently to mark the nominal plural. Such a hypothesis can be retained only if one could show why several independent changes produced so similar a result. In order for independent innovations to produce a similar form, one would have to have a similar source for them. It appears that there is such a source in those Chadic languages that have a -*Vn* suffix.

In many Chadic languages there is a particular form of demonstrative pronoun, genitive linker, independent pronoun, or similar morpheme related to the class of masculine nouns, which often contains a nasal consonant, usually an alveolar nasal, although sometimes it may be a velar nasal. The plural suffix -*Vn* could be derived from a form related to this marker. All the Chadic languages which have the -*Vn* marker do indeed have a form of the demonstrative masculine marker containing an *n*. In Hausa it is a genitive linker and stabilizer. In Bade there are pronouns and many demonstratives containing *n* (cf. Schuh 1975).

It is very likely that in a number of Chadic languages the feminine marker was also used in the formation of the plural, and that this was another source of plural markers that show similarity to one another, for example, markers involving -*k* or -*t*.

At present, I am unable to explain how and why masculine and feminine markers could be transformed into plural markers, but this is apparently what happened in Chadic languages. Outside of the Chadic branch of Afroasiatic, a similar phenomenon occurred in Semitic, in particular in Arabic, where the -*una* plurals were first an innovation as plural markers for masculine nouns and only later spread to cover both masculine and feminine nouns (cf. Kuryłowicz 1972:139).

Since it is impossible to reconstruct a common plural morpheme apart from /a/ and reduplication, one has to assume that the multitude of other morphemes occurring in various Chadic languages must be innovations, occurring after those languages split from Proto-Chadic and even after there was a split within the smaller branches of Chadic.

Footnotes

1 The forms in the singular are the underlying forms of the verb; they occur in this phonological form before some of the suffixes. The plural form is found in the imperative and some other paradigmatic forms of the verb.

2 There are similar restrictions on the form of the epenthetic vowel in Kanakuru (cf. Frajzyngier 1976).

3 The syllable boundary $ is phonetically realized as [?] due to a general phonological rule in Pero which inserts a glottal stop before all vowel-initial syllables. The V_2 of the plural form is a copy of V_1 when V_1 is [+high]. If V_1 is [-high], the V_2 of the plural cannot be predicted at the present state of analysis.

4 The following are the sources used for the particular languages: Dangla (Fédry 1971); Jonkor and Jegu (Jungraithmayr 1961/62; J. Lukas 1974/75); Kera (Karen Ebert, personal communication); Kapsiki (Smith 1969); Kotoko, Logone, and Buduma (Westermann and Bryan 1952); Tera (P. Newman 1970); Margi (Hoffmann 1963); Bachama (Carnochan 1970); Ga'anda (R. Newman 1971); Bade (R. Lukas 1967/68); Ron languages (Jungraithmayr 1965, 1970); Gisiga (J. Lukas 1970); Angas (Jungraithmayr 1963); Sura (Jungraithmayr 1963/64); Chip (Jungraithmayr 1964/65); Bole (J. Lukas 1971); Kanakuru (P. Newman 1974); Pero (Frajzyngier 1976 and fieldnotes); Musgu (J. Lukas 1941); Hausa (Russell Schuh's analysis in Welmers 1973; Frajzyngier 1965).

ON THE PROTO-CHADIC SYNTACTIC PATTERN

1. Introduction

The present paper is the first part of a projected two-part study of the proto-Chadic syntactic pattern.[1] It is concerned mainly with structures consisting of a verb, either transitive or intransitive, and a single argument. The second part will deal with constructions consisting of a verb and two arguments.

The purpose of this paper is to propose a hypothesis concerning the proto-Chadic syntactic pattern, to provide evidence for this hypothesis, and to point to some implications of the hypothesis for the historical and synchronic syntax of Chadic languages.

The problem of the semantic relationship between a transitive verb and a single NP with which it occurs is the central problem for the syntax of any language, since it ultimately determines the existence of other syntactic structures (or transformations), the presence of various grammatical morphemes (including inflectional) and is one of the first problems to be considered in the semantic description of verbs. This problem has not been explicitly dealt with in the comparative works, scanty so far, nor in the area of Chadic syntax or in the grammars of particular languages. All the analyses on which it might have had a bearing have assumed, although only implicitly, that the situation in Chadic languages is very similar to the situation in contemporary Indo-European languages.

Within the wider domain of Afroasiatic the approaches have been similar, with the notable exception of Diakonoff 1965:87, who claims that the proto-Afroasiatic verbal system was ergative and, following some studies of other ergative languages, states that in such a system "the point of view of the logical object is as much represented in the basic finite verbal form as is the point of view of the logical subject of the action." Diakonoff's support for the hypothesis is based on inflectional case markings in the Semitic branch of Afroasiatic. Later in the present paper Diakonoff's hypothesis concerning the ergative nature of proto-Afroasiatic will be shown to have merit for proto-

Chadic but his specific claims concerning the nature of this ergative system will be rejected.

Some of the issues discussed in the present paper have been dealt with in grammars of Chadic languages under the heading of transitivity, voice, and verbal extensions, including the causative.

2. Hypothesis
2.1 The possible models[2]

If the verb is inherently intransitive, i.e. it occurs with only one noun phrase e.g., 'come', 'fall', etc., the problem of the semantic role of the noun phrase in the clause does not arise. This role is fully determined by the verb and/or the lexical features of the noun.[3]

The situation is different when the verb has the inherent capability of occurring with two noun phrases, i.e., when the verb is potentially transitive. When such is the case, a language usually has a way of indicating the semantic role of each noun phrase and the semantic role of the single noun phrase which occurs with such a verb. In order to indicate the roles of the noun phrases languages resort to various strategies, such as inflections, adpositions, word order, etc. There is, however, one common element in those strategies: One role may often be unmarked, regardless of the means employed by a given language. This unmarked form is usually identical with the form that a noun phrase takes when it occurs with an inherently intransitive verb. Thus in most Indo-European languages the unmarked form is that of Agent.

In English it is best manifested in the pronominal system, e.g., 'I hit him' and 'I came' but 'He hit me'. In other languages which allow a potentially transitive verb to occur with one noun phrase it is even more overt, e.g., in Russian:

Ivan udaril
'Ivan hit'

Ivan ujexal
'Ivan left'

Now if in such a system a single noun phrase that occurs with a transitive verb has a different role from the one expected, this must be indicated somehow, e.g., by word order, inflectional devices, prepositions, etc. In most of the Indo-European languages this is accomplished by the use of passive constructions, reflexive constructions, case marking, or prepositions. I will call this nominative-accusative type Model 1.

In a second model the unmarked form of the verb and noun indicate Patient (rather than Agent, as in most Indo-European languages). Thus, if one were to use English words to illustrate the model, in the phrase 'John hit', 'John' would stand for a Patient rather than for Agent.

When the verb is inherently intransitive, the single noun phrase and the verb will be unmarked and the form of the construction will not differ from the construction consisting of a noun phrase and a transitive verb. And, in contradistinction to Model 1, when a single noun phrase that occurs with an inherently transitive verb is an Agent rather than the expected Patient, the language may have a means to indicate this. I will call this type of language Model 2. Thus in many ergative languages, the Agent is marked through inflectional devices, while the Patient or a single noun phrase in an intransitive construction remains unmarked.

2.2 The hypothesis concerning proto-Chadic

Contrary to the tacit assumption made in all previous studies devoted to Chadic, I would like to postulate that proto-Chadic was a Model 2 and not a Model 1 language. The proto-Chadic verbal system was characterized by a diathesis in which the unmarked noun phrase which occurred with a transitive verb was the semantic Patient, and not the semantic Agent as in present Indo-European languages and many present Chadic languages. Thus in proto-Chadic the construction consisting of NPp(atient) Vtr(ansitive) did not differ from the construction consisting of NP Vint(ransitive). The construction 'NPa(gent) Vtr' did differ from the above constructions, being marked by either morphological or syntactic means.

In the present paper I will reconstruct the means which were used to mark a single noun phrase as Agent in proto-Chadic. A corollary to the hypothesis that proto-Chadic was a Model 2 language is a hypothesis concerning the syntactic structure involving a verb and two noun phrases rather than one; that is, an Agent and a Patient, or controlling and non-controlling arguments). It may be postulated that in such a case the Agent would have assumed the position of the unmarked element. On the other hand, there is a possibility that such a construction was marked in the same way in which the construction NPaVtr was marked. The problem of the transitive sentence with two noun phrases will not be discussed in the present paper, since it constitutes the topic of another study. (cf. 'Marking Syntactic Relations in Proto-Chadic' further in this volume).

3. Evidence

The evidence presented here shows the presence of certain syntactic structures and morphemes in languages from three groups of Chadic, which are here claimed to constitute a common retention from the proto-Chadic syntactic pattern. The evidence will also point to the existence of certain morphemes which will be claimed to be innovations. Certain facts which cannot serve as evidence will nevertheless be introduced because of the frequent correlation of such facts with syntactic structures similar to the one postulated for proto-Chadic.

3.1 The syntactic pattern NPpVtr and the causative morpheme

As has been postulated in the description of Model 2 above, if the basic, unmarked construction has a Patient NP the language will have a device to indicate the case in which the single NP which occurs with the transitive verb is Agent instead of the expected Patient. In the discussion that follows I will therefore describe not only the presence of NPpVtr construction but also the existence and operation of the 'causative' or 'transitivizing' morphemes. I will assume Newman's 1977a classification of Chadic languages. The discussion will not cover the fourth branch of Chadic (Massa), because I do not have any data for this group.

3.1.1 West Branch
BOLE

      NPVint   isinko pete
                     'he is going out'

      NPpVtr   isinko ngora
                     'he is being tied'

In Bole in certain tenses or when certain extensions to the verb are present, e.g., the totality extension, a single noun phrase that occurs with a transitive verb represents Agent rather than Patient, e.g., *isi damatu woo* 'he swept it' (all examples Newman 1971:192). This phenomenon is rather frequent among Chadic languages and is important for a discussion of historical changes in the syntax. The transitivizing suffix in Bole is *-t*, e.g.,

      bol   'to break' (int)
      bol-t   'to break' (tr)

      dan   'to be saved'
      dan-t   'to save' (Lukas 1971:[4])

PERO

      NPVint
      ta   peto   bira
      Fut go out out
      'he is going out'

      NPpVtr
      Kurbe ta jigu-tu
      money Fut loss-ICP
      'money will be lost'

The causative transitivizing suffix in Pero is -*n*. As in many Chadic languages, it has two functions: Causative, i.e., 'causing x to do y', e.g., *pilu* 'buy', *pilu-n* 'sell' (i.e., 'cause to buy'), and transitivizing, e.g., *peto* 'go out', *peto-n* 'take out'. The causative marker in Pero is not a suffixed pronoun or zero anaphora marker, since it occurs even when there is an object, nominal or pronominal, e.g.,

> peto + tu +   n   bira   ka   te
> go out Vent. Caus. outside with her
> 'take her out'

DAFFO/BUTURA (a Ron language)

Jungraithmayr 1970:182 states that the verb in Daffo/Butura is neutral with respect to a transitive/intransitive distinction and that there is no difference in form between the one and the other, this distinction being reflected only in the form of the verbal noun. I take this statement of Jungraithmayr as indicating phrase NPVint, although I did not find appropriate examples to quote in this paper.

NGIZIM

In the imperfective aspect of Ngizim, when a single noun phrase which occurs with a transitive verb is Patient, the verb remains unmarked, e.g.,

> aa dlama bai
> 'it is not doable"

If, however, the single noun phrase is Agent, then the verb is marked with the suffixes -*w* or -*gu*, e.g.:

> naa dlama-k wana bai
> 'I won't do the work'

> naa dlama-w bai
> 'I won't to do it'

In aspects other than imperfective the NPVtr construction is apparently ambiguous and the noun phrase in such a construction may represent either Agent or Patient.

Ngizim has two morphemes, in complementary distribution, with a transitivizing function, -*naa* and -*du*, which are added to inherently intransitive verbs:

kwaana aa kalakta
'Kwana will return'

kwaana aa kalakta-du
'Kwana will return (it)'

dee bai
'he didn't come'

dee-naa am bai
'he didn't bring water' (Schuh 1972:30)

As one can see, there are several forms in Ngizim performing essentially the same function, viz., that of indicating presence of a second argument of a transitive verb.

3.1.2. Biu-Mandara Branch

TERA

The NPVtr construction represents a Patient in some cases, e.g.,

kimbili-a   waxi
'the pepper has been ground'

zlu-a ká zure
'the meat will be fried'

> zlu-a á zurte
> 'the meat is frying (being fried)' (Newman 1970:59)

Newman (op.cit.), however, gives the following sentence, which he says may be ambiguous:

> woy-a wa ruba
> 'the boy was injured' or 'the boy injured him/it'

The fact that 'boy' in the above sentence may represent a Patient is an important piece of evidence for the hypothesis being advanced in this paper, and the fact that it may represent an Agent as well, does not necessarily contradict it. Rather, it may be considered as an indication of changes in the verbal system of Tera. The intransitive sentences with a verb of motion have the same form as the above sentences, e.g.,

> Ali a gabte
> 'Ali is returning'

In the continuous tense, however, the noun phrase in the NPVtr structure always represents Patient. Were the noun phrase in such a construction to represent an Agent, the suffix -*an* would be added to the verb, e.g.,

> ta ndolar-an mu
> 'do you want (him)'

> tem a yobt-an
> 'we are dyeing (them)'

Newman (1970f) describes -*an* as a zero anaphora marker, and this description is correct in the sense that this suffix also occurs with prepositions in lieu of the head noun. However, its function in the clauses above can equally well be analyzed as marking the semantic role of the subject noun phrase as Agent, with an object not represented in the sentence at all.

GA'ANDA

The NPpVtr and the NPVint do not differ formally in Ga'anda, e.g.,

> NPpVtr
> e fel buteda (kade)
> 'the pot is cracked (up)'

> NPVint
> e in miiketenda (xa)
> 'the door opened (ip)'

The causative function in Ga'anda is performed by anaphoric pronouns referring to the semantic Patient and suffixed to the verb, e.g.,

> sen-men nafdi
> 'we know that man'

> sen -an-men nafdi
> 'we informed that man'

The suffix -an refers only to the third person. The following examples illustrate similar constructions with persons other than third.
Without anaphoric pronoun:

> na-i kwas weçe
> 'I (fut) unite you'
> 'I will unite you'

With anaphoric pronoun:

> na-i kwas-u-ta
> 'I will free you' (R. Newman 1971:41 and ff)

The formation of this type of sentence in Ga'anda may be considered an illustration of how this type of anaphoric pronoun for the third person came to carry a transitivizing function. One can imagine the following steps in the emergence of the new function:

Step One: there is a separate anaphoric pronoun for each person.
Step Two: there is only one anaphoric pronoun for all persons.
Step Three   the anaphoric function of the pronoun becomes secondary or is lost altogether and the form assumes the function of a transitivizer-causative suffix.

Compare the following sentences in Ga'anda which, being very similar to sentences in Pero and other Chadic languages, illustrate Step Three:

xiy-ince persa
'I bought a horse'

xiy-an-i persa kade
'I sold a horse (away)' (R. Newman 1971:44)

In the latter sentence it is clearly not a matter of anaphora, but of the causative function being included in the form -*an*.

MARGI

Although I did not find examples of the NPVtr construction in which the noun phrase represents a Patient in Hoffmann 1963, I assume that such constructions must occur in Margi. This assumption is borne out by Hoffmann 1963:115, where he states that in Margi the simple verb seems to be neutral in respect to transitivity. What it implies is that a verb does not change its form depending on the type of construction in which it occurs.

There is, however, a causative suffix -*ani*, one of whose functions is to make the intransitive verb transitive, e.g.,

hya   'to rise', 'to stand'

hyani   'to raise', 'to wake'

mbu   'to get better'
mbani   'to save', 'to cure'

Although the presence of the transitivizing suffix is not yet in itself evidence for the historical primacy of Model 2 I think that, in conjunction with the following discussion, it becomes a significant argument for the hypothesis advocated in this paper.

In Margi, as in a few other Chadic languages, there is an intransitivizing suffix which is derived etymologically from the noun *ker* 'head'. This suffix is in most cases added to the verbs which already have one extension, either the suffix *-ba* or the suffix *-na*. The property of these extensions is such that they transitivize the verb to which they are attached, a verb which was originally intransitive (Hoffmann 1963:153), e.g.,

mbu
'to hide' (INTR)

mbuna ker
'to hide' (INTR)

This points to an important fact that in the majority of cases the intransitivizing suffix is not needed, but is a device for indicating secondary intransitivity. The suffix is in fact called for when the verb has been made transitive by some morphological process.

GISIGA

Lukas's 1970 description of Gisiga is one of the most illuminating in the the whole of Chadic literature. The notions which Lukas entertained in his grammar are quite similar to the hypotheses being proposed in the present paper.

After saying that given the present state of our knowledge of Gisiga we cannot postulate morphemes specifically marking transitivity or intransitivity, Lukas 1970:58 states: "Ein Grundstamm, der seiner Bedeutung nach eine intransitive und eine transitive Funktion ausuben konnte, wird in der Regel als intransitiv verstanden, wenn er kein

Objekt hat, ist aber durch ein OP [object pronoun] oder ein nominales Objekt oder durch beide als transitiv gekennzeichnet."

In Gisiga, therefore, with only a few exceptions a single noun phrase occurring with a potentially transitive verb represents a semantic Patient and not an Agent. The transitivizing suffix in Gisiga is -*an* before a pause, and -*a* in other contexts, e.g.,

> 'i dum- le'
> 'I hid myself'

> 'i dum-a le
> 'I hid it' (Lukas 1970:59)

3.1.3. East Branch

At the time of writing this paper my data for this branch are very fragmentary and what little information I have is drawn from only from Dangla. In Dangla the NPVint construction does not differ from the NPpVtr construction, e.g.,

> mee a saw
> 'the chief is coming'

> boril tee
> lit., 'the iron of the hoe is eaten', 'the iron of the hoe is used'

Fédry 1971:XII states that all Dangla verbs, with a few exceptions, can be either transitive or intransitive, and transitivity is marked by the presence of complements. Therefore the situation is essentially the same as in the other Chadic languages discussed so far. It is interesting that Fédry describes the meaning of *na tee* as either 'he has eaten' or 'he was eaten'. Note that the verb 'to eat' is one of the few potentially transitive verbs which occur with Agent rather than Patient in Gisiga, e.g., *a zom* is 'he ate' rather than 'he was eaten'. It is very likely that a similar situation exists in other languages with respect to the verb 'to eat' and a few similar verbs, and I do not think it contradicts the hypothesis advanced in the present paper. The semantic features of verbs in combination with the semantic features of nouns preclude any kind of ambiguity. With such verbs as 'to eat' if a single noun phrase has the feature [+human] in normal usage it will be interpreted as Agent. It would be interesting to know the interpretation of a single noun phrase with the verb 'to eat' if this noun phrase had the features [-human] and [+animate]. Unfortunately I do not have examples of such sentences for either Dangla or Gisiga.

3.2. Historical interpretation

One of the questions which may arise in consideration of the NPpVtr is whether it is a retention from the system of proto-Chadic or an innovation, and consequently whether the starting point , that is the system of proto-Chadic, resembled the system of some modern Indo-European languages, or the system in many of the present Chadic languages. In other words, one has to choose between a direction of change from Model 1 to Model 2 or one from Model 2 to Model 1. Chart I, which summarizes the data presented for the Chadic languages above and also contains some data not yet discussed. The question marks in the chart indicate that my information for a given problem was inadequate.

CHART I

Branch	Language	NPpatient	Vtr Transitizer
West	Bole	yes	-t
	Pero	yes	-n
	Hausa	yes	-s/-r
	Ngizim	yes	-naa, -du
BiuMandara			
	Tera	yes	-an
	Ga'anda	yes	pronouns, an for 3 p.
	Margi	yes	-ani
	Lamang	yes	-na
	Gisiga	yes	-an/-a
	Bachama	yes?	-dv
East	Dangla	yes	? complements

It seems clear that the NPPatient Vtr construction could not have emerged independently in so many languages. As examples of other languages indicate, it is not 'natural' or obvious for a language to intransitivize by putting the semantic Patient with the transitive verb. Although it certainly may happen, its independent development in at least ten languages of the same family seems unlikely. Rather one must assume that the NPPatient Vtr construction in Chadic languages is a retention from the proto-Chadic system.

3.3 Transitivizing and intransitivizing devices
3.3.1 Transitivizer

As has been mentioned earlier, if the basic diathesis of the verb indicates Patient, the language may have some means to indicate that a single noun phrase occurring with a transitive verb is not a Patient, but an Agent. If we have reconstructed the proto-Chadic system as Model 2, we should be able to reconstruct the marker for the agentive noun phrase.

From Chart I it appears that there are at least two possible markers indicating presence of an agentive noun phrase, one consisting of (V)n(V) and the other of an alveolar stop, /t/ or /d/. Newman 1977 postulates this form to have an alveolar stop rather than a nasal. In the discussion of Ga'anda in the present paper it has been shown that an anaphoric pronoun can become a marker of agentivity of a single noun phrase. If one therefore assumes that the reflexes containing -n in various languages have their origin in the third person pronoun, one can assume that in proto-Chadic the original transitivizing morpheme had a form similar to (V)d(V) and that by the time of proto-Chadic this form was already being replaced by a form similar to (V)N(V) originating in the anaphoric pronoun. The above by no means constitutes the only possible way in which the transitivizing pronouns could have come to have a form containing a nasal consonant. As the reconstruction of the exact form of the transitivizing suffix is not of primary importance for the present paper, I will not dwell upon it further at the present time.

3.3.2 The problem of the *intransitivizing* marker

This section will consist essentially of a presentation of negative evidence regarding the hypothesis. In a Model 1 language, i.e., in a language in which the basic diathesis of the transitive verb indicates Agent, a morpheme is needed whose function would be to indicate that a single noun phrase occurring with a transitive verb is not an Agent but rather a semantic Patient. Such a function is performed in many modern Indo-European languages by so-called reflexive pronouns or by the passive construction, both of them marked forms. If the Chadic languages were consistent with Model 1 it should be possible to reconstruct a device or a morpheme which would have this function.

Intransitivizing morphemes exist in a number of Chadic languages. Newman (1971) considered the possibility that the intransitive copy pronouns (ICPs) might have been such markers. But, as has been shown in Frajzyngier 1977a the function of the ICP in Chadic is that of a non-stative marker rather than an intransitivizing marker. Moreover, it does not appear that ICP's had this function in proto-Chadic.

The functions of an intransitivizing morphemes (when they do exist) in a Chadic languages seems to be much more limited than the functions of intransitivizing morphemes in other languages (i.e., Indo-European). Often, the intransitivizing a verb is only one of several functions that the morpheme has. Thus in Hausa there are two 'grades' whose function is intransitive. Grade VII (ending in -*u*) has at least three functions, one indicating intransitivity, another indicating stative, and the third indicating the action well or thoroughly done. It is very likely that the intransitive function is not indicated by the form of grade VII but rather by a syntactic structure which consists of only a noun phrase and a verb, the noun phrase being the semantic patient.

In Margi, as has been pointed out above, the intransitivizing morpheme *ker* is added mainly to verbs which have been made transitive by suffixation of certain extensions to the verb.

In Kanakuru all intransitive constructions have an ICP suffix, even if the primary diathesis of the verb is intransitive. In many cases in Kanakuru the presence of ICPs as intransitive markers is redundant. In most Chadic languages the intransitive marker simply does not exist. The few forms that occur do not seem to be cognates and there is no possibility of reconstructing the proto-Chadic intransitive marker. The lack of an intransitive marker in proto-Chadic therefore supports the hypothesis advanced in the present paper by indicating that proto-Chadic could not have been a Model 1 language.

3.4 Plural verbs

The discussion in the present section, although is not intended as evidence, nevertheless supports the hypothesis. The value of this section lies in the correlation it shows in number agreement among the ergative languages and accusative languages. Among the ergative languages it is the semantic patient or subject of an intransitive verb that governs the agreement in number with the verb. Such is the situation in Avar[6], Blackfoot[7], and in Dyirbal (Dixon 1972:250), and Mel'cuk (1977:14). Among the accusative languages number agreement with patient rather than agent is rare.

Before going through a cross-language examination of plural agreement in Chadic, I will illustrate the phenomenon for a few selected Chadic languages.

KANAKURU

In Kanakuru there is a group of verbs which obligatorily agree in number with the direct object of a transitive verb or with the subject of an intransitive verb, i.e., with the semantic Agent. From the point of view of plural agreement, there is no distinction in Kanakuru between the object of a transitive verb and the subject of an intransitive verb. This fact alone supports the hypothesis of this paper about the ergative nature of proto-Chadic.

The formation of the plural stem in Kanakuru is similar to the formation of plural stems in other Chadic languages in that it involves gemination of the second consonant of the verb (Frajzyngier 1976 and 1977a). Compare the following sentences from Newman 1974:72:

wun boi kom	'they are shooting a rat'
shii bupe komen	'he is shooting a rat'
am bu-mai	'we will shoot (it)'
am bupe-mai	'we will shoot (them)'[8]

na dope donjini	'I tied the horses'
donjini wu dopo-wu	'the horses are tied'
dowi a dowe-ni	'the horse is tied'

| a muro-to | 'she died' |
| wu moto-wu | 'they died' |

The intensive form of the verb in Hausa is often triggered by the plurality of object (cf. Frajzyngier 1965). In Pero the only way to indicate the plurality of the Patient of a transitive verb or the subject of an intransitive verb is through the use of the plural from of the verb, as there are no plural forms of the noun.

BACHAMA

The plural form of the verb in Bachama is formed through an internal vowel change. As in Kanakuru, this form is triggered by either a plural Patient or a plural subject of intransitive verb, e.g.,

kcembeto a dimo
'the canoe sank'

keembyee a dyemo
'the canoes sank'

nda pir vuney
'he thatched the hut'

nda pyer vonye
'he thatched the huts'

The plural Agent does not trigger the plural form of the verb, e.g.

taa piira vuney
'they went and thatched the hut'

vs.

    taa pyaara vonye

    'they went and thatched the huts' (All examples from Carnochan 1970:102)

The following chart indicates the agreement system for plural verbs in some Chadic languages from the West and Biu-Mandara groups. For many languages I did not have the appropriate data, and in several languages, Logone and Tera, among others, no plural form of the verb seems to exist.

CHART II[5]

Language	Agreement with Agent	Agreement with Patient and subject of intransitive
West		
Hausa	no	yes
Kanakuru	no	yes
Bole	no	yes
Pero	no	yes
Sura	no	yes
Ron-Fyer	seldom	yes
Biu-Mandara		
Ga'anda	no	yes
Margi	no	yes
Lamang	no	yes
Gisiga	yes	no
Bachama	no	yes
Musgu	yes	no

The following conclusions may be drawn from this chart. First of all, it is obvious that the plural verb agreement with the Patient or intransitive subject cannot be an innovation, as it occurs in most of the languages. This type of agreement must have been a feature of proto-Chadic.

From the point of view of number agreement, proto-Chadic, like present-day Kanakuru, Pero, and Bachama, did not make a distinction between the categories of the object of a transitive verb, i.e., Patient, and the subject of an intransitive verb. The lack of this distinction is one of the features of ergative languages. Apart from the correlation with ergative languages, the real importance of this system of agreement may lie elsewhere.

The verb agreement system indicates a certain primacy of the relationship to which it applies. By primacy I understand an unmarked basic relationship between the noun phrase and the verb. This kind of relationship holds between the categories of subject and verb in Indo-European languages.

If one were to postulate the grammatical category of subject for proto-Chadic as a category which indicates the basic unmarked relationship, then the noun phrase standing in such a relationship could not be the semantic gent of the sentence. This of course, supports the hypothesis advanced in the present paper.

4. Evolution of the system

The various elements of the system which are present in contemporary Chadic languages and which have been advanced as evidence for the hypothesis do not always occur as a set in one language, and often a language will preserve one element of the system, e.g., the $NP_{Patient}V_{tr}$ structure, but will replace the other elements, e.g., instead of number agreement with Patient it will have agreement with Agent. It appears that none of the present Chadic languages preserved the proto-Chadic system in toto. The evolution in particular languages seems to be toward a system resembling a Model 1 language. In the following section I will briefly review trends in the evolution of each of the previously discussed features.

4.1 The structure $NP_{Patient} V_{tr}$

In certain languages such as Bachama this construction has disappeared completely and the noun phrase in the NPV_{tr} structure represents an Agent rather than a Patient.

In most of the languages the NP$_{Patient}$ Vtr structure, even though present, is restricted to certain tenses or aspects. In such languages and in the appropriate tense or aspect we generally find the following types of structures: (M in the structures below stands for the transitivizing marker, regardless of the phonological shape it assumes).

      a. Vint (NP)
      b. Vtr (NP$_{Patient}$)
      c. Vtr M(NP$_{Agent}$)
      d. Vtr (NP$_{Agent}$ NP$_{Patient}$)
      e. VtrM (NP$_{Agent}$ NP$_{Patient}$)

The above structures do not make any claim about the order of the constituents in the sentence. This does not mean that the order is not important for the structure of the sentence (in fact, the opposite is true) but I am not at present prepared to make any generalizations concerning the order. The important fact is that the form of M is the same in sentences of the type c. and d. Structures d. and e. are synonymous in most Chadic languages. The structure e. does not differ from transitive constructions in accusative languages, and it is this structure which I believe is an intermediate stage in the change from a Model 2 language to a Model 1 language. In structure e. the semantic relationship between noun phrases and the verb could be indicated by inflectional devices, prepositions, or word order. If the semantic role of the noun phrase in the structure e. is indicated by word order, as is the case in Chadic languages, one can easily imagine that deleting the Patient noun phrase produces the NP$_{Agent}$ Vtr structure.

But there is one important question to be answered before the above hypothesis is tested. This is the question of the relative priority of structures d. and e. On the basis of the data presented in this paper one can only speculate about the answer, and I would rather not do so at this time. I hope to have a satisfactory answer to the question after completion of synchronic and diachronic study of Chadic transitive sentences with two noun phrases.

4.2 The transitivizing marker

This marker is preserved in all Chadic languages, and it performs at least two functions, the causative and the transitivizing. So even if a language has changed from Model 2 to Model 1 one can still expect to find the causative marker cognate with the transitivizing markers in other languages.

4.3 Plural verb agreement

Plural verb agreement appears to be vestigial in most of the languages. In many languages (e.g., Hausa, Kanakuru) it is optional and in some languages it has disappeared altogether (e.g., Tera). Yet in some languages it is obligatory (e.g., in Pero and, possibly, in Migama). In most of the languages the proto-Chadic number agreement system has been replaced by a new system of agreement in which the controlling relationship is with an Agent rather than a Patient. Although in most languages this agreement is realized by preverbal pronouns, in some languages it is realized by changes in the verbal stem (e.g., in Musgu).

5. Conclusions

It has been shown that the proto-Chadic verbal system was characterized by a diathesis in which an unmarked noun phrase occurring with a transitive verb represented Patient rather than Agent. The evidence consisting of NP Patient Vtr constructions, transitivizing morphemes, and the verb plural agreement, has been gathered from a dozen Chadic languages, mainly from the West and Biu-Mandara branches.

It has been shown that most of the Chadic languages are evolving toward a system in which the basic diathesis indicates Agent rather than Patient. Presence of certain morphemes, e.g., transitivizing, and the lack of others, e.g., intransitivizing morpheme or passive construction, can be explained causally and not merely recorded as has been done before. One question, namely, why in Chadic languages the system is evolving from Model 2 to Model 1, remains unanswered at present.

Footnotes

1 The work on the present paper was supported by a grant from the Council on Research and Creative Work, University of Colorado. Moreover, the help from the University of Colorado for my attendance at the Third International Hamito-Semitic Congress is appreciated. I would like to thank Jean Charney, David Rood, and Eileen Weppner for the comments they made on an earlier version of this paper.

2 In the following discussion I have been greatly influenced by the excellent analysis of Dyirbal in Mel'cuk 1977.

3 This still may have to be further specified in languages in which the semantic feature [+willful] or [+control] is grammaticalized.

4 It is interesting that Hoffmann 1963:116 mentions that the derivational morphemes in Margi have a function similar to that of the derivational morphemes in Georgian, an ergative language.

5 The data for this chart and the discussion that follows, including Chart II have been taken from the following sources: Bole -- Newman 1971 and Lukas 1971, Pero -- Frajzyngier 1976, 1977a. 1977b, Hausa -- Frajzyngier 1965, Kanakuru -- Newman 1971, Lamang -- Lukas 1970 and Ekkehard Wolff, personal communication, Margi -- Hoffmann 1963, Bachama -- Carnochan 1970, Musgu -- Lukas 1936, and Gisiga -- Lukas 1970.

6 Keenan 1976. I am grateful to Jonathan Seely for pointing this out to me.

7 Allan Ross Taylor, personal communication.

8 As in many Chadic languages, the plurality of the object is indicated here by the form of the verbal plural only. Voiceless stops in intervocalic position in Kanakuru represent underlying geminated consonants (cf. Frajzyngier 1976).

ERGATIVE AND NOMINATIVE-ACCUSATIVE FEATURES IN MANDARA

1. Introduction[1]

Among the existing studies of Mandara[2], a Chadic language belonging to the Biu-Mandara branch (Newman 1977), there appears to be a gap in the description of the plural formation of verbs and also in the description of the function of the plural forms. The present paper, which is based on the Mandara dialect spoken in Pulka, is intended to fill this gap. The purpose of the paper, however, is not just to provide some additional information on this language, but also to show what can be learned about the history of Mandara and Chadic from the forms and functions of verbal plurals.

The syntax of plural verbs in the Mandara dialect spoken in Pulka and possibly in other dialects exhibits both nominative-accusative and ergative characteristics. While the former are represented by fully productive devices in the form of subject prefixes and infixes, the latter are manifested through traces of various plural markers whose distribution may be quite limited in the contemporary language.

The importance of the data from Mandara lies in the fact that ergative characteristics have been claimed for Proto-Chadic (cf. Frajzyngier 1983) and for Afro-Asiatic (cf. Diakonoff 1965). A detailed study of a particular language may contribute to the elucidation of the question as to whether those characteristics are innovations in a particular language or retentions from an earlier, possibly Proto-Chadic system.

2. Forms of verbal plural
2.1. Two paradigms of the verb

For the purpose of the present analysis the verbal paradigm in Mandara should be divided into two groups. The first group consists of just one tense which Mirt 1970/71 calls 'perfective' and which is formed through reduplication of the verbal stem. The subject pronouns and certain verbal extensions are then infixed between the two parts of the reduplicated verb. We can represent the perfective paradigm in the following formula: R-Pron-R, where R indicates the root of the verb and Pron indicates the subject pronoun.

The other group consists of all other tense/aspectual forms which are characterized by having the subject pronoun preceding the verb. The form of the imperative will constitute still a third group for it does not have any subject pronouns. Since the plural markers in the two paradigms are different, the following description will reflect the division into the two paradigms.

2.2. Perfective

Mirt 1970/71:39 postulates that in subject pronouns there occurs a plural suffix -ər. The marker -a- can not be considered a part of the plural marker since it also occurs in the singular forms:[3]

1sg	-an	1pl excl.	-anər
2sg	-ak	2pl	-akwər
3sg	-aa	3pl	-ar

The analysis of these pronominal forms indicates that first person pronoun is -n-, second person is -k- and the third person is unmarked. The plural suffix could be either -ər or just -r if one considers the possibility that shwa is an epenthetic vowel, whose occurrence here could easily be predicted by phonological rules inserting the vowel whenever a non-allowed consonant cluster could emerge. In the present paper I will assume, without providing further evidence, the form of this plural marker to be -r-. In the third person plural one would therefore have the category plural marked by -r- and the category person indicated by absence of any phonological markers.

The same plural marker occurs in the object pronouns which are suffixed to the verb. Compare the forms above with the following object pronouns, also from Mirt 1970/71:

		1pl incl.	-aməy
1sg	-əy	1pl excl.	-anər
2sg	-ak	2pl	-akwər
3sg	-an	3pl	-atɔr

The second device to form the plural is the reduplication of the whole verb. Mirt did not describe it for the dialect she studied but it occurs rather frequently in the Pulka dialect. Note that this reduplication precedes in derivation the formation of the perfective form of the verb. The perfective form of the plural verb formed through reduplication can be represented by the formula: R Pron R, where R represents the root of the verb.

The third device to form plural verbs involves the vowel *a* which either is added as a suffix to the verb or replaces the first vowel of the verb. The three devices will be illustrated in the next section.

3. Plural forms in perfective
3.1. The marker -r-

This suffix occurs in the Pulka dialect whenever the agent of the transitive verb or the subject of an intransitive verb is plural, e.g.:

1. pítà ɗa-ɗɗè
   P. go
   'Peter went'

2. pítà ntárà yàkúbú ɗa-rɔ́-ɗɗé
   P. with   Y.   go-Pl
   'Peter and Yakubu went'

3. gwá-xà   já-r-jì mátsámà
   elephant-Pl killed-Pl hunter
   'Elephants killed a hunter'

4. gwé   já-jì mátsámà
   elephant killed hunter
   'An elephant killed a hunter'

It is important to note that *-r-* in these examples is not a marker of person but rather a marker of number. Compare the following examples which illustrate the role of the morpheme *-r-*:

5. tsà-kù-r-tsé ɗà-kú-r-ɗè
   get up-2-Pl leave-2-Pl
   'You (pl) got up and left'

6. tsá-r-tsè ɗá-r-ɗè
   'They got up and left'

7. tsá-tsè ɗá-ɗɗè
   'He got up and left'

As the examples given above indicate, the infix *-r-* has nominative accusative characteristics, for its occurrence is determined by either the agent of a transitive verb or the subject of an intransitive verb. It is not affected in any way by the patient of a transitive verb.

3.2. Reduplication of the verb

Reduplication to mark plurality differs in several important respects from reduplication to mark the perfective, mentioned earlier in the paper. The most important characteristic of reduplication to mark plurality is the fact that it cannot be applied to every verb while reduplication to form the perfective is a very productive device, and appears to have no constraints as the the type of verb to which it can apply. As has been mentioned earlier, the reduplicated form indicating plurality serves as the base for the formation of the perfective form.

In sentences with intransitive verbs the reduplicated plural stem was given as an alternative form of the non-reduplicated stem. In each case reduplication occurred concurrently with the plural infix *-r-*, e.g.:

8. wúrà ɗá-ɗɗè
    man go-Perf
    'A man went away'

9a. wùrá-xà ɗá-r-ɗè
    'Men went away'

 b. wùrá-xà ɗàɗɗà-rɔ́-ɗáɗɗè
    'Men went away'

10. wùrá ŋáŋè
    'A man has run away'

11. wùrá-xà ŋàŋá-r-ŋàŋé
    'Men have run away'

There are also a few examples of the use of reduplication to mark plurality with transitive verbs:

12. wá-wà   gígálè
    shoot-Perf   rat
    'He/she shot a rat'

13. wá-rú-wà gígálè
    'They shot a rat'

14. wáwà-wáwà gìgálà-xà
    'He/she shot rats'

15. wàwá-r-wàwá gìgálà-xà
'They shot rats'

As examples (8)-(15) illustrate, reduplication as the marker of plurality in the perfective has ergative characteristics, for it occurs only when the argument to the verb is the plural subject of an intransitive verb, see (9b), (11), or the plural object of a transitive verb, see (14), (15). Reduplication is not affected, however, by the number of the agent of the transitive verb.

3.3. The marker /a/

This vowel marks plurality either when it is infixed after the first consonant of the verb or, alternatively, when it replaces the first vowel of the verb, e.g.:

16. gúw-à   m̀tsá-mtsà
    elephant-Def   die-Perf
    'The elephant has died'

17. gwá-xà màtsá-r-mátsà
    'The elephants died'

(The two forms for the word 'elephant' are phonological variants of *gwe* 'elephant'.)

18. ɗáugjè sá-msè
    D.   come-Perf
    'Daugje came'

19. ɗáugjè ántàrà   mùksá-nè sà-rɔ́-ms-à
    D.   with   wife-3 come-Pl-come-Pl
    'Daugje and his wife came'

Note that in (19) *-a* is a suffix to the verb rather than an infix. I do not have examples of the use of the vowel *-a-* as a plural marker with transitive verbs. The only example which I

have and which perhaps would be considered in this place involves suffix -*xa*. Compare
the following examples:

20. ca-r-cə   nəg nafa
     cut-Pl-Perf Dem tree
     'They cut this tree'

21. cá- xá- rà-   cá- xà náfà-xà ɓàɗámmè
     cut-Pl 3pl   cut-Pl tree-Pl   all
     'They cut all trees'

The reason the morpheme spelled -*xa* was taken into consideration in the discussion of -*a* is
the fact that -*x*- may be an epenthetic consonant inserted in the environment V ___ *a*. I include the examples (20) and (21) above very provisionally since the description of Mandara
is not yet available. Note, however, that even if the proposed analysis is later shown to be
incorrect, the form of the verbal plural will be identical with the form of the nominal plural
suffix -*xa*. If the proposed analysis is shown to be correct, again the form of the verbal
plural will be identical with the form of the nominal plural which then could be analyzed as
consisting of the vowel -*a*. Phonological identity of plural markers in verbs and nouns is a
very frequent phenomenon in Chadic languages (cf Frajzyngier 1977, Wolff 1977).

The following facts emerge from the discussion of plural markers -*a* and -*xa*: -*a* marks
the plurality of the subject of an intransitive verb and -*xa* marks the plurality of the patient
of a transitive verb. Neither of the markers is dependent on the agent of a transitive verb.

4. Plural forms in non-perfective paradigm

The non-perfective paradigm includes a number of tense and aspect categories, all of them
marked by various forms of subject pronouns which precede the verb. These pronouns
indicate either the subject of an intransitive verb or the agent of the transitive verb. The
system of subject pronouns is therefore nominative-accusative. The common forms of the
plural subject pronouns are as follows:

1 incl.	ma-
excl.	kwa-
2	kura-
3	ta-

But once again, as was the case in the perfective paradigm, the verb may be additionally marked for the category plural. Consider first intransitive constructions:

22. gwe   a   də mətsa
    elephant 3sg Fut die
    'An elephant will die'

23. gwa-xa ta   də matsa
    el.-Pl 3pl Fut die-Pl
    'Elephants will die'

As an example of the plural marker in transitive constructions I will provide paradigms of the verb 'to shoot' followed first by a singular object and them by a plural object. The aspect is 'progressive'. I have obtained it as a translation of the Hausa progressive aspect formed with -na:

	'shoot a rat'	'shoot rats'
1sg	ya-wwi gigale	ya-wwu gigala-xa
2sg	ka-wwu gigale	ka-wwa gigala-xa
3sg	a-wwu gigale	a-wwa gigala-xa
1pl incl.	ma-wwu gigale	ma-wwa gigala-xa
excl.	kwa-wwu gigale	kwa-wwa gigala-xa
2pl	kura-wwu gigale	kura-wwa gigala-xa
3pl	ta-wwu gigale	tra-wwa gigala-xa

The above paradigm indicates that there is a difference in the verbal form depending on whether the object of the verb is singular or plural. Moreover, when the verb is followed by a plural object the former ends in the vowel -a in all persons except first person singular when it ends in -u. Note, however, that even in the first singular there is a difference in the form of the verb depending on the number of the object. I have no explanation for the different forms of third person plural subject pronouns.

From the examples given above it is clear that -a- forms a part of an ergative system, for it occurs only when the subject of an intransitive or the object of a transitive verb is plural.

5. Historical explanation

Theoretically, there are only four possibilities for the reconstruction of a Proto-Mandara system:

(i) Proto-Mandara had only the nominative-accusative system and the contemporary instances of the ergative system constitute an innovation in the language.

(ii) Proto-Mandara had an ergative system of plural agreement and the existing nominative-accusative paradigms are innovations in the language.

(iii) Proto-Mandara had both nominative-accusative and ergative systems.

(iv) Proto-Mandara did not have either of the systems.

Since the discussion of (iv) cannot be substantiated by any available data it will not be pursued in this paper. In the discussion of possibilities (i), (ii), and (iii) I will consider morphological and syntactic devices involved in both systems. Whenever possible, both comparative data and internal reconstruction will be used. The discussion will start with the nominative-accusative system.

5.1. /-r/ as the nominative-accusative marker of plurality

5.1.1. Internal reconstruction

This marker is used only in one aspectual form, viz. 'perfective'. It is, however, also a marker of plurality of direct object pronouns. In fact, direct object pronouns cannot be phonologically distinguished form subject pronouns in the perfective. The only difference between them consists in the syntactic position in which they occur, viz. object pronouns are suffixed to the verb while subject pronouns are infixed. But, interestingly, the subject pronouns are infixed in between the reduplicated parts of the verb, so that in fact even the subject pronouns are suffixed to the verb, and then followed by the verb again. The set of subject prefixes presented in 4. shows -r- in the second person plural but not in the first or third person. This may indicate that -r- has been lost in other persons or that the second person marker has acquired it. If one accepts the second hypothesis, then internal reconstruction would strongly point to the possibility that the subject infixes were identical with object suffixes, and subject prefixes have been derived from the set of subject pronouns in Chadic (see Frajzyngier, 1982).

5.1.2. Comparative data

In closely related Cibak subject prefixes have -r- as the marker of plurality, e.g. *yar* 'first person plural', *dar* 'third person plural'. But again, as in Mandara, these forms are identical with the object suffixes.

Thus -r- as the plural marker cannot be an innovation in Mandara and must be a retention from an earlier system. It may even be a reflex of the plural marking morpheme -n- (cf. Frajzyngier 1977 and Newman and Ma 1966 for phonological justification for such reconstruction).

5.2. Subject prefixes
5.2.1. Internal reconstruction

One of the ways to investigate the history of subject prefixes through the method of internal reconstruction is to find out whether Proto-Mandara had subject prefixes or not. Since there is at least one verbal form, perfective, in which the subject pronouns are, in a way, suffixed to the verb, such an investigation is fully warranted. However, unlike independent pronouns in other Chadic languages (cf. Gouffé 1978), subject prefixes in Mandara do not bear markers that would enable us to reach a conclusion about their diachronic status in the language. The distribution of -r- in subject prefixes discussed above could, however, be considered an indication of their relatively recent emergence.

5.2.2. Comparative data

In many languages from the Biu-Mandara branch the suffixed paradigm is much more extensive than in Mandara. If one accepts the conclusion in Frajzyngier 1983 that the Proto-Chadic word order was VSO, and that the order of pronominal elements occurring with the verb was also VSO, then one could conclude that the subject prefixes in Mandara constitute an innovation. Such a conclusion, however, could not be used further in comparative research for it has been obtained through comparative data. (For an earlier discussion of the relationship between subject and object pronouns, mainly in Hausa, see Newman and Schuh 1974).

5.3. Reduplication
5.3.1. Internal reconstruction

Reduplication to mark plurality is used extensively in Mandara in adjectives in the predicative function. It can be reduplication either of the whole adjective or only of a part of it. Compare the following examples with the instances of reduplication given earlier in the paper:

24. ànnà bɔ̀lsɔ́-nà gyákkè
    Dem horse-Def large
    'This horse is large'

25. ànnà bɔ̀lsá-xà gyàk-gyákkè
    'These horses are large'

26. ágzàrá-ŋà cúcúkwà
    child-2sg small/Pl (cukwa 'small' Sg)
    'Your children are small'

5.3.2. Comparative data

Reduplication is one of the most widespread devices for marking plurality in Chadic and in Afroasiatic languages (cf. Frajzyngier 1977, 1979). Moreover, whenever it marks plurality in other languages it is most often plurality of action, plurality of the subject of an intransitive verb, the object of a transitive, verb but very seldom plurality of agent, i.e. of the subject of a transitive verb.

Thus, both internal reconstruction and comparative data indicate that the form and the function of reduplication constitute a retention in Mandara rather than an innovation.

5.4. The marker /a/

5.4.1. Internal reconstruction

The morpheme *a* occurs as the marker of the plurality of a subject of an intransitive verb in the perfective paradigm. It occurs as the marker of the plurality of both the subject of an intransitive and the object of a transitive verb in the non-perfective paradigms. If further study shows a connection between -*a* and -*xa* then there is also a related morpheme marking the plural in the nominal system. But even if such a connection is not found to be valid, nevertheless the distribution of *a* as either suffix or infix indicates that it is not an innovation but rather a retention from a once much more widespread system. Fluckiger states (p.c.) that *a* also marks plurality of action.

5.4.2. Comparative data

The morpheme *a* is another very widespread device to mark plurality in Chadic (cf. Frajzyngier 1977, and this volume). It occurs as an infix in three of the four branches of Chadic where it indicates plurality of both nouns and verbs. There is no doubt that in Mandara it constitutes a retention from an earlier system.

6. Conclusions

The present study has shown that two plural markers in Mandara, reduplication and infix-
ing or suffixing of *a*, have ergative characteristics. Moreover, the study has shown that
both markers constitute a retention from an earlier system. Comparative evidence indicates
that these two markers were already present in Proto-Chadic. Data from Mandara provide
an argument for the function of these two markers in proto-Chadic. Unless Mandara has
innovated in the function of the two markers, a possibility for which there is no evidence,
then their present function, as a retention from an earlier system, provides the evidence that
the function of reduplication and -*a*- in Proto-Chadic was to indicate plurality of the subject
of an intransitive verb, of the object of a transitive verb, and most certainly just plurality of
action (although the evidence for this was not provided in this paper). It is also very significant that there is absolutely no connection in Mandara between the occurrence of the two
devices and the plurality of the agent of a transitive verb. The data in Mandara thus provide
important evidence for the presence of ergative characteristics in Proto-Chadic.

An interesting fact about Mandara is the separation of the two systems by means of different grammatical devices. Thus the nominative-accusative system is realized through
subject prefixes and infixes while the ergative system is realized through reduplication and
the vowel -*a*-. It appears that in most Chadic languages such a separation of function does
not exist. Whether this characteristic is an innovation in Mandara or a retention from an
earlier system remains to be investigated.

Postscript

A subsequent work on Mandara, this time on the dialect of Mora, has revealed that the there
exist pairs of transitive verbs differing in number. The plural counterpart in such pairs
encodes plurality of object rather than plurality of agent, e.g.: *ìcá* 'slaughter, sg.' *ɗàtsà*
'slaughter, pl.'

27.   è-yc-ta   hlá
       3SG-slaughter.SG-PAST cow
       'he slaughtered a cow'

28.   à-ɗátsə̀-ta   hlá
       3SG-slaughter.PL-PAST cow
       'he slaughtered cows'

Footnotes

[1] Most of the data in the present paper were gathered during the Summer of 1981 in Maiduguri, Nigeria, as part of a larger project entitled 'Reconstruction of the Syntax of Simple Sentences in Proto-Chadic'. The work on the project was supported by a grant from the National Endowment for the Humanities. The trip to Nigeria was also supported by a grant from the Council on Research and Creative Work, University of Colorado. My language assistant was Mr. Philip N. Bugar, of Pulka, born in 1951. I would like to thank him for the patience and enthusiasm with which he worked. I would also like to thank Cheryl Fluckiger for answering my questionnaire and for making available some of the 'Mandara Pedagogical Grammar Notes'. I would also like to thank Paul Newman for many useful suggestions, and in particular for drawing my attention to the possibility that morpheme -r- may be related to -n-.

2 The following works on Mandara were consulted: Mirt 1969, 1970/71, Eguchi 1969, Whaley and Fluckiger 1980.

3 Since no phonological analysis of Mandara is available yet, the data are presented in a broad phonetic transcription. The following are the only special symbols I use:

       ə   high, back, unrounded vowel
       x   velar, voiceless fricative
       ɓ, ɗ   glottalized labial and alveolar affricates
       ts, dz voiceless and voiced alveolar affricates
       c, j   voiceless and voiced palatal affricates

MARKING SYNTACTIC RELATIONS IN PROTO-CHADIC

1. Introduction

In comparative studies of Chadic languages there is a gap in the fundamental area of syntax, viz., there are no attempts to describe how syntactic relations were marked in Proto-Chadic (PC). The purpose of the present paper is to provide an answer to this question.[1] This paper deals only with the distinction between subject and object, the term 'subject' designating either the subject of an intransitive or transitive verb. For transitive verbs, the term 'subject' always stands for the argument with the semantic role Agent.

The term PC is used here to indicate the product of reconstruction from the data available from contemporary languages. It is the stage directly preceding the split into the contemporary groups. By no means does this term designate the oldest possible form of PC.

The data for this study were taken from some 60 languages representing all four branches of Chadic as postulated in Newman's 1977 classification. The conclusions of this study would not be affected if one were to accept Jungraithmayr's 1978 classification (see Caprile and Jungraithmayr 1978) in which the Chadic languages are divided into three rather than four branches.

Some of the most widely used devices for marking syntactic relations in languages are: nominal inflection, pre- or post-positions, word order, and appropriate coding on the verb. Since the nominal inflection does not exist in Chadic, only the last three devices must be considered as possible retentions from PC. The rest of this paper will examine each of these devices in turn. For each, I will discuss its possible form, function, the change that he device has undergone, and some of the effects it might have had on other aspects of anguage structure.

2. Marking of syntactic relations on verbs

In some Chadic languages the verb stem, i.e. the root with its various tense and or aspect affixes, may also have markers whose occurrence is linked to the syntactic relation or semantic role of the following argument. This phenomenon will be illustrated with examples from Hausa without, however, any implication that other Chadic languages, when marking the syntactic relations on the verb, employ the same devices. In Hausa, when a Grade II verb is followed by a nominal object it is marked by the vowel -*i*.[2] When a Grade II verb is followed by a pronominal object it is marked by the long vowel -*ee*. When there is no direct object following the verb the final vowel of the verb is -*aa*, e.g.:

1. Awdu yaa sàyi dookìi
   'Audu bought a horse'

2. Awdu yaa sàyee shi
   'Audu bought it'

3. dookìn da ya sàyaa, faRii nèe
   'the horse that he bought is white' (Zima 1972:25, the transcription and translation as in the source):

What is interesting about these forms in Hausa is the fact that there is no functional explanation for the existence of the three markers. The identity of the morpheme following the verb is never in doubt and, in fact, Grade II is the only form that has this alternation. Other verbs do not change the final vowel when followed by a nominal object.

Chart 1 represents the distribution in Chadic of those verbal markings whose presence or absence depends on the nature of the argument following the verb. It also summarizes the occurrence of prepositions which will be described later.

CHART 1[3]

Morphological markers of syntactic relations

Language	Verbal Marker	Preposition
Hausa	Grade II verbs -*i* nom., -*ee* pron.	
Galambu	Vowel and tone changes before nominal D.O.	
Gera	Tonal changes before pronominal and some some nominal D.O.	
Kirfi	Perfective -*ko* ---> -*ki* and -*wo* ---> -*wu* before nominal D.O.	
Fyer	-*a* before nom.. D.O. (one class of verbs)	
Kulere		*ti* with some verbs *t* pronominal
Tera		*t* before some pron. D.O.
Glavda		*ka* and *ks* before nomin/pron.
Dghwcdc	Tonal changes on verb.	
Gisiga		*a* before pron. D.O.
Bachama	Tonal changes on verb	
Gude		*tə* before D.O., -*nə* before Subject.
Lamang		*ta*
Logone	Vowel change a --> e / __ nom., a --> i / __ nom./pron. obj.	
Dangla	In punctual perfect *a* class of verbs changes tone before object.	
Mokulu	Tonal change {H, F} --> L / __ nom. obj.	

Note that in most languages, as in Hausa, there is no functional justification for the occurrence of markers encoding the lexical category of the following argument. There is a notable exception, however, and that is Dghwede, where both subject and object can follow the verb. The distinction between the two is marked by tone alone. A low tone on the last syllable of the verb indicates that the following argument is subject, e.g.:

4. ´ à wàyə̀dù̀ dádà
   'the father rejected it'

5. ´ à wàyə̀dú dádà
   'he rejected the father' (Examples and analysis from Frick 1978:10).

The presence of markers of this type on the verb in languages from different branches of Chadic indicates that similar markers must have been involved in marking the syntactic relation of an argument with the verb in PC. The exact function of this device in PC cannot be described on the basis of synchronic descriptions for particular languages, for in most of them, as in Hausa, there is no functional load attached to the verbal markings.

It is not possible to reconstruct a single phonological form of the verbal marker, for at least two devices must have been involved: one, tonal changes on the verb and the other, vocalic changes. For neither of these devices does the amount of material available allow the reconstruction of its form with any degree of confidence.

3. Use of prepositions to indicate the role of arguments

As Chart 1 indicates, there are two prepositions that are involved in marking syntactic relations: one is *ks-* or *ka-;* it occurs only in Glavda, and therefore may be considered an innovation in this language. The other is a preposition which, for the time being, will be designated as *tV-*, for the nature of the final vowel has not yet been determined. The use of this preposition before pronominal arguments has been described in Frajzyngier 1982. It was shown there that in many of the languages involved the use of a preposition in marking the pronominal direct object is redundant and cannot be functionally justified by synchronic analysis. There are also languages in which the use of a preposition to mark the nominal direct object is redundant. One such language is Fyer, from the West Chadic branch. Certain verbs require that a nominal (as well as a pronominal) direct object be introduced by the preposition *ti*, e.g.:

6. yáà hénìn ti ló
   'I refused/declined the meat'

There is another class of verbs that introduces the nominal object with the particle *a*, which may be suffixed to the verb (examples and explanation from Jungraithmayr 1970:51, 73ff.):

7. mí ɗi-a ɓarès

'he saw his young one'

Some of the verbs that have the object marked by *a* are verbs meaning 'to see', 'surpass', 'give', 'catch', 'say', and 'hear'.

Again, as in the case of Hausa grade II verbs, there is no functional justification for these markers, since the role of the following noun is never in doubt.

In Lamang and Gude, however, the D.O. markers have a syntactic function, being the only markers of the nominal arguments. In Lamang (E. Wolff, p.c.) the preposition is used whenever there are no other means to identify the function of arguments when a fronting rule, the focusing device, is applied.

On the basis of available data it appears that prepositions were not a prime device to mark syntactic relations in PC. The main argument for this conclusion is the fact that the preposition tV, which marks a direct object, has been shown to be derived (Frajzyngier, 1982a) from a locative preposition most probably via the function of marking dative or benefactive.

In most languages, whenever the preposition tV marks the direct object, it also marks the dative/benefactive. The opposite, however, is not the case. There are many languages in which the dative/benefactive is marked by the preposition tV, but the direct object is not. Moreover, even in languages in which the direct object is marked by the preposition tV, this marking is a non-systematic device. For example, in Fyer, whether or not the direct object is marked by a preposition seems to depend on some as yet unspecified features of individual verbs. Similarly, in Tera, direct object pronouns are only sometimes marked by a preposition. In all Chadic languages the locative and dative, however, are always marked by prepositions (with the exception of certain verbs which take dative as their unmarked argument, such as the verb 'to give', and with the exception of nouns which have the inherent feature of locative). Thus, while the direct object in only exceptionally marked by a preposition, the benefactive/dative and locative are only exceptionally not marked by a preposition. These facts indicate the existence of the functional change by which the marker of locative became the marker of dative/benefactive and, in some languages, in certain syntactic contexts only, the marker of direct object.

If *tV* in PC was primarily the marker of the locative, then it could not also have been the primary marker of direct object. Prepositions were not, therefore, the primary means of marking syntactic relations in PC. The main argument against assigning this role to prepositions remains the fact that in all contemporary Chadic languages, the use of prepositions is redundant in the neutral word order. There remains, therefore, only one possible device for indicating the role of sentential arguments in PC: word order.

4. Word order

4.1. Possibilities and the nature of evidence

There are no studies devoted to word order in PC; nor are there any studies of word order in contemporary Chadic languages which use data from all four branches. Westermann and Bryan 1952 state that most of the Chadic languages have SVO word order. Schuh (1982) discusses word order in the West Chadic branch, and there are studies of word order in particular languages, mainly, as in Schuh's work, in connection with focusing devices, such as Hoskison 1975, Jarvis 1981, and grammars too numerous to list. None of these works, however, makes any claims concerning word order in PC.

In the known Chadic languages, the main device for indicating the syntactic relations of agent and patient is word order. Most of them indicate agent by its position before the verb and patient by its position after the verb, resulting in the SVO word order. In some languages, however, the neutral word order is VSO. The term neutral refers to a sentence in which the only function of its form is to indicate the relationship between the verb and its arguments. A non-neutral word order is the one which indicates some other semantic relation, such as new versus old information, focus, topic, emphasis, etc. The term neutral is different from the term basic, for the latter may sometimes involve statistical considerations, such as frequency of occurrence. It is also different from the term underlying, which belongs to the transformational model of linguistic description.

The languages that have neutral VSO order all belong to the Biu-Mandara group of Newman's classification. They are all from the A sub-branch of this group: Ga'anda, Hona, Glavda, Guduf, Dghwede, Lamang, Gude, and Podoko. The question to be resolved is whether the neutral word order of PC was SVO or VSO. An immediate answer would be that SVO was the neutral word order in PC, and that in some languages of the Biu-Mandara group this order was changed to VSO. The justification for such an answer is the often-found argument that it is much more likely for one branch to have innovated than for two or three branches to have innovated in such a way that the product of the innovation is the same in each case. This type of argument amounts to nothing more than a weak statement of probability, given the number of branches of Chadic, three or four, depending on the classification one accepts.

This argument is not very persuasive for yet another reason. When dealing with word order, we deal with the same 'segments' (S, V, and O), and the only innovation possible is a change in the sequential ordering of these segments. Starting with the same word order in two or more languages we may find the product of independent innovation to be exactly the same, i.e., once again the two languages will have the same order, but different from the word order they used to have at some earlier stage. The possibility of having identical products of innovation increases when the change in word order is caused by the same functional considerations, such as emphasis, 'theme' vs. 'rheme' distinction, etc.

What is going to be considered as evidence in such a study is not a trivial question, for we do not have written records old enough to be of any value in the reconstruction of PC. In lieu of direct evidence, I propose the use of explanations, which provide reasons for the change from one word order to another, and which would eventually provide a reason for the existence of some of the redundant markers of syntactic relations in contemporary Chadic languages.

4.2. Arguments for SVO as the neutral word order in PC

If we accept that SVO was indeed the PC word order, we must find an explanation for the VSO order in some of the languages of the Biu-Mandara group. The first thing that comes to mind is some rule by which the subject was moved to the position immediately after the verb. Movement rules, or, alternative word orders, are known in Chadic languages, and they are almost always triggered by focusing, topicalization, or some other semantic factors, often described in the literature as 'emphasis'. In most of the Chadic languages, the alternative word order results from placing the focused, emphasized, or topicalized element in initial position. Only in a few languages is the position of emphasis other than initial. Some of these languages are: Kanakuru, Pero, Bade, Ngizim, from the West Branch, and

Musgu from the Biu-Mandara branch. A common characteristic of the focusing devices in
these languages is the position of the focused subject at the end of the sentence. Compare
the following pairs of neutral and focused sentences in Kanakuru:

8. Balau à at ɗenoi
   'Balau ate peanuts'

9. at ɗenoi Balau
   'Balau ate the peanuts' (Newman 1974:63).
   (All prepositional phrases including I.O. in Kanakuru follow the focused subject.)

In Musgu, the focused construction has virtually the same form, viz., the focused subject at the end of the sentence, e.g.:

10. à sì-ŋ-kì s áa (àtɔ́ŋ) pay
    'it is the chief who gave it to you' (pay = chief)

11. à sɔ̀-ŋ-àa sí à tɔ́ní áp-à
    'it is my father who gave it to me' (Meyer-Bahlburg 1972:195); lit., 'he gave it
    to me it is my father' (Henry Tourneux p.c.).

It thus appears that the subject occurring at the end of the sentence constitutes a part of
the clause 'it is x'. What is involved, therefore, is a periphrastic device by which the subject is introduced by a separate clause.

It is quite possible that the postposed subjects in other languages, usually introduced by
a particle, derive from phrases similar to the one exemplified in Musgu. The evolution of
the derivation of the postposed subject construction in these languages would then have the
following history (X designates subject, Y designates object):

Stage 1	Stage 2	Stage 3	Stage 4
X verb Y ------->	Pro verb Y it is X ------->	Pro verb Y X ------>	verb Y X

One cannot postulate this derivation as anything more than a hypothesis because the
crucial stage 2 is attested only in Musgu. The change from stage 3 to stage 4 would have

occurred as the result of a reanalysis of the function of the phrase 'it is' from copula to marker of a focused subject. Note, however, that Harries-Delisle 1978 claims that all emphatic clauses derive from equational sentences.

In Ngizim and Bade, the postposed subject is marked by a preposition consisting of an alveolar nasal and a vowel, as in for example the Duwai dialect:

12. dɛ̀c   nə̀ Sáaku/Múusá
    come
    'Saku/Musa came' (Schuh 1982, 3.1.)

13. tlə́rmə̀-g   zə̀nítìi   nə̀ níidə̀m
      tear my gown   wood
    'wood will tear my gown'

This preposition has been replaced in some dialects by other markers, but Schuh reconstructs it as the focused subject marker for Proto-Bade-Ngizim.

In Pero, the focused subject occurs at the end of the sentence and, if it is nominal, it is preceded by the particle *nin*. Pronominal focused subjects are also postposed, but they are not preceded by any particle.

Schuh 1982 claims that subject postposing must have been a Proto-West Chadic focusing device, since the two subbranches that have it, Bole-Tangale and Bade, are very distant from each other, and therefore could not have developed the same word order independently. This reasoning suffers from the methodological error discussed in 4.1. There is no reason why several languages with the same word order could not undergo the same change, resulting in an identical word order different from the original one. One could argue that focusing devices similar to those shown above for Kanakuru, Bade-Ngizim, Musgu, and Pero might have given rise to the VSO order found in some of the languages of the Biu-Mandara group. But there is a serious problem with this hypothesis. In all the languages in which focusing is achieved by postposing the subject, the focused subject always occurs after the object, never before it. Thus, accepting the hypothesis that the neutral word order in PC was SVO would imply that in some languages this word order has become VSO. The only movement rules that we have attested in contemporary SVO Chadic languages are movement toward the end of a sentence, viz., SVO --> VOS, or toward the beginning of a sentence, viz., SVO --> OSV for object focus. No language has a rule by which SVO becomes VSO.

Thus, although most Chadic languages now have SVO order, while only a few have VSO, we can find no explanation by which SVO could have become VSO. One has, therefore, to examine a statistically less likely hypothesis, viz., that the neutral word order in PC was VSO, and that it was eventually replaced by the SVO order found in the majority of contemporary languages.

4.3. Arguments for VSO as the neutral word order in PC

Again, the main argument for this word order will be the availability of an explanation of how VSO could have become SVO. We will be looking thus at a mechanism which would have moved the subject from the position following the verb into the position preceding the verb.

While it is expected that in an SVO language the focus position for the object will be the beginning of the sentence, it is not obvious that this should also be the focus position for the subject. And yet this is exactly the case for most of the languages examined (those described in 4.2. are exceptions).

The subject is usually focused by putting a particle after it. Hausa is in this respect a typical language, e.g.:

    14. nii nèe na tàfi
        'It is me who went'

    15. daanaa nèe ya kaawoo làabaarìi
        'It was my son who brought the news' (Kraft and Kraft 1973:358).

The information provided by the constituent in focus denies an assumed presupposition of the hearer and provides instead the 'correct' information, which is always new information. This conception of the focus function is not always explicitly stated in the consulted descriptions of Chadic languages. It is nevertheless supported by the translation of the examples to be found in the descriptions. Thus, in Musgu:

16. a sá-a mbày ɗà tɔ́ni
    'c'est lui qui m'a donné le manioc'

17. à yìmà ɗà àtɔ́ŋbàrú
    'c'est la variole qui l'a attrapé' (Meyer-Bahlburg 1972:195).

In most of the languages that have the VSO neutral order, subject preposing is used for subject focusing. Compare the following examples from Lamang, Gude, Ga'anda, and Hona:

18. Tuwake mbəɗəb t ogo
    'a sheep changed into a goat' (Lamang, Wolff 1980:72).
vs. neutral:
19. mbəɗəb tuwak (ta) ogo

-e is the focus marker and *ta* is the object marker whenever the identity of arguments is in doubt. The neutral sentence is a presumed form, confirmed by E. Wolff (personal communication).

Gude: In a neutral construction, the subject is marked by the preposition *ne* and the object is marked by the preposition *ta*. When the subject is focused it precedes the verb and occurs without the preposition. Compare (20a.) neutral, and (20b.) with the subject focused:

20.a. agi   bələ-nə John tə bwaya endzii
      Aspect kill   J.   leopard now
      'John is killing a leopard now'

   b. John   ci   a-bələ bwaya əndzii
             Aspect
      'John is killing a leopard now'

There is also another focusing construction in Gude, in which the subject, which is also preposed, is followed by the postposition *ne*. (Examples and analysis from Hoskison 1975:228).

Ga'anda and Hona, which belong to the same subgroup of the Biu-Mandara branch, appear to have a split system in which both word orders are allowed. Thus, in the progressive and future tenses, the neutral word order is SVO, while in the past tense, the neutral word order is VSO. Ga'anda (R. Newman 1972:69-71):

SVO

21. ngət ce   awun pukomnda sə tə   xafta
    I   shoot you rabbit   for with arrow
    'I am shooting a rabbit for you with an arrow'

22. na wat-an 'yə + i + ta kaɗə kə xeera
    Fut the fire burn me   away on hand
    'The fire will burn me on the hand'

VSO

23. tləf + incə ndə kə inda
    Perf hit I   him on head
    ' I hit him on the head'

The emphatic construction in Ga'anda differs from the neutral construction in having the emphasized element at the front of the sentence, e.g.:

24. ø xiy- incə cemscə cap ---> ngət ø   xiy-cə cemscə cap
    Aor buy I   chicken two   I Aor buy rel chicken two
    'I bought two chickens' (Analysis and examples from R. Newman 1972:131).

The focusing mechanism in Hona consists of putting the subject at the beginning of the sentence and marking it with the particle *ni*. Compare the following sentences (in broad phonetic transcription, from my field notes):

25. wúɗ   íyà   à   húkàsúɗ
    return mother Loc market
    'my mother returned to the market'

26. íyáa nì wúɗə á húkàsúɗ
    'it is my mothcr who returned to the market'

Hona also has subject fronting without any implied focus. The alternative, with fronted subject in the past tense, was given without any additional semantic interpretation. Thus, (25) had an alternative:

27. ìyà wuɗ húkàsúɗ
    'my mother returned to the market'

Compare also the following pairs cach apparently having the same meaning:

28. fànáŋ núnà   wánà
    wash my wife child
    'my wife washed my child'

29. núunà fànánd wánà
    'my wife washed my child'

30. ngwàlán pàshín-nà   tlú-díyà
    finish   fiiend mine meat-Def
    'my friend finished the meat'

31. pàshín-nà   ngwàlán tlú-díyà
    friend mine finish   meat-Def
    'my friend finished the meat'

The importance of the data from Hona rests in the fact that one may have the subject in the front of the sentence, without any additional marker and without any implication of it being in focus. Hona, thus, presents an intermediate stage between a language that has VSO order in the neutral sentence, and SVO in the focused construction, and a language in which SVO has become the neutral construction. This intermediate stage, however, is consistent with either direction of change, viz., from SVO to VSO or from VSO to SVO.

There is only one VSO language in which the reported focus position for the subject (and for all other arguments) is not sentence initial. According to Jarvis (1981), Podoko, which she analyzes as a VSO language, has two possible word orders. One is VSO, the only possible order in the tense which she calls Monologue Perfective, the tense that occurs in the narrative. The other order is VOS, and it occurs in the Dialogue Perfective and in the Imperfective. According to Jarvis, there is no possibility of focusing a constituent through a change of word order in the Monologue Perfective, i.e., the VSO order cannot be disturbed. Jarvis does not describe means for focusing a constituent in the Monologue Perfective.

In the Dialogue Perfective and in the Imperfective, the focus position is the one following the verb. Since Jarvis says that in the Dialogue Perfective and in the Imperfective the VSO order is also possible (no examples given, however) it would appear that, in many cases, there is no distinction between focused and non-focused subjects. Compare the following sentence, given as an example of a focused subject in Dialogue Perfective:

32. a təla   mala
       cook mother my
       'my mother cooked it'

The evidence that the above sentence is an example of a focused construction is provided solely by the fact that it is a response to a question:

33. A təla wa sləɓə ma
       cook who meat Int
       'who cooked the meat?'

It is important to note that the function of this 'focus' construction is radically different from that of the other 'focus' constructions described previously for other languages.

In the case of Podoko, we are dealing with the position of arguments in the answer to a question; in the case of other Chadic languages, we are dealing with contrastive emphasis. The structures are not only different in form, but also have different functions. Whatever the function of the constructions described as 'focus' in Podoko, the movement rules that are involved are VSO --> VOS resulting from the movement of object.

There are, however, in Podoko examples of the SVO word order in 'conclusion sentences at the end of paragraphs and in purpose clauses, both with a special subject pronoun', e.g. (Jarvis, 1981):

34. Ngaye təla sləɓa
         I   meat
    'and so I cooked the meat'

35. A taka yə te   sləɓə la
         I cook meat not
    'I was not cooking the meat'

It appears, therefore, that there must have been some movement rules in Podoko which
moved the subject from the position after the verb to the position preceding the verb.
Although the amount of material available on Podoko does not allow us to state what these
rules were, it appears that the data in Podoko support the hypothesis about the change from
VSO to SVO neutral word order.

When, in a VSO language, an argument is moved into the front position, there is really
no way to determine its semantic role, for both subject and object can be focused in this
way. Therefore, one would expect there to be some other means, apart from the word
order, for indicating the role of the arguments whenever the word order is disturbed. In the
consistently VSO languages, such as Lamang and Gude such markers do occur. Thus, in
Lamang and Gude, the direct object is marked by a preposition tV. In Glavda it is marked
by a preposition ka, which also marks the indirect object.

If one were to take the situation in these languages as similar to the one that occurred in
PC one would expect to find some traces of these additional markers in some presently
non-VSO languages. The redundant syntactic relations markers listed in Chart I could be
taken to constitute such traces. In particular, the widespread use of the preposition tV to
mark the direct nominal object with some verbs in Fyer, before pronominal object in a
number of West Chadic languages, such as Scha, Kulere, Fyer, and some Biu-Mandara
languages, such as Tera, is evidence of an earlier system of marking syntactic relations.
When the order was changed to SVO, the function of these markers became redundant, and
they have been preserved only as lexical characteristics of some verbs. The above is the

first explanation for the redundant markers that has been offered either for a single language or for comparative Chadic.

Tone and/or final vowel changes on the verb may be also taken to be old markers of syntactic relations markers, whose functional load became insignificant after the changes in word order were completed. There is no lack of evidence that the tonal/vowel changes in the verb were involved in marking syntactic relations. Among the present VSO languages, only Dghwede uses tone differences in verbs to mark the role of the following argument.

We thus have in most VSO languages a construction that may give rise to an SVO syntax, viz., the focusing construction. Note that in the SVO languages no construction that would have given VSO word order could be found. The presence of the SVO order in focus constructions is not, however, in itself, an explanation of why this order became the neutral word order for most Chadic languages. Although one can conclude that there must have been a reanalysis of order from 'emphatic' into 'neutral', we do not have an explanation of why such a reanalysis occurred if indeed this was the reason for the change. One such reason may be the fact that the construction occurs so frequently in the language that new generations of speakers would consider it to be basic, and hence neutral. There are no well documented cases in which the mere frequency of occurrence would have been the cause of reanalysis.

When a construction X has a semantic function Y, for it not to be interpreted as a marker of this semantic function there must be some other reason besides the mere fact that the construction occurs frequently. One such reason may be the existence of another construction in the language, formally similar to the construction X but not having the semantic function Y.

There appears to be more than one construction in Chadic languages which not only could have motivated the required reanalysis, but in itself could have caused a change from the VSO to the SVO word order. Such are the structures involved in the formation of the future tense, progressive aspect, and possibly some non-past tenses.

In more than one Chadic language the future tense is formed through the use of a form of the verb meaning 'to go'. The progressive aspect in Chadic (an non Chadic languages as well) is often formed through the use of the verb meaning 'to be', 'to sit', etc. In this type of construction the verb 'to go' or 'to be' is the main verb and whatever follows it is its complement, which is another verb, often nominalized, with or without its own complement. We have, therefore, the following structure for the future tense or progressive aspect in the VSO languages:

| verb | subject | verb | (subject) | object |

[go/be]

The second occurrence of the term subject is in parentheses, for it is not altogether clear that this subject must occur, since it already occurs after the verb 'to go'. So we already have the object following the verb in what is, semantically, the main proposition of the sentence. The verb 'to go' very soon is not perceived as a verb anymore, but rather as an auxiliary and eventually as a grammatical morpheme indicating future. And thus we have a situation in which the order of elements becomes Fut-subject-verb-object. This scenario of events involving the future tense is not inconsistent with the scenario described earlier in which the change of word order was seen to come about via the focusing process. Instead, each process reinforces the tendency toward word order change presented by the other process. The justification for the two processes contributing to the change of word order is the following: the subject in the VSO neutral word order is moved to the front of the sentence for focusing. The construction indicating the future tense also has the subject before the main verb, i.e. in the same position as in the focusing construction, and yet it does not serve a focus function. The presence of the same word order, once to indicate that the subject is in focus, and in another context, without this indication, affects the reanalysis of the word order in question from marked to the unmarked. In this way, what was a marked word order, indicating an element in focus, becomes a neutral word order.

Is there evidence that indeed the future tense was formed with the verb 'to go'? A random check of three branches of Chadic shows that in each branch there are languages whose future tense marker is etymologically related to the verb 'to go'. The best known Chadic language, Hausa, forms future with the marker za, which is agreed to be related to zoo, je 'to come, go' (cf. Newman and Schuh 1974). A similar situation exists in a number of other Chadic languages. Although it is possible that a number of Chadic languages developed the future form simultaneously through the use of the verb 'to go', that does not rule out the possibility that the same construction was also used in PC.

Chart II presents the result of a random check of individual languages to determine whether or not the verb 'to go' is used to form the future tense.

CHART II

Potential sources of the future tense

Language	Future	'go'
Hausa	zaa-	zo, je, za
Angas	met	met
	(before sentential objects only)	
Ngizim	ya	ya
Mandara	da	d-
Daba	va-ka	va
Logone	l	ul
	(sporadic)	
Musgu	ga	ga
Dangla	aa	daa?

As mentioned before, it appears that in these same languages the progressive aspect was also formed through the use of an auxiliary verb such as 'to be', 'to stay', etc. and the formation of progressive could also have contributed to change of word order, in essentially the same way as the future tense formation.

The hypotheses concerning the formation of the future tense and VSO word order in PC also contribute to the explanation of some of the unusual facts in contemporary Chadic languages. One of these is the form of the future marker in Hausa. Unlike the other tense aspect markers, the future is formed through suffixation rather than prefixation of pronouns to the tense marker. The question why this should be so has puzzled a number of Hausa scholars, and a number of interpretations of this fact have been proposed. Thus Newman and Schuh 1974 reject the Parsons 1960/61 analysis of the future tense formation through the suffixation of subject pronouns to the verb 'to go'. They also reject Gouffé's 1967/68 analysis in which the pronouns are treated as object pronouns. Instead they propose that the unusual form of the future tense formation is due to the suffixation of Intransitive Copy Pronouns. However, in Frajzyngier 1977 it has been shown that the Intransitive Copy Pronouns are not syntactic devices devoid of semantic function. Whenever they occur, the sentence has a very specific meaning, most often indicating a sudden change of state, the beginning of an action, etc. While the ICPs occur sporadically in Hausa, and in very specific environments, Newman and Schuh would have them occurring regularly after the verb 'to go' when it serves as the marker of the future. There is no reason, at least Newman and Schuh do not give one, for which a marked construction were to be frozen and used as a future marker. Instead of this proposal by Newman and Schuh, I believe that it is simpler to consider the future tense formation as an instance of the preservation of the old word order, in which the unmarked construction consisted of the verb (in this case 'go') and the following subject pronoun. What has been frozen is not a marked construction with the Intransitive Copy Pronoun, but rather the syntax of the neutral sentence, in which the subject followed the verb.

5. Conclusions

I have attempted to reconstruct the system for differentiating between subject and object in PC. Three devices were taken into consideration: (1) the marking of syntactic relations on verbs; (2) the use of prepositions; and (3) word order. In those languages in which these devices are used, the first two are used sporadically and, in most cases, redundantly. Only word order has the non-redundant function of differentiation between the subject and the object of a transitive verb.

Two word orders used in contemporary Chadic languages: SVO and VSO, the first one being the most frequent. Two hypotheses concerning PC word order were examined: first, that the neutral word order in PC was SVO and that it eventually became VSO. The second hypothesis was that the neutral word order was VSO and that it eventually became SVO in the majority of the contemporary languages, presumably via the changes in immediate descendents from PC. In no Chadic language could a mechanism be found for effecting the change from SVO to VSO. The only alternate word order in SVO languages is VOS. With respect to the second hypothesis, there were at least two mechanisms that could bring about an SVO word order from VSO.

These mechanisms are (1) subject focusing by fronting and (2) the future tense and possibly progressive aspect construction. In the latter, the verb meaning 'to go', followed by its subject, occurs at the beginning of the sentence. The lexical meaning of the verb is eventually replaced by its grammatical function, and thus what was once the subject of the preceding verb becomes the subject of the following verb, producing the word order SVO.

In view of the fact that there is no mechanism to explain the change from SVO to VSO, and that there are at least two mechanisms to explain the change from VSO to SVO, the hypothesis that the neutral word order in PC was VSO seems to be preferable to the hypothesis that it was SVO.

The VSO hypothesis helps to explain the presence of the now redundant direct object markers in a number of contemporary languages. The VSO hypothesis also explains the unusual sequence of morphemes in the future tense formation in Hausa.

Footnotes

1 The work on this paper was supported by NEH Grant No. 000259802095, for the study of the Proto-Chadic Simple Sentence. Attendance at the Colloquium was made possible by support from the NEH grant, the University of Colorado, and the Seminar für Afrikanische Sprachen und Kulturen, Hamburg University.

I would like to thank Scott DeLancey for remarks on this paper and Michael Serwatka, Research Assistant on the Project, for help in the research and editing of this paper. I would also like to thank Daniel Barreteau, Elizabeth Jarvis, Herrmann Jungraithmayr, Michka Sachnine, Theda Schumann, Henry Tourneux, and Ekkehard Wolff who generously shared with me their knowledge of various Chadic languages by filling out a questionnaire on Chadic syntax. Elizabeth Jarvis and Russell G. Schuh have kindly provided me with pre-publication versions of their papers. I have benefited from the remarks made by participants during the discussion of this paper at the Colloquium.

None of the many people who helped in one way or another is responsible for the reasoning or conclusions contained in this paper, to say nothing about the errors of analysis. Those are my sole responsibility.

2 Analysis and terminology from Parsons 1960. For alternative analyses of the verb-final vowel in Hausa and other Chadic languages, see Newman 1975 and Frajzyngier 1983b.

3 The following are sources used for this Chart and for Chart II to follow later in the text: Hausa: Parsons 1960; Galambu, Gera, Kirfi: Schuh 1978; Fyer, Kulere: Jungraithmayr 1970; Glavda: Rapp 1966; Dghwede: Frick 1978; Gisiga: Lukas 1970; Bachama: Carnochan 1970; Gude: Hoskinson 1975; Logone: Lukas 1936; Lamang: Wolff 1980 and personal communication; Dangla: Ebobissé 1979; Angas: Burquest 1973; Ngizim: Schuh 1971; Mandara: Mirt 1969/70; Daba: Mouchet 1967; Mokulu: Lukas 1977.

ON THE INTRANSITIVE COPY PRONOUNS IN CHADIC

1. Introduction[1]

The purpose of this paper is to propose an analysis of the rules that govern the occurrence of ICPs in some Chadic languages. The specific goal of this paper is to explain the function of the ICPs in the verbal system of the Chadic languages and to show the relationship between this type of suffix and some other formatives with which it forms a system.

The term 'intransitive copy pronouns' (proposed by Newman 1971) designates pronouns suffixed to a verb, and having the same features for number, gender, and person as the subject of the sentence, as e.g. in Kanakuru:

1. Basha à ga-to məna

   enter-ICP house

   'Basha entered the house' (where -to, 3f pronoun agrees with Basha, a feminine proper name) (Newman 1974:23)

Newman (1971:189) postulates a rule which states that in certain tenses, viz. the perfective, relative perfective, subjunctive, and imperative, when the construction is intransitive, the ICP is obligatorily suffixed to the verb. This rule is retained in Newman (1974:23), and the class of intransitive sentences is specified as containing simple intransitives with motion verbs, and agentless sentences with subject having semantic role of object. Newman stresses that the notions 'transitive' and 'intransitive' apply to sentence types and not to classes of verbs. If this is so, the above rule for Kanakuru appears to add a redundant feature to sentences that are fully specified by some other means. Thus, the rule describes what happens in Kanakuru but does not explain why it happens.

In Pero, a related language belonging to the same branch of Chadic, the ICPs occur as well. But the rule that Newman has postulated for Kanakuru is not valid for Pero; specifically, Pero verbs of motion do not require an ICP, e.g.:

2. mákúl-kò
   wander about-Perf
   'he has wandered about'
   but not *mákkùl-k-ee-nì
                     Perf. ICP

3. nì-cúg-ínà
   1Sg- fall down-Perf.-Vent.
   'I have fallen down'
   but not *nì-cúg-ín-ee-nò
                     ICP

Sentences with motion verbs are not the only intransitive construction in which the ICPs do not occur, e.g.:

4. nì-cín-kò
   1Sg-sleep-Perf.
   'I slept'

Thus, in Pero an intransitive construction does not automatically require an ICP suffix.

2. Analysis of the ICPs in Pero
2.1. ICP with intransitive verb

From the data collected, it appears that the ICPs in Pero (as in Kanakuru) occur only when the sentence consists of V and a single NP (locative, time, and instrumental NPs are not taken into consideration). The above it constitutes the first condition for the occurrence of an ICP suffix in Pero. All the examples in this section will serve to illustrate this point.

2.2. No ICP with objective

If an inherently transitive verb, i.e. one whose syntactic frame is [A,O], occurs with object only, the second condition for the occurrence of an ICP is met, e.g.:

5.a. péngúrò   'get something back, retrieve something'
  b. pìngìr-g-ée-nì
        Perf. ICP

6.a. nì   ɓélò-kò   jírè   vúró-ì
    1s break-Perf. branch tree-Def.
    'I broke the branch off the tree'

  b. jók   ɓél-k-ée-tò
    chair   Perf.-ICP(3f)
    'The chair got broken'

7.a. túkkò jándè
    hide yam
    'Hide the yam'

  b. tuk-t-ée-ji
    hide-Vent. ICP(2f)
    'Hide yourself'

However, not all sentences that are intransitive and contain an inherently transitive verb require an ICP. Consider the following examples, all with a transitive verb and only one argument:

8. dúè ìv-áanì
    bird catch-Stat.
    'The bird is caught'

9. mín-ì   wúll-ánì
   beer-Def. brew-Stat.
   'The beer is brewed'

In the above examples, the verbs have to be interpreted as stative. The following is there-fore postulated as the third necessary condition for the suffixation of ICPs in Pero.

2.3. ICP with change of state and inchoative meaning

The ICPs in Pero indicate a change of state. They never occur in stative sentences such as (8) and (9). The difference between sentences (10) and (11) is the one between a stative and inchoative meaning.

10. yé   dígè ícc-aánì
    inside pot dry-Stat.
    'The pot is dry'

11. yé-dígè íccé-k-ée-tò
                  Perf. ICP(3f)
    'The pot dried'

12. nì-tà-íccò dígè
    [ǹdèéccò dígè]
    'I will dry the pot'

If the verb is inherently stative, then by adding an ICP suffix, one obtains the meaning of entering the state, i.e. it has an inchoative meaning. An example of this distinction in English may be the pair 'to be seated' and 'sit down'. The following is an example from Pero:

13. ni-d-ínà   tù gbandum
       Perf. Loc.   (no ICP)
    'I lived in Gwandum'

14. ní-dí-jï   tù gbandum
     Cont.   (no ICP)
  'I live in Gwandum'

15. nì-wàn -nà   fílíà nì-nd-ée-nù
     come Perf.   1s Conj ICP
    'I came to Filiya and settled'

2.4. The stative suffix -ánì

Sentences (8)-(10) illustrate one of the functions of this suffix, which can be described as adding the stative meaning to the non-stative verbs. The meaning of this type of sentence is 'X is in the state of Y', where Y consists of the semantic components of the verb. A few more examples of this type of sentence are given:

16. yá ɓwè núɗɗ-ánì
    inside gruel stirr-Stat
    'the gruel is stirred'

17. yá kú-nò kpákàl-ánì
    inside head-1Sg bald-Stat
    'my head is bald'

18. ló   ní-ánì
    meat cook
    'the meat is cooked'

There are a few other functions of this suffix in Pero, some of them related to its stative meaning, but they do not have a bearing on the system which is described in this paper.

2.5. 'Causative' suffix -*n*

If the unmarked frame of the verb consists of an affected argument only, then, if the verb has to occur in the syntactic frame [A,O], a morpheme -*n* 'causative' is suffixed to the verb and the object of the verb may be introduced by the preposition *ka*, e.g.:

> 19. cékkú-tò-n   dóè
>   be lost-Pl-Caus   everything
>   'lose everything'

> cf. kúrbè tà jígú-tù
>   money Fut be lost-Vent
>   'the money will be lost'

> 20.a. íllό-n   kà   né
>   get up   with   1Sg
>   'get me up'

> b. pétò-kò-n   bírà
>   go out-Perf-Caus   out
>   'he took it out'

> cf.   pétò-kò bírà
>   'he went out'

The 'causative' suffix has some other functions in Pero but they do not pertain to the system under consideration.

2.6. Summary of the system in Pero

It appears that the crucial information for the operation of the ICP suffixes as well as the stative and the causative suffixes in Pero is the inherent semantic and syntactic properties of verbs. Among the syntactic properties, the only important information is whether the verb occurs with one argument or with two arguments, V (NP, NP). The only semantic information that is important is whether the verb is inherently stative or not. Thus, one can postulate the following types of verbs in Pero:

Type	I	II	III
Stative	+	-	-
V (NP)	+	+	-
V (NP, NP)	-	-	+

Note that if a verb is [+ stative] it will be [+ V (NP)]. Some examples to illustrate various types of verbs:

Type I:	cékò	'be lost'
	dì	'be seated'
	cínà	'sleep'
	cétò	'stand'
Type II:	ámbò	'climb'
	pétò	'go out'
	wátù	'go, walk'
	wállò	'wander about'
Type III:	vúndò	'cook'
	pílù	'sell'
	cúbù	'show'

The use of any of the above verbs in the syntactic frame different from its inherent frame or in the semantic frame different for the inherent value of the feature stative requires addition of a suffix. Thus, a verb of type I, used in the semantic frame of type II will require addition of an ICP. If the verb is of type II, its use in the syntactic frame of type III will require an addition of the suffix -n. The same rule operates when a verb of type I has to occur in the syntactic frame of type III. If the verb of type III has to occur in the frame of type I, the suffix -ani is added. It appears that Pero, cannot have a verb of type II occur in the frame of type I. Thus, the pair 'to go' and 'gone' does not have an equivalent in Pero.

There are several verbs in Pero that appear to have the property of belonging to more than one type, and it appears that because of this, speakers sometimes apply to them the rules outlined above and sometimes not. The following is an example of such verbs: *íccò* 'to dry' was said to belong to type III (cf. sentences 10-12). However, there are sentences that indicate that this verb may be treated as belonging to type II, e.g.:

> 22. dígè íccò-kò
>   pot   dry-Perf
>   'the pot dried' (no ICP, no stative suffix)

Interestingly, along with two different syntactic classifications goes a semantic distinction. Sentences (10)-(12) indicate a pot which had had water in it, while (22) indicates a freshly made clay pot.

3.   Analysis of other Chadic languages[2]

The following analysis has a twofold purpose: it aims to find out whether the system proposed for Pero has equivalents in other Chadic languages, and second, to determine the functions of the ICPs in other languages. The data are from some twenty languages from the West, Biu-Mandara, and East Branches of Chadic, arranged according to the Newman's classification of (1977). My conclusions have to be treated as very tentative for several reasons. First, I did not have adequate data for the languages from the East Branch, and none for Masa, which Newman (1977) considers to be the fourth branch of Chadic. Second, sources for other languages, excellent otherwise, were sometimes not very helpful as far as the ICPs are concerned. Several writers admitted that they did not understand the meaning and function of the ICPs, or stated that the use of the ICPs is redundant.

3.1. West Branch, Subbranch A

Hausa

Hausa preserves only traces of the ICPs, used only with the verbs *je* 'go' and *zo* and *ya* 'come' (cf. Newman 1971:194). Newman claims that "at a not too distant period in the past, Hausa intransitives in Aux 1 were regularly and systematically marked by a fully operative icp agreement system." I will return to this hypothesis later in this paper. For the time being, it is important to find out which verbal forms have taken over the function or functions that used to be indicated by ICPs. The reason for seeking an answer to this question is not only the fact that there are some traces of the ICPs, but also the fact that Hausa has the other elements of the system described earlier in this paper. Thus, it has a causative suffix *-as* (grade V in Parsons' classification), which, among other functions, changes an inherently intransitive verb into a transitive. There are at least three forms available in Hausa to indicate stative: one of them is the verbal form ending in *-u* (Parsons' grade VII), e.g. *tàarú* 'collect, assemble', *jèerú* 'line up', *ràbú* 'part', etc. (Parsons 1960/61:25). Another is the use of so-called participial forms of the type *dàfáffée* 'cooked' as predicates and finally the use of deverbal stative nouns (Parsons' VANS) as in the following sentence:

23. sú   nàa   kàamé   dà   ɓàràay
    they Prog. arrest   Assoc. thieves
    'they have the thieves under arrest' (Parsons 1961:121)

It seems that the prime candidate to complete the system is the verbal form ending in *-a* and having the tonal structure for the disyllabic verb [LH] (Parsons' grade III). A perusal of the grade III forms in Parsons (1960/61) and Parsons (1971/72) did not turn up a verb in this grade that would have stative meaning.

Kanakuru

The main function of the ICPs in Kanakuru appears to be that of changing inherently transitive verbs into intransitive verbs. Compare the following examples:

24. nà por panda
    'I took out the mat'

25. nà poro-no
    'I went out'

But since the ICPs have to be added to all intransitive constructions, they cannot be analyzed as intransitivizing suffixes only. Thus, all the intransitive verbs of motion have this suffix, e.g.:

26. à do-to
    'she came'

When such a verb is used in a transitive construction, the ICP is retained, e.g.:

27. à do-to-nu
    'she brought it'

The stative in Kanakuru is formed by the suffixation to the verb stem of the nominalizing suffix -*ma* and a pronoun which differs from the ICP, e.g.:

28. wo-nàa til-mo-nò u
    'I am not burnt'

29. shìjì jaŋ-ŋa-jì
    'you (f) are cured'

Newman (1974:34) provides several arguments for not equating ICPs with the pronoun set occurring in stative constructions. Although I am not going to deal with this problem in this paper, it should be noted that the phenomenon of suffixing the pronouns to the adjectives is frequent. It occurs in at least two branches of Chadic, having been noted in Ngizim, Margi, and Kapsiki, to mention just a few languages.

Bolanci
In Bolanci a structure of the form V + *jii* ('body') + possessive pronoun changes a transitive verb into an intransitive, e.g.:

30. ɓól-áa-jìi-nì
    'it will break'

Lukas (1971:12) has noted that the same type of construction is used with intransitive verbs, and he considers the ICPs in this usage to be redundant, e.g.:

31. pet-è-jii-tò
    'she went out'[3]

Bolanci has another construction in which an inherently transitive verb occurs with only one NP, e.g.:

32. 'ŋ-gówú-wo
    'I was hit'

33. 'ŋ-gowá
    'I will be hit'

34. 'ŋ-gówú-woo-yíi
    'I have hit it'

Lukas (1970-72:132) states that the lack of the morpheme *yíi* with transitive verbs is a marker of passive. We will come across similar constructions in other languages later on.

The stative in Bolanci is formed by suffixing possessive pronouns to the verbal noun, e.g.:

35.a. motá-ni
      'he is dead'

   b. ɓolá-ni
      'it is broken'

    c. mi"ya ganda-su
      'the people are lying down'

Bolanci has also a transitivizer -*t*-, used with inherently intransitive verbs, which apparently
is restricted to only a few verbs (Russell Schuh, personal communication).

    Unfortunately, I was not able to determine from Lukas (1970/72) and Lukas (1971) the
difference between the so-called passives of the structure NP Vtr and the intransitive constructions of the type NP Vtr + *jii* + ICP. Since Bolanci has a construction specifically
indicating stative, it would seem that the difference between NP Vtr and NP Vtr +*jii*+ ICP
cannot be the one between non-stative and stative. However, there is still another possibility. If the stative construction in Bolanci is limited to the present tense only (or, if it is
tenseless, which is a more likely situation), then the difference between the so-called passive and the stative construction will be only one of tense, i.e. the passive construction
would replace the stative in all tenses but the present. The difference between the 'passive'
and the construction with the ICP might be one between stative and non-stative. Although
the data in Lukas (1970/72) do not contradict this hypothesis, nevertheless, it should be
checked on a larger body of data.

Ron languages

In Fyer, the object suffixes are often attached to intransitive verbs, and Jungraithmayr
(1970:50) describes their function as "reflexive medial", which implies, in my understanding, an inchoative meaning.

    Bokkos has remnants of an intransitive marker -*at*, e.g. *bukàt* 'trip', *hatat* 'turn (intr.)',
sunat 'dream'. That the suffix -*at* is not productive is indicated by the fact that verbs which
have this suffix do not have counterparts without it. In monosyllabic verbs, ICPs have a
non-stative meaning. Compare the following examples (Jungraithmayr 1970:118):

    36. tì   -í   fót -a yá
        Tns.-1Sg. lose-2Sg. completely
        'I have lost you'

    37. tì-í fót-un
            1Sg
       'I hid myself'

38. tì-í fôt

   (stative)

   'I am lost'

Note that in Bokkos, as in Bolanci, the lack of any overt object marker with transitive verbs is an indicator of an intransitive construction. In the case of Bokkos, this construction has a stative meaning, judging from the examples given by Jungraithmayr [1970].

3.2. West Chadic, Subbranch B

Ngizim

Schuh (1972:28) considers ICPs as the allomorphs of the totality extension which are suffixed to intransitive verbs. So it would appear that the only thing that the ICPs in Ngizim have in common with the ICPs in languages described so far is the fact that they occur in intransitive constructions. But the primary function of ICPs in Ngizim appears to be different. However, Ngizim does have other elements of the system closely linked with ICPs in languages described so far. Thus, if verbs that are inherently intransitive (Schuh calls them "basic intransitives") are used in a transitive construction, a transitivizing suffix -náa or -dù is added.

   Stative predicates can be derived from verbs by adding a prefix dá to the verbal noun, e.g.:

39. akəraucin da-jiba

   'the thieves are caught'

Schuh (1972:80) states that statives derived from intransitive verbs may take the totality extension, i.e. ICP, e.g.:

40. ii dar'yi-gaa

   I   ICP

   'I am standing'

The usage of ICPs with such verbs as 'to stand', 'to sit', and 'to lie down' is a convincing indicator that the function of the ICPs here was not that of totality, but rather inchoative, similar to the function of ICPs in several other languages. That this function is no longer primary is indicated by the fact that ICPs are preserved in the stative construction.

Finally, verbs that are inherently transitive may either be used in intransitive constructions without any markers of intransitivity or with the ICP as in any other intransitive verb.

3.3. Biu-Mandara Branch, Subbranch A

Tera

The stative marker in Tera is -an, similar to the stative in Pero. That this is not an accidental similarity is shown by the fact that the same form that indicates stative in both languages indicates 'zero' anaphora as well, e.g.:

> 41. mban xəs-an
> 'the belly is swollen' (Stat.)

> 42. tem á yoɓt-an
> 'we are dyeing (them)' (zero anaphora)

There is an OV construction in Tera, similar to Bokkos, e.g.:

> 43.a. woy-a wá ruba
> boy   injure
> 'the boy was injured'

> b. zu-a ká zurə
> 'the meat will be fried'

Intransitive verbs in Tera may take an ICP, e.g.:

44. koro-a   wà   xa   varan   xa

    donkey-Def   Perf   sat   himself   down

    'the donkey sat himself down'

Newman (1970:49) says, "I am unclear about the semantic difference between [this] sentence and [(45)]":

45. koro-a wà xa ɣa

    'the donkey sat down'

As a possible explanation, one could postulate that the verb *xa* 'to sit' is inherently stative, and therefore the inchoative is realized by an ICP suffix. Thus, the only function of the ICP in Tera would be that of changing a stative verb into a non-stative. There is, however, an obstacle for the proposed analysis of Tera: Newman (1970:61) gives the sentence:

46. Ali xar-an ɣa

    'Ali is seated'   (Stat.)

which would at the first sight contradict the hypothesis that the verb *xa* is inherently stative. In order to resolve the problem, we would have to know if there are sentences similar to (46) in other tenses, e.g. in the past or future. If there are not, then (46) does not contradict the hypothesis. The system of grammatical relations in Tera would include the ICP to indicate inchoative and passive to indicate intransitive and stative. Stative and passive would supplement each other in the system of tenses, in which stative is not marked for any tense.

Margi

The ICPs in Margi are suffixed to the intransitive verb followed by a possessive linker. Hoffmann (1963:209) states that they are frequently suffixed to the verbs of motion. The fact that they are suffixed to the verbs meaning 'lic' and 'sit' indicates that they might have had an inchoative meaning. Compare the following example quoted by Hoffmann (1963:209) (ICPs bold)

47. dɔ́ í shádú gà lì írí mádləmà **gɔ́ndà** gà pìdà **gɔ́ndà**
'and the squirrel went in under his shelter and lay down'

The causative suffix -*ani* has, as in most other Chadic languages, two functions: one Hoffmann describes as "cause person or thing to do (the accusative verb)" and the other is clearly transitivizing, e.g.:

48. hyà   'to rise, to stand up'   hyànì   'to raise, to wake up'
    mdzù   'to spoil (intr)'   mdzànì   'to spoil (tr)'

The participle, formed through reduplication, may be used as a predicate. From the examples provided by Hoffmann (1963:165), it appears that if a verb is inherently [-stative], the participle will be [+stative], e.g.:

49. ŋwìvù   'to become thin, lean'   ŋwìŋwìvù   'emaciated, lean'
    'ùl   'to dry (intr)'   'ùl'ùl   'dried, dry'
    ŋgyù   'to burn (intr)'   ŋgyìŋgyù   'burnt'

A transitive verb may occur with only one NP, without any marker of intransitivity.

4. Summary

4.1 The functions of the ICP

There appear to be differences between the functions of the ICPs in the West and Biu-Mandara branches. In the West branch, ICPs have both intransitivizing and inchoative functions. They can be added to inherently transitive verbs, changing them into intransitive and probably inchoative, and they can be added to intransitive stative verbs, changing them into inchoative. In the Biu-Mandara branch, they can be added to intransitive verbs only, changing them into inchoative in those languages in which the system is productive.

The claim that intransitives in Hausa were at one time marked by a fully operative ICP agreement system cannot be defended in the light of the data from Pero and other languages. If Hausa had a system of ICP agreement, its function might have been either to indicate inchoative or intransitive or both, but it was not a system to mark redundantly every intransitive construction. The situation in Kanakuru seems to be unique among Chadic languages in that the ICPs are obligatorily added to the verb in every intransitive sentence.

There seems to be yet another function of ICPs in Chadic. In a number of languages from both the West and the Biu-Mandara branches, a set of pronouns is added to predicatively used adjectives. This set of pronouns differs from the ICP set if a language has one. I am not able now to say whether there is any relationship between these two phenomena.

4.2. Grammatical/semantic functions marked in Proto-Chadic

It appears that Proto-Chadic had a system to indicate the following grammatical and/or semantic functions in a sentence:

a. transitive   b. stative   c. intransitive   d. inchoative

These elements are realized by various means in different languages, but regardless of the means, one can still detect the existence of the system. ICPs realized the inchoative and the intransitive functions; stative was realized by several means including a morpheme of the form *an(V)*. Inherently intransitive verbs could be made transitive with a 'causative' morpheme which can be found in most of the present day Chadic languages.

Footnotes

1 Work on this paper has been partially supported by a grant from the Council on Research and Creative Work, University of Colorado, for the study on passives. I would like to thank David Rood and the participants in my seminar on passives for the comments they made on this paper. Special thanks are due to Russell Schuh, who read the previous version of this paper, provided important information on Bolanci and Ngizim and comments on the rest of the paper. Any errors and mistakes are my sole responsibility.

2 Sources for particular languages are mentioned in the text. I have followed the systems of transcription used in the sources cited. For Pero, I have used my own field notes.

3 Russell Schuh [p.c.] indicated that the gloss here should be 'she will go out'.

'CAUSATIVE' AND 'BENEFACTIVE' IN CHADIC

1. Introduction

In several Chadic languages a suffix is added to some verbs when they occur in a sentence containing a dative or a benefactive argument. This suffix is often analyzed or referred to as a 'benefactive' or 'dative' marker. The following example from Hausa illustrates the occurrence of the marker -s (realized as [s], [r], [d], [n] and [m]). This example and the ones to follow it are typical for other Chadic languages as well.

1. yaa zaaɓ-ar wà 'Audù dookìi
   he choose Ben horse
   'He has chosen a horse for Audu' (Gouffé 1962:192).

The same form of the verb is also used in other contexts. One of these contexts is a causative construction, meaning 'to cause X do Y', e.g.:

2. naa hawar /hau dà 'Audù dookìi.
   'I made Audu mount the horse.'

3. naa gana-d dà shii takàrda.
   'I made him see the letter' (Gouffé 1962:190)

The third context in which the marker occurs is in the transitivizing construction, e.g.:

4. 'an fita-d dà shii sàrautàa.
   'He has been turned out of office'
cf.

5. yaa fîta sàrautàa.
   'He has quitted his official position'

6. yaa tsaya-d dà mootàa
   'He stopped the car'

cf.

7. mootàa ta tsayàa
   'The car stopped'

Most of the scholars working on Hausa were implicitly assuming one underlying function for all of the cases listed above and for several other cases that will be described later in the paper. There were also some explicit statements concerning the function of the 'causative' morpheme. Parsons 1962:265 states that "with most causatives that correlate with intransitive primary grades there can be little doubt about the function, which is quite simply causative (sic!), or, as I would rather put it, putting the actor-action relationship a stage further back. . . ." Gouffé 1962 states that one of the functions of the causative form is transitivizing. The same function is postulated in Frajzyngier 1977a. Newman 1983 rejects the implied or explicit unity of function as illustrated in examples quoted above, and claims that the identity of form is a result of the merger of two different morphemes, which was made possible by some so far unexplained historical processes.

Among scholars working on other Chadic languages the fact that the same morpheme was used in the benefactive construction and in the causative construction did not elicit an explanation or even a commentary. The notable exception is Margaret Skinner 1979 who states: "Since returning from the field, I have wondered whether or not it is a mere co-incidence that the benefactive and causative markers are identical in form". She does not, however, pursue the topic any further.

In the present work I will propose a hypothesis concerning the function of the 'causative' marker. This hypothesis will explain the diverse uses of the marker in various Chadic languages. I will also postulate that such a marker was part of the grammatical system in the Proto-Chadic.

2. Hypothesis

In the grammatical system of Proto-Chadic there existed a morpheme whose function was to indicate that the verb has one more argument than it is allowed to have in its unmarked form. The argument thus added could be any of the primary arguments of the sentence, viz. agent, patient or dative/benefactive.

The role of the added argument was not marked on the verb but rather through a system of prepositions and/or word order. In particular, the hypothesis states that the 'causative' morpheme had the following sub-functions, all resulting from the main function as stated above:

2.1. Signalling that an inherently intransitive verb, i.e. a verb which occurs with one argument only in its unmarked form, has now two arguments. The formula for Proto-Chadic would be: Verb-Causative Agent Patient. For many modern languages the formula for this type of sentence is: Agent Verb-Causative Patient. This function of the 'causative' morpheme is illustrated by examples 4. and 5.

2.2. Signalling that a transitive verb, which in its unmarked form occurs with an agent and patient has now an additional agent, which causes the relationship between the unmarked agent and patient. This is the Parsons' "putting the actor-action relationship a stage further back." This sub-function is illustrated by example 2.

2.3. Signalling that although no argument is overtly specified in the sentence, there is in fact one. The 'causative' morpheme functions as an anaphoric pronoun, referring to an argument presumed to be known to the hearer. The formula for this sub-function is : Verb-Causative Agent Patient/Dative. Note that either the patient or the dative may occur, but not both.

2.4. There was a syntactic rule in Proto-Chadic which could be formulated in the following way: When a verb occurred with three rather than two arguments, and it was not an inherently three-argument verb, such as 'tell, give', etc., two syntactic possibilities existed for realizing a sentence. One possibility was that the order of constituents was: Verb Patient Benefactive. In such cases the benefactive argument was marked by a preposition. The other order was: Verb Benefactive Patient. When this order were to be realized (for whatever reasons, semantic, stylistic, or pragmatic) the verb had to have a marker of additional argument, the causative marker. The two orders with appropriate markers had the following form:

     a. Verb Patient Prep-Benefactive

     b. Verb-Causative Benefactive Patient.

3. Nature of evidence

3.1. Theoretical considerations

The evidence for the hypothesis will be based on the following theoretical assumption: To prove that a proto-language had a morpheme X with the function Y incorporating various sub-functions it is enough to show that in contemporary languages there is a morpheme which has several of the sub-functions of Y. Although it is possible that the same grammatical function emerged independently in several languages, occurrence of the same morpheme in several sub-functions in a number of languages constitutes an argument against its being an innovation and hence constitutes an argument that it is a retention from a proto-language. There is also a possibility that a given morpheme has been borrowed. Once again, however, its occurrence in several seemingly unrelated functions constitutes the evidence against its being borrowed. Note that the evidence as described above does not necessitate a phonological similarity between the morphemes involved in several languages. Phonological similarity may of course be an additional indication of the fact that morphemes in question are cognates and therefore may constitute retention of the morpheme and its functions from the proto-language. Both types of evidence will be sought in the present paper.

3.2. Choice of languages

Chadic languages are classified into either four groups (Newman 1977) or into three groups (Jungraithmayr 1978). Newman's classification will be used here. Ideally one would like to have data on languages from all four groups. Unfortunately syntactic descriptions are available for only three groups, West Chadic, Biu-Mandara, and East Chadic. There are not enough data available on syntax of languages from the Masa group.

    Data from the East Chadic group do not support the proposed hypothesis; there is simply no causative marker recorded in grammatical descriptions of these languages. However, there is a considerable amount of data from the West Chadic and Biu-Mandara branches to support the hypothesis. The question remains whether this should be considered sufficient evidence that indeed the form together with its functions constitutes a retention. Accepting the classification into three rather than four branches will make an interpretation of retention a more likely one. Accepting classification into four rather than three branches may allow for innovation in the two branches. I think, however, that the actual evidence available for the two branches together with some information available for Masa, a member of the fourth branch, will argue for retention of the morpheme and its functions from Proto-Chadic. In what follows I will provide a detailed analysis of data for some languages from the West Chadic and Biu-Mandara branches and then I will provide a chart showing the distribution of causative and benefactive markers on verbs in all branches of Chadic.

4. Analysis of data
4.1. Ga'anda

In Ga'anda, the form of indirect object pronouns is *-an-* for third person, *-u-* for second person and *-i-* for first person. The data will illustrate the role of the markers in adding various arguments. In all examples that follow the character 'ə' (shwa) stands for the central high vowel.

Addition of Agent

8. a. ə fin wata
      fire
      'The fire ignited'

   b. ə fin-án-fee wata
      someone
      'Someone ignited the fire'

9. a. ə saki lawlawat-an
      book   Def.
      'The book was lost'

b. ə saka-án-i lawlawat-an
   1sg
   'I lost the book'

The verbs in 8-9a. are inherently intransitive, i.e. they occur with one argument only without any additional markers. This argument becomes grammatical object and semantic patient in the transitive construction as represented by the b. sentences.

An agent, may, however, be added to a transitive construction and in such case we deal with a causative construction par excellence, viz. with the construction having the meaning 'cause somebody to do something', e.g.

10. a. ə rək nda nafɗa
       3pl   man
       'They chased the man away'

    b. ə rək-an-nda nafɗa
       'They had the man chased away'

11. a. sən-mən nafɗi
       'We know that man'

    b. sən-án-mən nafɗi
       'We informed that man'

12. a. ə xiy-incə pərsa
       1sg horse
       'I bought a horse'

    b. ə xiy-an-i pərsa kaɗə
       'I sold the horse'

Examples 11 and 12 represent the constructions frequent in Chadic languages in which addition of the causative marker to the verb 'to know' produces the semantic equivalent of the English 'to inform' and addition of the causative to the verb 'to buy' produces the semantic equivalent of the verb 'to sell'. Although the interpretation of similar constructions in Chadic as Causative has been put in doubt by Newman (1983) it is in fact perfectly consistent with functions of causative constructions in other languages. Quite simply, one more argument is added to the sentence.

Dative/benefactive

The terms dative and benefactive are used interchangeably in the present work for in fact no grammatical distinction exists in the languages quoted between recipient of an object (dative) and beneficiary of an action (benefactive). In the existing literature on Chadic languages, including the grammar of Ga'anda, no explanation is provided as to why there should be a dative/benefactive marker on the verb whenever there is a dative/benefactive argument in a sentence. R. Ma Newman (1971) gives the following examples of the use of -an- in the benefactive construction:

13. ə shiy-án-nda yata kutiran
        3pl food chief
    'They begged the chief for food'

14. ə mbu'-án-i yarɗa i -kutiran
    1sg tell   thief Prep-chief
    'I told on the thief for the chief'

Instead of the claim that the marker -an- in 13 and 14 represents the dative morpheme, I would like to propose that it indicates presence of one more argument apart from the one that would be expected for a given verb, or in other words, one more argument apart from the argument whose occurrence is predictable given the inherent characteristics of a verb. Thus in 14 yarda 'thief' is not a natural argument of the verb of 'saying', for it is not what has been said but rather the topic of the verb of 'saying', the object that one talks about. The evidence for this interpretation is provided by example 15, in which a verb of 'saying' is followed by the direct object:

15. ə mbu'incə ndikt'an i-kutiran
    1sg tell news Def Ben
    'I told the news for the chief'

In 15, both arguments *ndikt* 'news' and *kutiran* 'chief', are inherently natural arguments of the verb of saying.

In 13, the morpheme -*an*- could refer to either the direct object or the indirect object. Which one it is, can be determined only after one has conducted a test in which the verb 'to beg' would be tested for occurrence with each one of the arguments separately. Unfortunately, no such tests are available.

4.2. Hona

The 'causative' marker in Hona is the suffix -*n*.

Transitivizing function
    16. a. nà lúdì àxwárà
            Fut shirt dry
            'The shirt will be dry'

        b. xwárá-ŋ núnà lúdì
               wife
            'My wife dried the shirt'

        c. nà núnà àxwárà-ŋ lúdì
            'My wife will dry the shirt'

    17 a. hárnà   kə́ndə̀
           hand-1sg cure
           'My hand got well'

b. kə́nà-ŋ líkítà hárnà
    doctor
'A doctor cured my hand'

As in most Chadic languages the Hona equivalent of the verb 'to sell' is derived through the addition of the causative marker to the root meaning 'to buy' e.g.:

18 a. ni-hi bərma
     'I will buy yam'

    b. ni-heŋ bərma-ɗ
        away
      'I will sell yam'

19 a. támgà hí bə̀rmá
     'You used to buy yam'

    b. támgì hé-ŋ bə̀rmá-ɗ
      'I used to sell yam'

Hona does provide good evidence for the hypothesis that the causative marker is in fact nothing else but a device to indicate that there is an additional argument in the sentence. Compare 20 with the preceding sentences:

20. hé-ŋ kéké-ɓa
    buy   bicycle Vent
    'Buy him a bicycle'

If the function of the suffix -ŋwere to indicate causation one would expect the meaning of the verb in 20 to be 'sell'. As it is, the suffix indicates simply the presence of another argument, which is a third person pronoun. In this sentence the added argument is benefactive. But the same suffix can be used to indicate presence of a patient rather than benefactive, e.g.

21 a. tsú lábàrà
     'Tell a story'

   b. tsú-ŋ
     'Tell it'

Thus, the data from Hona clearly indicate that the function of the 'causative' marker is addition of one more argument to the number of arguments that the verb may take in its unmarked form. Marker of an additional argument is identical with the pronominal argument of the verb.

4.3. Pa'anci

In Pa'anci the 'causative' marker is -*ei*, realized as -*e* before consonant initial complements. M.Skinner 1979:133 states that this is also the marker of benefactive.

Benefactive:

22. má   kər-e Binta tin
    I+Compl steal   it
    'I stole it for Binta'

Transitivizing:

23. a. ná mba
     'He went out'

   b. ná mb-e dla
     'He took the boy out'

   c. ná mb-e tli
     'He took them out'

24. a. í zaa
   'She entered'

   b. í zei
   'She put [something] in'

25. a. má bəla
   'I returned'

   b. má bəleyi
   'I took it back'

In examples 23-25 b. and c. the function of the morpheme -e is to indicate that although the verb is inherently a one-argument verb there is an additional argument in the sentence. The function of -e in 22 is exactly the same although in this case the verb 'to steal' is inherently transitive. But the argument that follows the verb is not the direct object, which would normally be expected after this verb but rather an indirect object. Therefore, -e indicates that there will be one more argument in the sentence.

4.4. Ngizim

Two morphemes in Ngizim have the function of either adding an argument to a sentence or marking the presence of an additional argument. These morphemes are -du which occurs when there is no argument following it (hence it functions as an additional argument) and na which occurs when there is an object following it. The two morphemes are involved in the following sub-functions. (The following data organize according to various sub-functions listed at the beginning of the paper rather than according to the two markers involved.)

Transitivizing:

26 a. dee bai
     'He did not come'

   b. dee-naa am bai
      'He did not bring water'

27 a. kwaana áa kalakta
      'Kwaana will return'

   b. kwaana áa kalakta-du
      'Kwaana will return it'

In 26, we deal with an intransitive verb and the addition of the suffix -naa indicates that there is another argument present in the sentence. In 27, the verb is also intransitive and the suffix -du is the only indication of an additional argument. This role of -du is further supported by the following examples containing a benefactive argument:

28. bar-d   ii dəgəm
    give-Ben   chief
    'He gave it to the chief'

29. nàa rama-d ii-ci
                    3Sg
    'I will tell him'

30. nàa ya ná viyai-d ii-kəm
    go   2Sg
    'I will go and wash it for you'

In 28-30, -d has the anaphoric function, it refers to an argument that is not explicitly stated in the sentence but which nevertheless is part of its semantic structure. The marker d occurs, however, also when the patient and a benefactive argument are present in the sentence. Compare 31-33 with 28-30:

31. ná rauree-d ii-tu   atu
    1Sg call   Ben-3f 3f
    'I called her for her'

32. ná bar-d ii-kun dəvu
    1Sg give road
    'I have given you (pl) the means (the road)'

33. áa nii-d ii-ci kare
           Ben 3m load
    'He will take loads to him'

Note that in 31-33 the direct object follows the benefactive argument rather than the verb. I would like to postulate that the position of D.O following the I.O. is the main cause for the verb having the additional argument marker. The benefactive argument in Ngizim is marked by the preposition *ii-* and it can be added to any sentence. If, however, the benefactive argument follows the verb, a signal is inserted that there is also some other argument following. The above hypothesis concerning the occurrence of the additional argument marker is supported further by the following sentences in which the direct object follows the verb and is in turn followed by the benefactive argument: As predicted by the hypothesis, there is no causative marker.

34. à taatk(i) aci ii magəraf
            3m   visitor
    'Show him to the visitor'

35. na ram laabar ii nən
    'I told the news to the man'

36. zaata-naa aw ii Zaara
    'She pounded guinea corn for Zara'

37. Baaba dà bari wunya-gəri ii Mai Səleeman
    'then Baba gave his daughter to mai Suleman'

38. á baren daġwda ii gazgara-gaa
money   brother-1sg
'give money to my brother'

An important conclusion from the examples containing the benefactive argument can be drawn. Although sentences in which the benefactive argument occurs do have the suffix -*d*, the function of the suffix is not to indicate the presence of the benefactive argument, but rather, the presence of an additional argument, which more often than not is the direct object. According to the hypothesis presented in the present paper there should also be cases in which -*d* would signal presence of an additional argument, which could be benefactive. However, in the data presented in Schuh 1972 I could not find such examples. The suffix -*na* may also occur in sentences containing a benefactive argument. The only example I found is with an inherently intransitive verb *nii* 'to go', e.g.:

39. náa nii-naa akši ii mii -kši
3pl   mother
'I will take them to their mother'

Conclusions concerning Ngizim

The markers -*d(u)* and -*na* signal the presence of a direct object in sentences in which no direct object is overtly marked and also in sentences in which it does not follow directly after the verb. These markers indicate the presence of a direct object when the verb is inherently intransitive, for with the inherently transitive verbs there is no need to signal presence of a direct object, it being expected in a sentence because of the inherent properties of the verb.

5. The origin of the 'causative' marker

5.1. Newman's hypothesis.

In the existing literature on Chadic languages only one hypothesis has been proposed concerning the origin of the 'causative' marker, viz. hypothesis presented by Newman (at the International Colloquium on Chadic Linguistics in Hamburg, 1981, published 1983).

Newman (1983) states: "Proto-Chadic had an Efferential verbal extension *də [which] combined the two elements 'Action Away' and 'Transitivizer'. . . In some present-day languages the extension has its functions; in others the extension has shifted and expanded its semantic range in one manner or another. But, given the Efferential concept, the system in all the present-day languages can be historically related in a natural way."

The only falsifiable question in this statement is whether or not the marker of movement away and the marker of transitivizing are indeed identical or at least derived from each other. The evidence that Newman brings in support of his hypothesis does not in fact indicate that the hypothesis is correct. The evidence consists in indicating that in several languages certain verbs which have the transitivizing marker may also indicate the movement away. The choice of examples here is not very convincing. Thus for Karekare (the causative marker in this language is -tu) four verbs are given as examples of a transitivizing function (nzara 'drip', nzaratu 'pour away', dənu 'warm', dəntu 'warm up something') and two of movement away. One of those indicating the movement away is the verb dəbatu 'sell' (for which no form without the suffix -tu exists) and the other is rakatu=raku 'drive away', where the marked and unmarked forms have the same meaning. Data from other West Chadic languages Ngizim and Pa'a do not support the hypothesis proposed by Newman for they simply do not indicate movement away as the meaning of the causative suffix. The evidence from the Biu-Mandara languages consists of some examples from Gisiga, Kotoko, Kapsiki, Higi, and Bachama. Of these, the appropriate morphemes in Bachama (de) and Gisiga (de) have only a transitivizing/causative function, and hence in no way support the hypothesis about the 'motion away' being a function of the 'causative'. In addition there is no evidence that Gisiga de is morphologically the same as the 'causative' marker in the other languages, for it is not a suffix but rather a separate particle. According to Lukas 1970 the meaning of this particle is 'with', a preposition which often introduces objects of causative verbs in Chadic. Kotoko examples (only two were found) also support the transitivizing function only, viz. hal 'burn' (intransitive) vs. haldə 'burn smth'. The other example appears to have no bearing on the problem, viz. yin 'know' vs. yində 'know how, be able'. Examples from Kapsiki illustrate the use of the 'movement away' suffix -mte, which however is not a transitivizing morpheme for it can be added to inherently transitive verbs, e.g. kəle 'take (one thing)' vs. kələmte 'take away (one thing)'. The only examples that may lend some support for Newman's hypothesis are the ones quoted from Higi, such as ndal 'throw' vs. ndalna 'throw away', ngyə 'burn' (v.i.) vs. ngyəna 'burn something', dəl 'buy' vs. dəlna 'sell'.

Therefore, although ten languages are quoted as allegedly providing the evidence for Newman's hypothesis, actually only one language has the type of examples that could be considered as evidence. But evidence from one language is not enough to postulate that 'movement away' and 'transitivizing' were once two functions of the same morpheme in Proto-Chadic, because the situation in one language may represent equally well an innovation as well as retention from a proto-language. Instead of Newman's hypothesis, I would like to propose an alternative hypothesis of the origin of the causative marker.

5.2. 'Causative' and the third person pronoun

As was indicated for Ga'anda the marker of 'causative' and 'benefactive' for third person is identical with third person pronoun. Such a use of the pronoun is a natural way to add an argument, because the addition of a pronoun is in itself an addition of an argument. It is therefore necessary to examine whether the same device for addition of an argument is used in other Chadic languages. In the Chart I have included three grammatical functions that are usually described as separate morphemes in various grammars, viz. the 'benefactive' marker on the verb, the 'causative' marker and the third person pronoun. The purpose of this chart is obviously to show that rather than having three different morphemes one is dealing here with the same morpheme. The term 'the same' morpheme' may have two interpretations in the present work: one diachronic, viz. indicating that the morphemes are historically related, and the other synchronic, meaning that the morphemes are identical. Languages in which no marker occurs in the sentence containing a benefactive argument and no marker occurs in the causative construction were not included in the chart. No elimination was made, however, if the third person pronoun was different from the two markers. The chart is organized according to classification in Newman 1977, and languages chosen represent three out of four branches postulated in this classification. As the chart shows, whenever the 'benefactive' and the 'causative' functions are marked by the same morpheme, this morpheme is invariably derived from the third person singular pronoun. In most of the languages the pronoun is masculine but in Masa it is feminine. This fact, however, does not undermine the hypothesis stated. We do not know enough yet about the marked and unmarked characteristics of the gender distinctions among pronouns in various Chadic languages. What appears to be a functional extension of the pronoun is not even an extension, for the pronouns are used in exactly the same way in which they are used when serving as direct or indirect objects.

CHART 1

Language	'Benefactive marker'	'Causative marker'	3 p.pronoun
Bolanci	-in	-t	taa (f)
Pero	-n	-n	-n
Kanakuru	----	-nu	-n(i)
Ngizim	-d ,-naa	-d,-naa	da (subj)
Ga'anda	-an-	an-	-an-
Higi	-----	-na	
Bachama	-----	-də	ndu
Masa	ta	ta	ta (f)

Having shown that the causative marker in Chadic is derived from the third person pronoun it is necessary to address the other problem, viz. sporadic meaning of the motion away that may be found associated with this morpheme in some languages, such as Higi.

There is ample evidence in Chadic that the two functions were realized by two separate morphemes. Compare example 12 b. from Ga'anda, where the causative is marked by -an- and the 'movement away' is marked by kadə occurring at the end of the sentence. Similarly in Hona, examples 18 and 19 b. where the causative is marked by -n and the 'movement away' is marked by -d occurring at the end of the sentence. Virtually the same situation obtains in several other languages in which the directional markers occur at the end of the sentence rather than as suffixes to the verb. We have thus established that the 'directional marker' and the causative marker are separate morphemes.

It is necessary now to establish a connection between the transitivizing meaning and the directional meaning indicating the motion away. In several verbs, the lexical meaning of the transitivized form may pragmatically involve motion away. This is especially true for such verbs as 'to sell', 'to inform', 'to teach'. These verbs occur with the motion away suffix, as it is the case in Ga'anda and Hona. It is therefore quite possible that in some languages a functional merger might have occurred in which the two functions came to be realized by one morpheme. Higi may possibly be an example of such a language.

The proposed hypothesis concerning the origin of the causative marker explains not only its transitivizing function and causative function, but it also explains its function in sentences containing a benefactive argument. Newman's hypothesis about the 'movement away' and the 'transitivizing function' being represented by one morpheme in Proto-Chadic does not explain the use of the 'causative' morpheme in sentences containing a benefactive argument.

6. Explanation for the 'causative' in Hausa

The data from Hausa were not quoted in the discussion of the evidence, because the causative form of the verb in Hausa has been the subject of intensive discussion and there is no non-controversial analysis that could have been quoted in support of the proposed hypothesis. The following section will propose a new analysis of the facts in Hausa, providing two explanations: one for the use of the causative forms in sentences containing benefactive argument and second for the origin of the causative marker in Hausa. The explanations provided will constitute a test of the validity of the hypothesis proposed for Chadic.

6.1. Current explanations

Parsons 1971 assumed that the basic form of the causative marker in Hausa is -*s* and that the other forms that are encountered, such as -*r*,-*n* and -*d* are derived from it, presumably, through phonological processes independently attested in Hausa, such as: s ---> r /___$, ($ stands for syllable boundary), r ---> n /_____n, and r/n/s ---> d /___d. This assumption was accepted also by other scholars even before Parsons' paper although there are few explicit statements concerning the nature of phonological rules involved. A notable exception to this general assumption is expressed by Newman 1977a. where he claims that -*n* is not derived from -*r* or some other form underlying the causative marker but rather is a remnant of a completely independent morpheme, which he calls 'destinative'. He also claims that the phonological rule involved was n ---> r rather than r ---> n . Newman also claims that the causative form of the verb as it occurs in sentences containing a benefactive argument is in fact an instance of the destinative extension to the verb. If this form have merged with the 'causative' construction, it would explain the occasional -*r* ending on verbs that one finds in this syntactic environment, as illustrated in example 1 at the beginning of this paper, quoted here again for the ease of reference:

1. yaa zaaɓar wà Audu dookìi
   'He has chosen a horse for Audu'

The evidence that Newman brings for his hypothesis is both synchronic and comparative. The comparative analysis suffers from a major error. The Hausa causative forms as occurring in the clauses containing a benefactive argument are compared with the ventive forms in other languages, indicating movement toward the speaker. Thus from Pero, Newman has taken the ventive form -*ina* rather than 'causative' form -*n*. The verbal forms were thus compared with complete disregard to the syntactic environment in which they occur. The compared forms were therefore not comparable if the aim of the comparison was to prove the identity of the -*n* variant of Hausa causative marker with the ventive form of the verb in other Chadic languages. What should have been compared were the verbal forms occurring in the same syntactic environments, such as illustrated in chart 1. While the -*n* ending would nicely fit into the chart, showing that it is a cognate of the other forms which also end in a nasal consonant, the ending -*s*, which is considered to be the basic causative marker, would not. The comparative evidence as presented by Newman for his claim simply cannot be considered as evidence.

The synchronic evidence provided by Newman consists of several examples in which the causative ending in sentences containing a benefactive argument is -*n* rather than -*r* or -*s*. But there are examples in which the ending is -*r* and there are examples in which it is -*s* and for these examples Newman does not provide any explanation. The change r ---> n is attested in Hausa independently, e.g.: *birni* ---> *binni* 'walled city', *murna* ---> *munna* 'joy', *mutuwar nan* ---> *mutuwan nan* 'this death' (Abraham 1959:156). There is, however, no independent evidence for the change n --- >r and Newman does not provide any either. Therefore Newman's proposal claiming that 'there is little reason to relate the r/m D-forms to the causatives' (Newman 1977a:291) cannot be accepted for the lack of evidence. His claim that -*n* is derived from the Proto-Chadic destinative **in* has to be rejected because of the methodological error in comparative analysis.

6.2. The new explanation

Although most linguists working on Hausa did assume identity of the causative form as used in transitivizing process and as used in sentences containing a benefactive argument no explanation for this fact was provided. Let us consider in what circumstances the causative is used in sentences containing a benefactive argument. Newman 1977a states that it is used in Grades 2, 3, and 7, e.g.:

40. yáa némám másà
    'He sought it for him' (Grade 2)

41. yáa túubám mínì
    'He apologized to me' (Grade 3)

42. yáa 'áukám mátà
    'It befell her'   (Grade 7)

I would like to propose that the role of the causative ending in all of its uses in Hausa is exactly the same, viz. to add one more argument to a clause, or to indicate that there is one more argument in the clause whenever the argument that follows the verb is other than expected, given the inherent properties of the verb. Zima 1972 proposes the following description of the ability of various Grades to occur with direct and indirect objects:

Grade 1. direct object, indirect object.
Grade 2. direct object only.
Grade 3. indirect object only (with some special features).
Grade 4. direct object, indirect object.
Grade 5. causative object, indirect object. (This is the form with the causative marker)
Grade 6. indirect object (rare), direct object.
Grade 7. indirect object (rare).

The occurrence of the 'causative' marker correlates with the ability of the verb to occur with one or more than one argument. Grade 2 accepts only the direct object. Therefore, whenever this form of the verb occurs with the indirect object following it, the verb has the marker -*s* to indicate that there is one more argument following. The same applies to grade 3 and grade 7. This constitutes the synchronic evidence for the function of the causative morpheme in Hausa.

The comparative evidence consists of the simple observation that the same form in other languages discussed in this paper occurs in exactly the same environments, viz. when the verb is intransitive but an object follows it, when the verb is transitive but there is no overt object present, and when there is a benefactive argument which follows the transitive verb.

What would appear to be a counterargument to the proposed hypothesis is the form of the 'causative' marker -*s* which obviously cannot be considered a cognate of other causative markers as listed in Chart 1. But in fact the form of the marker provides an additional argument for the proposed hypothesis. As has been shown for some Chadic languages, the 'causative' marker is derived from the form of the third person singular pronoun. The third person singular masculine pronoun in Hausa is *$*sV$, such as *sa, shi* (palatalized because of the following high front vowel). Interestingly, this form is not cognate with the third person pronouns in closely related West Chadic languages. But quite obviously it is related to the causative marker. We can therefore add to Chart I the following entry for Hausa:

Hausa	'Benefactive marker'	'Causative marker'	3 p. pronoun
	-s	-s	s

The proposed hypothesis, explains therefore why the same form of the verb occurs in several seemingly unrelated environments and also explains the origin of the verbal ending. As a footnote to this paper it is worth noticing that in comparative studies involving Afro-Asiatic languages (e.g. Greenberg 1966) the causative form of the verb in Hausa was related to causative *s* in Berber and in some other languages. In view of the proposed explanation this similarity must be considered rather accidental.

The connection between /s/ as a marker of the 'causative' and the variant with [n] may require some additional information apart from the simple phonological rule involving assimilation of [r] to [n] in front of [n], because there are environments in which the variant [n] cannot be explained by assimilation as in the following example from Taylor 1959:101 quoted from Newman 1977a:294: *sanan wa* 'inform'.

I would suggest that -*n* endings which cannot be explained by assimilation to the initial nasal of the following word constitute a remnant of the demonstrative or some other type of pronoun in Hausa. This is not an ad hoc explanation for in the present day Hausa there are several traces of demonstrative pronouns containing -*n*, such as the definite marker for masculine nouns -*n*, demonstratives *nan* and *can*, etc. For West Chadic the third person masculine pronoun is more likely to be reconstructed with an alveolar nasal rather than with the *s* that occurs in present day Hausa.

Footnotes

[1] The work on this paper was sponsored by the National Endowment for the Humanities grant Nr.RO-00259-80-2095 entitled 'Structure of simple sentence in Proto-Chadic'. The help of the N.E.H. is gratefully acknowledged. I would also like to thank Scott DeLancey with whom I discussed certain aspects of this paper.

[2] In the above formula the VSO order is assumed for the Proto-Chadic for the period preceding its split into three or four groups. For the justification of this assumption cf. Frajzyngier 1983a and the present volume. In contemporary languages which have the SVO word order the position of the causative marker is the same as in the VSO languages, viz. following the verb.

[3] The following are sources for the languages examined: Ga'anda -- Ma Newman 1971, Hona -- my own fieldnotes collected in the Summer of 1981, Pa'anci -- M. Skinner 1979, Ngizim -- Schuh 1972, Kanakuru -- Newman 1974, Bolanci -- Lukas 1970, Pero -- Frajzyngier 1989, Masa -- T.Schumann, P.C., Hausa -- as stated for each example, Bachama -- Carnochan 1970.

[4] The analysis of data follows the one presented in Frajzyngier 1977a and differs in several respects from the one proposed in Schuh 1972.

ENCODING LOCATIVE IN CHADIC

1. Purpose and scope of the study

The aim of this study is to provide a first attempt at the reconstruction of the system in Proto-Chadic for encoding various semantic notions loosely characterized as locative. Individual grammatical devices will be reconstructed only when necessary to provide support for the reconstruction of the general patterns.

The study includes locative stative clauses and clauses involving a verb of movement. Both types of clauses contain all the grammatical devices to encode the locative, but the description of one type has no bearing on the description of the other. The two types are described simply because they exist in the grammatical systems of Chadic languages. The data are drawn from some thirty languages.[1]

The major sections of the study are stative locatives, verbal extensions, and the prepositional phrases, which differ significantly from their equivalents in IE languages. An overall view of forming locative constructions is provided in the summary.

2. Stative locatives

By stative locatives I understand expressions equivalent to English 'X is located in/at Y'. They can be independent clauses, such as 'John is at home', or phrases such as 'at home' in 'I saw John at home', e.g.:

   1 a. dàdərwaixà à-m Káanò
        father   Prep.
        'My father is in Kano'

   b. Pita àmbálvà à-m mákárántà
      learn   school
      'Peter studies in school' (Mandara, field notes)

The only interesting question with respect to stative locatives is whether they had or did not have a copula in Proto-Chadic. Because a copula occurs in some languages and not in others, the question to be answered is whether the locative copula is an innovation or a retention. In the majority of contemporary languages there is no copula in locative sentences. The general form of such sentences is SUBJECT PREP-NP, e.g.:

  2 a. takini goro panda
       shoes under mat
       'the shoes are under the mat' (West, Kanakuru, Newman 1974:32)

    b. Kúɓər Cácá ləg   àgá Làsà
                 near (prep.) with
       'Kubur Caca is near Lasa' (Central, Margi, Hoffmann 1963:239)

    c. wə apəy-à
       he up- Loc
       'he is up' (East, Kera, Ebert 1979:189)

    d. dz á   mbwà
       he Prep room
       'he is in a room' (Cibak, Hoffmann 1955:143)

Although in the three branches most languages form stative locatives without a copula, there is at least one language, Bolewa, that appears to have a copula in locative sentences, and Fyer, a Ron language, has a morpheme that may be analyzed as a locative copula, e.g.:

  3 a. sùɓá-nò   à kò réwè
       shirt-1sg   on tree
       'my shirt is on a tree'

cf. b. zéetì sùɓá gà   kó réwè
    put shirt Prep on tree
    'put a shirt on a tree' (Bolewa, field notes)

4 a. yít-a-ǹ tá á
    she-Cop?-Prep there
    'she is there'

  b. ma-á -na
    he-? -here
    'he is here' (Fyer, Jungraithmayr 1963:78)

Jungraithmayr op. cit. mentions the possibility that the function of /a/ is linked with the locative preposition {a} with the meanings 'at, in', although no examples are given of the unambiguously prepositional function.

The possibility that the locative copula in Bolewa and Fyer constitutes an innovation rather than a retention has been discussed in Frajzyngier 1986. It is supported by the following arguments: It is more likely that one branch of West Chadic, Ron, has innovated and that the majority of languages preserved the Proto-Chadic system. Claiming that the majority of languages have innovated would require an explanation of why they have innovated in exactly the same way. In languages that have locative copulas one often finds copulas in equational sentences as well. Yet among the languages examined, only in the Angas group and in Ron is there an equational copula identical with the locative copula or with a preposition, e.g., in Mupun:

5 mùn a nèn   kàmkàm
  we Cop people teaching
  'we are teachers'

But even in those languages equational like sentences without a copula are very frequent, e.g., Mupun:

6 mùn ɓál
  'we are strong'

In most languages the equational sentence does not have a copula, e.g.:

7 mùr cìbòk
   'we are Cibak' (Hoffmann 1955:143)

We see then that Chadic languages historically do not exhibit a copula in locative stative sentences, and that those languages that do so today have innovated.

3. Directional locatives

3.1. Grammatical devices available in Chadic

In contemporary Chadic languages the notion of locative is realized by at least four different grammatical devices:

   (1) DEICTICS
   (2) VERBAL EXTENSIONS
   (3) SERIAL VERB CONSTRUCTIONS
   (4) PREPOSITIONAL PHRASES

   Serial verb constructions, verbal extensions, prepositional phrases, and phrase final particles may co-occur. Some languages have all four devices; others have only some of them. However, if two devices have exactly the same function, such as indicating the same direction of movement, etc., they will not co-occur in the same environment. In what follows I will discuss the function of each of these devices and the possibility of reconstructing the device for P.C.

3.2. Deictics

Deictic locative markers are similar to I.E. deictic adverbials with the general meaning 'here', 'there', etc. In Chadic the deictic markers occur in sentence final position and they indicate the direction of movement with respect to the speaker or to some other previously defined place, e.g.:

8 gwàr ɗə́ wùr sù sə́
   man REl 3sg run there
   'the man who run away' (Mupun)

These markers occur in languages of the Angas subgroup of the West branch, and in Hona, Ga'anda, and Cibak of the Central branch. In the languages listed above, the place of speech, 'here', is marked by sə and the place away, 'there', is marked by several devices, including ɗi. If we assume that the subgrouping of Chadic languages based solely on phonological data obtained by lexical comparisons is correct (cf. Newman 1977, Jungraithmayr 1978), then we will be justified to conclude also that sentence final particles were part of the P.C. grammatical system. The phonological near identity of devices in two branches is unlikely to be a product of independent innovation. The phonological similarity of the clause final markers, however, may be a reflex of the same source from which these markers have developed. In particular, for at least one language, Mupun, it has been shown that clause final deictic and anaphoric locative markers are ultimately derived from verbs 'to go' and 'to come' (cf. Frajzyngier 1987 and the present volume). A similar origin of clause final particles in languages of the Central branch could then explain the phonological similarity of the markers.

3.3. Locative extensions and serial verb constructions

There already exists relatively abundant literature on verbal extensions in various Chadic languages as well as some comparative studies (cf. Mirt 1971, Lukas 1971, Newman 1983). The following is just an example of a typical locative extension:

9 a. yaa fit-oo
     3sg go out-Vent
     'he came out to here'

cf. b. yaa fìta
    'he came out' (Hausa)

Serial verb constructions have attracted the least attention in synchronic descriptions of contemporary languages, but they are nevertheless rather common, e.g.:

10 n-dùul àkwàatí-nə́ sín jì sə̀
   1sg- pull box Def give come here
   'I pulled the box in here' (Mupun)

Constructions involving movement to and from involve verbs rather than prepositions before the locative NP in Mupun, Pero (West), Mandara (Central), e.g.:

11 a. dá nkà dəm màkàrántà
     go-1sg-Neg go school
     'I did not go to school'

cf. b. pítà à dəm kánò
     Peter Aux go Kano
     'Peter went to Kano' (Mandara, field notes)

I have shown (Frajzyngier 1987 and present volume) that ventive and centrifugal verbal extensions are derived from a specific type of serial verb construction. There are two pieces of evidence for this hypothesis. Locative extensions and serial verb constructions with a locative function do not co-occur in Chadic languages. The other piece of evidence rests on phonological similarity between locative verbal extensions and verbs 'to come' or 'to return' from which the extensions are derived historically. Therefore, for the purpose of reconstructing the system of encoding the locative in P.C., I will treat these devices as two historical stages of the same grammatical form.

In a number of languages prepositions and the deictic locative markers may be attached to the verb, thus forming verbal extensions. Compare the following examples in which, due to the aspect differences, the same semantic notion is expressed in one case by a ventive extension (12 a.) and in another case by a prepositional phrase (12 b.), with the same form of the extension and the preposition:

12 a. ᵞkəs-atsa   mayə́ həyə́ sə   Múra
      take-to-here I   corn under Mora
      'I carried the corn here from Mora'

b. A ᵞkəsə həyə́ yá ᵞtsa sə   Múra
     V.m. take corn I   here under Mura
     'I am carrying the corn here from Mora' (Podoko, Jarvis 1983:314)

The functions of the locative extensions can be divided into two groups; one oriented with respect to the speaker or some other previously defined place, and the other, for the lack of a better term, "non-speaker oriented." The first group consists of two forms; the ventive, always marked, and the non-ventive, unmarked form. The ventive indicates that the action occurred at some place away from the speaker with a subsequent movement toward the speaker. The non-ventive form does not indicate movement away from the speaker but rather is unspecified with respect to the direction, e.g., *saukoo* 'arrive here' vs. *sàuka* 'arrive (somewhere else)' (Hausa, Hodge and Umaru 1963:268). There are, however, languages with three-way contrast; ventive, centrifugal (efferential in Newman 1983), i.e., action away from the speaker, and the unspecified direction, e.g.:

13 a. 'à zá yà
       'he carried (it)'

b. 'à zə-gre   báyá   dà gàyá
     carry-away mother Prep house
     'the mother carried it off into the house' (Dghwede, Frick 1978:.20)

c. nánà tlùwe zè -dəgre   gè
      meat carry-toward
      'here is the meat I brought' (ibid. p. 21, all glosses mine, Z.F.)

The ventive/centrifugal extensions frequently occur with the verbal root having the general meaning 'to trade'. The suffixes then specify whether the transaction is that of selling or buying, e.g.:

14 a. ɓə́lmà nam tə̀ zə́r nì   tárà ɗə́l-ɓà
       yam Dem Rel boy Def   trade-Vent
       'the yam that the boy bought'

   b. ɓə́lmà nam tə̀ zə́r nì   tárà ɗə́l-ntà
      'the yam that the boy sold' (Cibak, field notes)

The second group contains all other extensions, such as movement upward or downward. These extensions are not oriented in relation to the speaker and indeed may be oriented in relation to the object, as is the case in Mandara (cf. Mirt 1969/70). The extensions
of the second group occur only in the Central branch. In some languages, such as
Dghwede and Gude, the extensions from the two groups can be combined, e.g.:

15 ndərə   'climb'
    ndərə-gərə   'climb down'
    ndərə-gi   'climb up'
    ndərə-və   'climb to that place'
    ndira   'climb toward speaker'
    ndira-gərə   'climb down toward speaker'
    ndira-gi   'climb up toward speaker' (Hoskison 1983:100)

One of the questions that must be answered concerning extensions is whether the two
functional groups, viz., extensions oriented toward the speaker and extensions that are
non-speaker oriented, should be considered as two distinct structural sets or merely as
members of the same structural set with different semantic values. The second question
that must be answered is which locative extensions occurred in the P.C. verb phrase.
    Unlike extensions that are non-speaker oriented, extensions oriented with respect to the
speaker are not easily derivable within each language. The following example shows the
form of verbal extensions and their possible sources in Dghwede.

16   Source   Extension
     sə̀gé   'foot'   -sə̀gè   'underneath'
     gré   'head'   -gré   'away from'

We thus have the first argument for the existence of two sets rather than one. Moreover, the co-occurrence of the extensions of the two groups, as in Gude, would provide an additional argument for the distinction between the two sets.

We can also make a distinction between the two sets based on a relative chronology of their emergence. Set A, oriented with respect to the speaker, is older than set B. This conclusion is again based on the fact that the origin of the markers of set B is transparent; they are synchronically derivable in each language from some other morphemes (cf. ex. 16 above). The set A markers are not synchronically derivable (except for languages that have innovated recently, such as Dghwede), and they can be reconstructed only through comparative study (cf. Frajzyngier 1987, and present volume.)

There appear to be no compelling reasons to postulate the existence of extensions belonging to set B in Proto-Chadic, because the markers are synchronically derived in each language. In Frajzyngier (1987, and present volume) it is argued that extensions of set A did not exist in Proto-Chadic either. The main argument against reconstruction of Set A extensions for Proto-Chadic is based on the fact that they are derived diachronically from directional verbs of movement or synchronically from prepositions, as is the case in Podoko, as illustrated by example 12 above.

The function that is performed by the locative extensions of sets A and B was most probably performed in P.C. by the morphemes and constructions from which the contemporary extensions derive, viz., by words indicating spatial or geographical location (up, down, North, South, etc.) and by serial verb construction in which the direction of movement or action was indicated by appropriate verbs, as is still the case in the Angas group of the West branch, and in the Bura group of the Central branch, e.g.:

17 a. wùr d́él sé   dɔm jìpáarí
   3m pass go away go to Jipaari
   'he passed by [here] on his way to Jipaari'

   b. mó kà   lè   án ájì féer
   3pl ascend put 1sg grade four
   'they came up and put me in grade four'

    c. mó sìam lè án   ájì féer
       descend
     'they came down and put me in grade four'

    d. mó də́m   lè   án ájì féer
        go
     'they put me in grade four' (Mupun)

18 n-yít   tùl   sé   n-də̀m már
   1sg-leave home depart 1sg-go field
   'I went from home to the farm' (Mupun)

19 a. à azrá sí vì
      go   come
    'come home'

    b. à zrá   lí vì
       go   go
     'go home' (Cibak, field notes)

I do not know all the conditions that were necessary for a serial verb construction to become a verb-extension construction. But one of the factors that constitutes an obstacle to such a change is the word order of the directional verb with respect to the other verb in the clause. The change from a directional verb to an extension occurred when the directional verb followed the non-directional verb. It appears that the change did not occur in languages in which the directional verb could occur either before or after the non-directional verb, as is the case in Mupun.

4. Prepositional phrase

4.1. Hypotheses

In contemporary languages (cf. Chart) there are several locative prepositions, for such meanings as 'at', 'to', and 'from'. The first question to be answered in this section is:

How many locative prepositions were there in P.C.? The second question is: What was the function of preposition(s) in P.C.? The answer to one question can be falsified by the answer to the other.

I would like to propose that in Proto-Chadic there was only one locative preposition {a}. I would like to propose that the only function of the locative preposition in P.C. was to indicate that the following NP is a locative phrase; i.e., it denotes the place at which something happened, toward or from which the movement is directed. Note that although this hypothesis may sound trivial, the function of the locative preposition in Proto-Chadic would actually differ significantly from the functions of locative prepositions in I.E. languages, which not only indicate that the following NP is a locative complement, but also indicate the spatial configuration of an event with respect to some argument in the sentence, such as 'below', 'above', 'inside', 'outside' of an object. Note that hypotheses similar to the ones stated above have been already stated for individual Chadic languages. Hoffmann 1963:237 postulated for Margi: "Generally speaking, Margi local prepositions do not indicate whether the place mentioned is the starting-point or the end of movement, or whether it is the location of an object. Similarly to [wū] ár may mean 'on', 'on to' or 'down from'." Similarly Newman 1974:24 stated that Kanakuru does not overtly distinguish 'to' from 'at' phrases. The two statements above may be considered to provide some support for the proposed hypotheses for Proto-Chadic. But much stronger evidence will be presented next.

4.1.2. The evidence
4.1.2.1. The nature of the evidence

Grammars of various Chadic languages often give separate forms for the prepositions meaning 'at', 'to', and 'from' as illustrated in the Chart. We have to proceed, therefore, with the reconstruction of what for the time being appears to be as three different prepositions. If we can show that instead of the three different prepositions there was only one, then the hypothesis about the number of prepositions in P.C. will be proved. If we can show that the preposition was {a} rather than something else, then the hypothesis about the form of the preposition will be proved. If we can show that {a} was used in many different contexts, such as indicating 'in', out', 'to', etc., then the hypothesis about the locative function only of this preposition will be proved. Here then is an attempt at reconstruction of, for the time being, three different prepositions.

4.1.2.2. Stative preposition 'at'

There is little doubt that this should be reconstructed as /a/. The tones should probably be left open, as the morpheme has different tonal values in different languages. There are several languages in each group where the stative preposition is other than /a/. Thus in Pero it is {ti}; in Mupun, {n} with a few petrified instances of {a}; in Bole, {ga}; and in Angas, {ka}. In the Central branch and East branch we can see morphemes that could be cognates of the above, such as Kapsiki {te}, Masa {tá}, Lamang {n}. There can be no doubt that {a} should be reconstructed as the stative locative preposition, and the forms {tV} and {n} should be considered as innovations. It is also possible that the innovations {tV} and {n} occurring in some languages could have all come from the same source. I will discuss the problem of the possible sources in section 5.

4.1.2.3. Directional 'to'

There is more variation in the form of the preposition 'to' than of the preposition 'at'. There are essentially three possible candidates for the reconstruction: /n/, /tV/, and /a/. Of the three, /a/ is by far the most frequent form because it occurs in three out of four branches. One would therefore postulate /a/ as the preposition occurring in constructions involving directional locative complements. As in the case of stative locatives, one also has to postulate that various innovations involving /a/ and /ti/ had only two sources, one for /a/ and the other for /ti/. What is important, however, is the fact that we reconstruct the same form /a/ to occur as both stative and directional locative complements. Even when we have some marker other than /a/, frequently the same marker is used for both kinds of complements, e.g.: Bole /ga/, Pero /ti/, Mupun /n/, Podoko /da/.

4.1.2.4. Directional 'from'

The most interesting fact about the equivalents of the preposition 'from' is that quite often
there is no preposition at all. When, however, a preposition occurs, it is either some form
of /dV/ or /a/. We can reconstruct both of these possibilities, but we must also allow for
the possibility that there was no preposition meaning 'from' in P.C. A hypothesis concerning the form /dV/ will be offered in a later section Postulating /a/ as a morpheme occurring
in directional locatives provides sufficient argument for the claim that there was only one
locative preposition.

4.1.2.5. Summary of the reconstruction of prepositions

If we have to postulate that the same preposition occurred in constructions meaning 'at',
'to', and 'from', then the preposition could not have the separate meanings 'at', 'to', and
'from' but rather had a general locative meaning indicating that the following argument is a
locative phrase, as in the following examples from two languages:

    20 a. wúɗ íyà à   húkàsù-ɗ
        mother return Loc market-Dist.
        'My mother returned to the market'

      b. ɓaíɓà à   húkàsù
        'I came from the market'

      c. tsáwdi à   Maiduguri
        'I stayed in Maiduguri' (Hona)

    21 a. wùr wáa   á   n-Kaguu
        he return Foc Prep-Kaguu
        'He returned from Kagu'

b. wùr wáa   séet   də́m a n-Kaguu
   he   return go-away go
   'He returned to Kagu' (Mupun)

The notions of direction were realized by some other devices, in particular by the serial verb constructions discussed earlier.

4.2. Non-redundancy of the locative function

Now that it has been shown that there was only one preposition in the P.C. and that it had only one function -- locative, it is important to observe that the preposition was used only when the locative function was not implied by the inherent features of either the nouns or the verbs involved in a construction. When the locative function was implied by nouns or verbs, the preposition was not used.

Locative constructions in many Chadic languages allow us to classify some nouns as inherently [+LOCATIVE] and others as [-LOCATIVE], with a possibility of the existence of nouns that have no inherent value for this feature. [+LOCATIVE] are all names of towns and villages. [-LOCATIVE] are all animate nouns, but also those objects that are not salient enough to serve as point of reference.

The data from languages in all branches indicate also the existence of two types of verbs with respect to locative constructions. Certain verbs of movement inherently also indicate unique direction: Thus equivalents of 'go' and 'come' in many Chadic languages require a locative complement without any preposition. When a [+LOCATIVE] noun occurs as a complement of a directional verb of movement, it is not marked by any preposition. The evidence for this hypothesis consists of the fact that there are prepositionless locative complements in all branches of Chadic, e.g.:

22 a. à w tupə-moro Shelen
    they-Fut send-her
    'they will send her to Shellen' (Kanakuru, Newman 1974:25)

b. pa 'yá dzaa Tekí
then I go
'then I went to Teki' (Kapsiki, Smith 1969:92)

c. dìbìnìm ten kóore kúpòr
tomorrow I go
'tomorrow I am going to Kupor' (Kera, Ebert 1979:199)

d. nam i suk-ŋa
he goes market-Def
'he goes to the market' (Musey, Platiel 1972:86)

e. mó wáa kano
they return
'they returned from Kano' (Mupun)

The occurrence of this type of construction in all four branches of Chadic cannot be attributed to similar innovations, but rather represents a retention of the P.C. type.

A preposition would occur only when the verb is not [+MOVEMENT], and therefore the noun would have to be marked as a locative rather than as some other complement.

23 a. gami à tukwe-ni la gawi
ram Aux hide-ICP in room
'the ram hid in the room'

b. à wui gami la gawi
'he put the ram in the room' (Kanakuru, Newman 1974:25)

If the noun is a [-LOCATIVE], as is the case with all animates (and pronouns referring to them), then in the locative function it must be marked by a special morpheme, which in some languages is cognate or even identical with a lexeme meaning 'place'. This phenomenon is noted in languages from all groups. Thus in Kanakuru it is *yǐ* 'at place of', in Ngizim the added word is *rai* or *rii* (medially) 'place', e.g.: [3]

24 ná dée-w gaaɗa-k nya ii Barno ii rii-k   Seehu
   'I came to Bornu to Shehu' (Schuh 1972:66)

25 a. wùr sé   dᵊm pᵊ́ màt   dè kᵊ́ dée sᵊ́
      he go-away go-to Prep woman Rel Asp be there
      'He went to that woman over there'

   b. *wùr sé dᵊm   màt dè kᵊ́ dée sᵊ́ (Mupun)

Note that 25 b. is ungrammatical because the locative complement is not preceded by
the morpheme pᵊ́, which may be related to the lexeme pee 'place'.

In other languages the locative marker for [-LOCATIVE] nouns may be derived from
other lexemes such as 'body' or 'mouth', e.g.:

26 wáat-nà cìg tójè
   go-Vent body horse
   'he/she came to a horse' (Pero, field notes)

In Logone when the object is human it must be marked by a preposition, e.g.:

27 a. nd u wagᵊr ga gᵊnᵊm
      I   went   to woman
      'I went to a woman'

   b. nd u wágᵊr u (a'á)
      'I went to the village' (Lukas 1936:54)

In Kera, when the locative complement is a person, it must be preceded by a 'relator'
gèr or sár.

4.3. Spatial relationship

If the preposition {a} marked only the following noun as a locative argument, then how were the spatial relationships such as 'in', 'out', 'under', 'behind', marked?

As in a number of languages from the area, these relationships were marked by the names for parts of the body, which preceded the noun. The form of the locative complement with a spatial specifier was therefore the following:

> a + Spatial Specifier + N
>   [-Place]

Constructions with spatial specifiers derived from names of parts of the body are present in the majority of contemporary Chadic languages, and the following examples from Angas (Burquest 1973) are fairly typical:

28 a. Musa ka-ke   kì -lu
        M. at-head of-hut
        'Musa is on top of the hut'

   b. Musa ka-ɓwlìn kì lu
                     back
        'Musa is behind the hut' (p. 139)

   c. Musa sìit n-ɗin-lu
           go   in-inside
        'Musa entered the house' (p. 163)

5.   Other prepositions

In this section I will offer an explanation for some of the prepositions that occur in various languages (cf. Chart) but are not postulated as having a prepositional function in Proto-Chadic.

5.1. From names of body parts to prepositions

There are two sources for the prepositions. One source has been pointed out already in
some synchronic descriptions. The spatial markers that originated from terms for body
parts became reanalyzed as prepositions. For this to have happened at least two other processes must have occurred. The construction "spatial marker-NP" became grammaticalized
and acquired a form different from the similar possessive construction "term for part of
body-NP". In Kanakuru, where all prepositions derive from parts of the body, the differentiation applies to the constructions with *ko* 'on' and *yó* 'at the foot of' where the differences are marked by tone, e.g.:

> 29 a.   à wúi kó -ró
>   'he put it on her'

> cf. b.   kó -ró
>   'her head' (Newman 1974:91)

The other process that must have occurred is the loss of the preposition *a*. I cannot say
with any certainty what the relative sequence of these processes was. But since not all
constructions "spatial marker-NP" differ from constructions "body part NP", quite possibly the loss of the preposition preceded the structural changes in the construction.

5.2. From verb to preposition: the origins of {tV} and {dV}

Two of the most frequent prepositions that remain to be explained are {tV} and {dV}. The
explanations I provide have not been proposed in any synchronic description, and they are
more speculative than the explanations provided for the prepositions derived from spatial
markers. I hope that this discussion will provoke some other explanations.
    I would like to propose that the preposition of the form {tV} derives from a verb of the
same form and that the meaning of this verb must have included a notion of 'stopping at,
in'. The evidence for this hypothesis consists of the fact that in many languages there is
such a verb. In Mupun, it is the verb *ta* 'to fall, stop by'; in Kanakuru there is a morpheme

ɗa that Newman describes as 'via' and that is used in exactly the same function as Mupun *ta*. In Gude it is the verb *taŋi-* 'cross, cross over'. Compare also Hausa *ta* 'via'.

Concerning the preposition *dV*, which usually has the meaning 'from', I would like to propose that it derives from the verb *dV* 'go' that occurs in Lamang, Mofu, Ngizim and in many other contemporary languages. There is only one problem here but it is serious; there are no indications that in many of these languages the verb involves the meaning of 'going from'. Only in Hoskison 1983:173 we find a statement that *dəmə* means 'go in or out'.

Thus, in Chadic as in many other languages, the original locative expressions would have had a form of a serial verb construction of the type 'X goes stops at Y' for constructions that eventually gave the preposition *tV* and 'X goes leaves Y' for constructions that eventually gave the preposition *dV*.

The process of change from verb to preposition is well documented in other language groups, e.g., in Kwa by Lord 1973, in Chinese by Li and Thompson 1981.

6. Recapitulation of all systems

The role of marking direction 'to' or 'from' was carried not by prepositions but by serial verb constructions, and later in some languages by speaker-oriented extensions. We therefore have systemic motivation for the existence of the two types of grammatical devices. The same kind of argument can be used as systemic evidence for the existence of serial verb constructions and eventually extensions indicating movement 'upward', 'downward', etc.

The serial verb constructions must have existed already at the P.C. stage to provide a more precise realization of those notions that were not realized through the system of prepositions.

The stative locatives were marked in P.C. by apposition of subject and locative, which was marked by the preposition *a*. Note that this marking was important, because in the absence of the preposition the sentence would have been interpreted as equational (cf. Frajzyngier 1986).

The directional locative complement was not marked when the verb was inherently directional. In other circumstances, the locative complement was marked by the same preposition as in stative locative sentences.

Nouns that were inherently [-LOCATIVE], such as all animate nouns and the pronouns referring to them, were made locative through the addition of special morphemes, sometimes derived from lexemes meaning 'place'.

The spatial reference to the locative complement was marked through the set of markers derived from the names of body parts, or locative adverbs. Note that the system of locative marking in Chadic is not unusual in the world languages and actually is quite similar to the system in Thai described in Kolver 1984.

An important implication of the study is that different elements of grammatical structure constitute a system in which the properties of one element motivate the existence of another element. The fact that prepositions are not marking direction motivates the existence of serial verb constructions and verbal extensions, or alternatively, the existence of serial verb constructions and verbal extensions motivates the limited function of preposition.

LOCATIVE PREPOSITIONS

Language	at	to	from	PLACE marker	Copula
Hausa	à	zuwa	daga	wuri/waje	na
Bole	ga	ga	ka	0	0
Pero	ti	ti	Verb	pudi(place)	0
Kanak	lá	0	0	yı(place)	0
Angas	ka	n	0	0	0
Mupun	n	a	0	a	0
Ngizim	àa	ìi	dà	raì	áa
Pa'a	á	0	daga(H.)	0	0
Tera	0	nə	0	Yes	a
Ga'anda	ə, kə	0	0	0	0
Hona	a	a	a	0	0
Cibak	ka, a	a	0	Ʋ	a
Margi	a	a	a	(yes)	0
Kapsiki	te	0	0	kwa	0
Mandara	àm	dəm (go)	0	0	0
Podoko	da	da	da	0	0
Lamang	-n, má	-dá	ɳ	0	0
Mofu	á	á	dà (from,in)	0	0
Zulgo	a	a	0	0	0
Gisiga	i	i, a	0	0	0
Gude	a	a	də	0	0
Logone	na	ga	na	0	0
Munjuk	a	a	a.pár	0	0
Kera	a---a	a a	Body parts	0	0
Musey	0	0	0	0	a
Mesme	á	á	0	0	0
Masa	tá	Verbs of movement			

Footnotes

[1] The work on this study was supported by the Center for Applied Humanities, University of Colorado and by NSF Grant Nr. BNS-84 18923. The data were taken from the following sources: Kanakuru -- Newman 1974, Bole -- Lukas 1971, my own fieldnotes, Pero -- Frajzyngier 1989, Angas -- Burquest 1973, Mupun -- my own field notes, Ngizim -- Schuh 1972, Pa'a -- M. Skinner 1979, Tera -- Newman 1970, Ga'anda -- Ma Newman 1971, Hona -- my own field notes, Cibak -- my own fieldnotes and Hoffmann 1955, Margi -- Hoffmann 1963, Kapsiki -- Smith 1979, Podoko -- Jarvis 1983, Lamang -- Ekkehard Wolff, p.c., Mofu -- Daniel Barreteau, p.c., Zulgo -- Haller et al. 1981, Gisiga -- Lukas 1970, Bachama -- Carnochan 1970, Gude -- Hoskison 1983, Logone -- Lukas 1936, Buduma -- Lukas 1936, Munjuk -- Henry Tourneux, p.c., Kera -- Ebert 1979, Mokilko -- Herrmann Jungraithmayr, p.c. and Lukas 1977, Mesme -- Fischer 1980, Musey -- Platiel 1972, Masa -- Theda Schumann, p.c., Zime -- Michka Sachnine, p.c. My profound thanks to all colleagues who generously shared with me their knowledge of various languages.

I would also like to thank an anonymous reader of a previous version of this paper for the careful checking of my quotes and to a referee of the *Journal of West African Languages* whose comments prompted me to change the organization of the paper.

I use the term West to refer to West Chadic, the term Central (proposed by Jungraithmayr 1978) to refer to Central Chadic (Newman's 1977 Biu-Mandara), East to refer to East Chadic, and Masa to refer to the Masa branch.

[2] For a description of change from preposition to the equational copula, see Frajzyngier 1986.

[3] The phenomenon of having a special morpheme to mark the inherently non-locative nouns as locative complements is by no means an exclusive property of Chadic languages. Thilo Schadeberg has pointed out to me the existence of the same phenomenon in Bantu languages.

VENTIVE AND CENTRIFUGAL IN CHADIC

1. Aim and scope of paper

Locative verbal extensions, occurring in a number of Chadic languages, are considered by many to be a typical characteristic of this branch of Afroasiatic. The initial aim of this paper is to propose sources from which the locative extensions in Chadic are derived. The second aim is to propose, for the first time, reasons for the emergence of the locative extensions in Chadic languages. I will conclude by showing that locative extensions may not have been a feature of the Proto-Chadic grammatical system.

The two most frequent extensions are ventive (centripetal), indicating movement toward the speaker or the place of speech, and centrifugal, indicating very generally movement away from the speaker or the place of speech,[1] e.g.:

1 a. a- səkəm-ára slú í   kwàskwà -yá
      he-bought-Egr meat Prep market-Egr
      'He bought meat at the market and brought it here'

  b. ì-dé-áhà á dzékwiŋ
      I-go-Ingr Gen then
      'I will go then there' (Haller et al. 1981:47)

In many languages there are also other extensions indicating movement upward, downward, in a westerly or an easterly direction, etc. I will be concerned in this paper only with the ventive and centrifugal. The reason behind this limitation is that for the two extensions I can postulate hypotheses supported with a considerable amount of evidence. Possible sources of other locative extensions will be indicated but not elaborated on. In Chart 1, I list the forms of ventive and centrifugal extensions in some thirty languages.[2]

2. Sources of locative extensions

2.1. Hypotheses

Hypothesis I: One source of locative extensions in Chadic is the verbs of movement 'return', 'come in', and 'come' for the ventive, and 'depart' and 'go' for the centrifugal extension.

Hypothesis II: Another source is prepositions and phrase final locative markers that came to be attached to the verb by a process that has yet to be explained.[3] Some of these sources have been previously proposed and documented for individual languages, e.g., Hoffmann 1963, Mirt 1970/71, Wolff 1983.

2.2. Arguments for hypothesis I

2.2.1. From a verb to the ventive extension

2.2.1.1. Evidence based on retention

On the basis of data presented in Chart 1, it is not possible to reconstruct only one form of the ventive extension. Within West Chadic there are at least three forms that can be reconstructed: For the Bole-Tangale branch there is the pair $*-t(V)$ non-perfective and $*-(V)n(V)$ for the perfective forms. The two markers are portmanteau morphemes encoding both aspect and direction. Both forms can be reconstructed as occurring already at the stage of Proto-Bole-Tangale. In the remaining languages, Hausa has -oo and Ngizim has -ee(-w) and -ina.

In the Central branch the most widely distributed are forms containing [wa]. They occur in several clusters of the A branch of the subgroup.

I would like to propose that the suffixes -wa and -a occurring in several languages of the West and Central branches, and the ventive marker -oo in Hausa ultimately derive from the verb *wat, which in the West and Central branches had one of the three meanings: 'return', 'come', and 'come in'. The arguments for this proposal follow.

Of the two available attempts at reconstruction of the lexicon in Chadic, only Jungraithmayr and Shimizu 1981 propose *wt as one of the roots they reconstruct for the gloss 'come'. Newman 1977 proposes *ya, but several examples he gives contain [w] as the initial segment. For the verb 'return' Newman 1977 postulates *ma (Jungraithmayr and Shimizu 1981 do not reconstruct this verb). I have taken the entries for 'return', 'come', and 'come in' in Kraft 1981 and excerpted those glosses that are of interest in the present paper. The results are found in Chart 2. Note that in the West and Central branches, [w] appears to be the first segment of all three verbs in different languages. Note also an interesting coincidence: the occurrence of [w] as first segment of the three verbs stops at the same branch where the occurrence of [w]/[a] as ventive markers stops. Concerning the ventive marker [t] in the Bole-Tangale branch, notice that the distribution of [t] as the initial consonant of the verb 'to come in' and 'return' equals in my sample the distribution of [w] in those verbs. Hence it is very likely that the ventive marker {tV} also derives from the verbs 'come' and 'return'.

2.2.1.2. Phonological plausibility

The explanation of phonological changes may serve as an additional argument in support of the proposed hypotheses. I will illustrate the process for the ventive form only, because it displays the most differences from its alleged source.

On the basis of data presented in Chart 2 we can reconstruct the verb 'to come' in Proto-West and Proto-Central branches as *wVt, similar to the form postulated by Jungraithmayr and Shimizu 1981, with the medial vowel most probably being [a].[4] Since the verb had a grammatical function, it was eventually reduced to just the first two segments, or even the first segment. Note that phonological reduction involved in grammaticalization is independently confirmed by studies of grammaticalization in other languages, cf. Heine and Reh 1984, Lehmann 1985, Bybee and Pagliuca 1985. After the verb was reduced, it became a suffix to the preceding verb. In the process of suffixation in many languages, the labial glide [w] was deleted by phonological rules, which do not allow a /Cw/ cluster for most consonants. As the result of this reduction, we have just the vowel [a] as the ventive suffix. In some cases the labial glide became a mid rounded vowel, a phonetically very plausible change.

2.2.1.3. Evidence based on innovation

Although the evidence for the derivation of ventives from the three verbs is considerable
(the number of languages quoted for each gloss is equal to the number quoted for a single
gloss in either Jungraithmayr and Shimizu 1981 or Newman 1977), I think that even better
evidence can be obtained from languages in which the ventive has a form different from the
one reconstructed above. In Munjuk (Tourneux 1978 and p.c.), Kera, and Zime (Sachnine
p.c. and Kraft 1981), the ventive marker happens to be also the first consonant of a verb
'to come, return', e.g.:

Language	Ventive	Possible source	
Munjuk	-si	su	'come'
Kera	-dà	dèyè	'arrive (there)'
Zime	-fi	fon	'return'

Given this correlation in the three languages it is unlikely that the similarity between the
extension and the appropriate verb of movement is accidental.

Lack of cognates in the same language, if indeed none can be found, can be explained
also by postulating that after a verb becomes a grammatical morpheme, especially after it
becomes an affix in at least one environment, it ceases to function as an independent lexical
item having the same meaning or the same form as before. This would account for the fact
that languages that have an extension derived from *wVt do not have this form for the verb
'to come'. Compare in this respect the Hausa entry for 'return'. One of its meanings is
'turn', an obviously related meaning, as demonstrated by examples from English, Russian
(*vernut'* 'return', *vertet'* 'turn') and many other languages. The change of form is illustrated by ventive extensions in Logone, Munjuk, and Zime, where the extension has a different vowel from the one contained in the verb that presumably served as a source.

2.2.1.4. Summary of arguments

Let us summarize the arguments in support of the hypothesis that in a number of languages
the ventive extension derives from one of the verbs meaning 'return' or 'come': In a num-

ber of languages the form of the ventive suffix can be plausibly derived from a verb *wat* meaning 'return' or 'come'. In several languages in which such a derivation is not possible, the ventive suffix is phonetically similar to the verb 'come' or 'return'. We can consider therefore as proven the hypothesis that in many Chadic languages the ventive extension derives from one of the verbs involving motion toward speaker.

2.2.2. Centrifugal extension

The only West Chadic language for which a centrifugal extension has been postulated is Hausa (cf. Newman 1983). In the Central, Eastern, and Masa branches there are several markers of the centrifugal which do not allow reconstruction of a single phonological form of the marker.[5] But it is possible to reconstruct two functions of the sources from which centrifugal markers are derived. The first source are the verbs 'to go', and the second source is the preposition 'out', as illustrated for Mandara in ex. 4. The marker {-*ɗ*} in Hona and in several other languages may be related to the form *ɗə 'go' reconstructed for Proto-Chadic in Newman 1977. For some other languages I have obtained the following correlations:

Language	Centrifugal	Possible source	
Logone	-li	l	'go'
Margi	-ba	ba	'go out'
Munjuk	-fu	fuki	'leave, move'

We have once again a high correlation between the markers of centrifugal and the verb 'to go'. I consider that these data constitute evidence for the hypothesis that a number of centrifugal markers are cognates with the verb 'to go'.

2.3. Arguments for Hypothesis II

There is a fundamental difference between extensions derived from verbs and extensions derived from prepositions. While the former represent a process of diachronic develop-

ment, the latter are a product of a synchronic rule, by which a preposition or a locative adverb becomes attached to the verb, e.g., in Podoko:

   4 a. ykəs-atsa mayə həyə sə Múra
          carry-Ven.
          'I carried the corn here from M.'

      b. A ykəsə həyə yá ytsa sə Múra
          'I am carrying the corn here from M.' (Jarvis 1983:314)

The phonological similarities between the extension and the appropriate prepositions are
considerable, e.g., in Mandara:

          Extension   Source
          əm 'in'   <   ám 'in'
          tə 'out'   <   átə 'out' (excerpted from Mirt 1971)

Although it is easy to show that some extensions derive from prepositions, as has been
convincingly shown in Hoffmann 1963: 119-149, Mirt 1970/71:13-37 and Wolff
1983:109-25, it is by no means easy to find a motivation for syntactic rules by which the
same morpheme serves once as a preposition and another time as a verbal extension. In
languages in which this occurs the constraints are linked to different tenses and/or aspects.
And as in example 4 from Podoko, the completive aspect tends to involve verbal extension.
This may well be linked with the fact that the completive is usually formed on a verbal base
while non-completive, on a nominal base (cf. Wolff 1979).[6]
   Note that although similar phenomena have been known in Indo-European (including
English), mainly in the development of preverbs, (cf. Meillet 1937, Kuryłowicz 1964,
Vaillant 1966 for Slavic), they have not been satisfactorily explained, i.e., we still do not
know why a given morpheme, such as an adverb, occurs in some instances before the
verb, and eventually becomes a preverb, and in other cases before a noun, and becomes a
preposition (a scenario described in Kuryłowicz 1964).

3. Explanation

3.1. What needs to be explained?

If one accepts the hypothesis that locative extensions derive from verbs, then quite obviously there must have once been a construction consisting of two verbs, with the second verb eventually becoming an extension. This is the stage where all explanations usually start; e.g., Heine and Reh 1984 opt for one of the models proposed in Lord 1975 whereby some verbs become part of a verbal compound, then lose their semantic content and eventually become affixes. Although this is a plausible mechanism to explain the change, the initial stage of this process, viz., the existence of verbal compounds, remains unmotivated. What we really do not know is why there were structures consisting of two verbs to begin with. Hence in this work I would like to start with a stage that has not been previously considered in studies of verbal extensions.

I will try to provide an answer to the following, questions which to my knowledge have not been asked previously: Why did the verbs 'return', 'come', 'come in', 'go', become locative extensions? Why has the process occurred in some Chadic languages and not in others? The explanations that I will provide for Chadic may not be valid for other languages, but perhaps the method proposed, viz., that of looking for a functional justification, may be of some use in explaining the processes of grammaticalization going beyond the formation of verbal extensions.

3.2. Functional-systemic explanation

There are at least two cognitive elements that may be involved in the conceptualization of movement. One is the notion of the manner of movement lexicalized in such verbs as 'run', 'swim', 'jump'. The other is the notion of direction. This may be oriented with respect to one or more points of reference. For these points of reference I will retain the now traditional labels 'goal', 'source', and 'path'. Direction may be lexicalized, e.g., 'go' and 'come' (6a) but also grammaticalized, i.e., encoded in the grammatical system of the language. A frequent grammaticalization of direction will involve use of adpositions (e.g., 6b) and/or case inflections (6c).

6 a. P. came happy. (lexicalized direction)

   b. P. returned from Africa. (Grammaticalized direction with an adposition)

   c. P. vernulsya   domoy   (Grammaticalized direction through inflection)
       return-Refl home-Loc
       'P. returned home' (Russian)

Quite often the speaker, as the point of reference, is lexicalized in a few verbs of movement, such as 'go' and 'come' in English, and the speaker as the point of reference appears to have been similarly lexicalized in Chadic (but see discussion in Newman 1977: 27). Most other verbs of movement do not have an inherent point of reference.

The reasons for the emergence of locative extensions must be sought in the Proto-Chadic grammatical system, and in particular in the means that were available for the expression of direction with verbs of motion. According to Frajzyngier 1987a and the present volume, at a certain stage P.C. had only one locative preposition, whose sole function was grammatical, specifically to indicate that the argument following it is locative. Unlike prepositions in contemporary I.E. and several Chadic languages, this preposition did not indicate the direction of the movement. None of the contemporary Chadic languages has nominal inflection to indicate direction, and therefore there are no grounds to reconstruct nominal inflection as occurring in P.C., which relied on word order for marking semantic roles of the arguments (cf. Frajzyngier 1983).

Given the above conditions, viz., lack of directional prepositions, lack of nominal inflection, and the fact that directional verbs (such as 'come', 'go') were oriented with respect to only one argument, e.g., goal or source of the movement, there were no grammatical devices in P.C. to mark direction with respect to the other point of reference. The second verb of movement therefore comes to perform exactly the same function as prepositions in I.E. languages, that of orienting the movement with respect to the other point of reference. Hence, when verbs of movement started to appear with other verbs in a clause, the function of the verbs of movement became grammatical as well as lexical. Which verb was chosen to perform a given function depended on the verb's lexical semantic features. The appropriate construction in those Chadic languages that at present have ventive and centrifugal extensions derived from verbs had the form:

Verb1   Verb2
[-directional]   [+directional]

In the majority of languages that did have such a construction, V2 became an extension. There are, however, some instances in which V2 is retained as a full verb as in example 8 from Cibak and 9 below from Mupun, e.g.:

8. trá tá   gà trá sì   krá
   leave Prohib 2SG leave come back
   'Leave and don't come back' (Cibak)

An interesting fact about the ventive extension is the distinction between the perfective and non-perfective forms. This distinction is present in at least two branches, in the Bole-Tangale group of West Chadic and in several subgroups of the Central branch. This distinction is not accounted for by the fact mentioned earlier that the completive aspect is formed on the verbal base and non-completive on the nominal base. Although I have no explanation that I could support with any evidence, I would like, however, to offer the following speculation, as a hypothesis to be confirmed or rejected by future work. Among the several verbs that gave rise to the ventive extension, one might have been inherently completive, and another might have been either inherently non-completive or unmarked for this feature. For the Bole-Tangale branch, the perfective ventive *-(v)N(v)* marker would derive from the inherently completive verb. The only indication that there was a verb of the form *(v)N(v)* with the meaning 'come' is in Schuh 1972: 16ff, but there is no indication of its value for the feature [completive]. And as I have no information about the completive feature for any other hypothetical sources of the ventive extensions, I consider the above as just a hypothesis.

Interestingly, there is no differentiation in West Chadic into completive and non-completive centrifugal extension.

3.3. Why locative extensions did not develop in all languages?

Since a motivation existed for the emergence of locative extensions in many Chadic languages, it becomes especially interesting to ask why locative extensions did not develop in some language groups. It is very likely that we may obtain different explanations for different languages. For the time being I would like to propose just one such explanation for Mupun, a language from the Angas subgroup of West Chadic. In this language there is only one locative preposition {n-} whose sole function is to indicate that the following argument is locative. Hence there are no prepositions to indicate direction. Instead direction is indicated by verbs, in constructions reminiscent of serial verb construction in Kwa languages, e.g.:

> 9. wu   ji   wul   n-kaano
>   2pl come arrive Prep-Kano
>   'you(pl) arrived in Kano'

In fact all indications of direction, such as movement downward or upward, or on a level plain, are indicated by separate verbs, such as *dɔ́m* 'go (on a level plain)', *sìam* 'go down', *kà* 'go up'.

There is in Mupun the verb *wà* 'return', whose unmarked 'internal' argument is the source of movement, i.e., the place from which one returns, e.g.:

> 10. n-   wà   n   jòs
>   1SG-return Prep Jos
>   'I returned from Jos'

Functional equivalents of ventive constructions are formed in Mupun with this verb, e.g.:

> 11. a. wùr wà   sèt dúurì
>   he   return eat yam
>   'He ate a yam somewhere and came here'

cf. b. wùr sét dúurì
'He ate a yam'

c. wà mù sìam n- máŋ fòtó ɗəmù páspòrt nə
return 1SG go down Prep take photo REL passport Def
'We went down to take a photo for the passport and returned'

In many instances the meaning of such a construction includes more than just the direction toward the speaker, and very frequently there is a notion of doing something again, e.g.:

12.a. mò wà ráŋ tàkàrdá
3PL return write letter
'They again wrote a letter'

cf. b. mò ráŋ tàkàrdá
'They wrote a letter'

13.a. wùr wà lá màt mpó
3SG return marry woman another
'He again married another woman'

cf. b. wùr lá màt mpó
'He married another woman'

As can be deduced from the above examples, the functional equivalents of ventive in Mupun have the following form:

Verb 1   Verb 2
[+directional]   [-directional]

Hence the construction is drastically different from the one postulated for languages where the ventive became part of the morphology of the verb. It is very likely that the main reason why the morphological ventive marker did not develop in Mupun is the fact that the directional verb indicating return to the place of speech occurs before, rather than after, the non-directional verb.

4. Can locative extensions be reconstructed for Proto-Chadic?

The fact that we know where the locative extensions come from does not imply that they did not exist in P.C. The process of reanalysis of directional verbs as locative suffixes might well have happened already at the P.C. stage.

Since the ventive and centrifugal occur in some, but not in all, languages we have two possibilities: (1) P.C. had ventive and centrifugal extensions, and they were subsequently lost in some languages. (2) the two extensions did not exist in P.C. but rather emerged independently, not only after the split into the major branches of Chadic but even more recently, after the split into the smaller subgroups or individual languages within each branch.

The only argument in support of the hypothesis that locative extensions developed at the P.C. stage may be the fact that they occur in three branches of Chadic. This is, however, a purely typological argument. As reported in Heine and Reh 1984, such extensions developed in a similar way in Bantu (Guthrie 1971) and already in Niger-Congo (Voeltz 1977) and in Kxoe, a Khoisan language (Koehler 1981). Thus there is no good argument to postulate the existence of the locative extension in Proto-Chadic.

There are, however, several arguments against the existence of the extensions in P.C. The first is the fact that the forms of ventive and centrifugal extension are not cognate across languages. And since in particular languages they are cognate with the corresponding verbs, that would imply a process of reanalysis whereby speakers would periodically replace the form of the ventive with a new morpheme derived from the appropriate directional verb. Indeed, assuming that the ventive form is derived from the P.C. verb 'return', 'come' would force us to postulate a process of degrammaticalization whereby in Mupun, and most probably in other languages of the Angas group, an affix became detached from the verb and became an independent lexical item. Although such processes are possible, they are exceedingly rare (Lehmann 1985). In addition, for the Angas group we would have to postulate that the newly emerging directional verb has assumed a new position. Finally, we have the problem that in many languages locative extensions appear to be cognate not with verbs but rather with nouns and prepositions indicating direction. For these forms we would have to postulate that the locative extensions derived from verbs were replaced by extensions derived from nouns and prepositions -- a possible but rather complex process without any motivation to justify it. We have therefore at least four different problems, each requiring an ad hoc explanation.

If, however, we postulate that the locative extensions emerged after the split into subgroups within each branch of Chadic, then the only problem that we have to deal with is to explain why this process has happened independently in several subgroups. Usually in attempts at reconstruction such independent innovations are rejected as being unlikely. In this case, however, we can justify them by pointing to the identical initial stage consisting of two verbs with the second verb having a grammatical function.

5. Conclusions

I have shown in this paper the following: (1) Locative extensions in Chadic languages derive from one of three sources: a. verbs of movement (ventive and centrifugal extension), b. locative preposition, and c. nouns indicating direction. (2) The development of ventive and centrifugal extensions was conditioned by the syntactic position that the directional verb occupied in a clause. If the directional verb followed the main verb of the clause then there was a possibility (but by no means a necessity) for the locative extension to develop. The syntactic conditions were also one of the factors that prevented the emergence of locative extensions in some languages. If the directional verb preceded the main verb, the ventive and centrifugal extensions did not develop. (3) The occurrence of the directional verb was motivated by the properties of the grammatical system of P.C., and in particular by the fact that this system did not contain grammatical devices to indicate direction of movement with respect to the second reference point. Locative extensions did not exist in the P.C. grammatical system.

The following questions remain unanswered: (1) What syntactic processes allowed for the fusion of prepositions with preceding verbs? (2) Why was there a distinction between the perfective and non-perfective form of the ventive extension?

CHART 1

	Ventive		Centrifugal
	Perf.	Imperf.	
Hausa	-oo		---
Bole	-n	-t	---
Pero	-ina	-tu	---
Kanakuru	-tu		
Angas	---		---
Mupun	---		---
Ngizim	-ee(-w)	-ìiná	---
Pa'a	---		---

Tera	Locative prefixes to the verb.		
Ga'anda	---		--- Clause final locative particles
Hona	-ɓa		-ɗ (Clause final)
Cibak	---		-bà
Margi	-wá (in)		-bá
Kapsiki	(rich system of locative extensions, but no ventive or centrifugal)		
Bana	"		
Mandara	"		
Podoko	-atsa		-á (and many other extensions)
Dghwede		-d	--- (other extensions present)
Lamang	-gha	-aa	-b -be (Perfective)
Mofu	-wa		
Zulgo	-ára		-áha
Gisiga	-awa		---
Daba	-aha		
Bachama	-a		
Gude	-a		
Logone	-o		-li
Buduma			-li

Munjuk	-si	-fu

Tobanga	-ga	
Kera	-dà	-ná
Mokilko	-o	-e

Masa	-áya	-áysa

CHART 2

Language	'return'	'come'	'come in'
Hausa	waiwaya		
Pero		wat-na	
Tangale		wanna	
Cip	wa	wul	
Ankwe		wul	
Karekare	taw		
Dira			te
Geji			tewi
Bulli		warru	wərgu
Seya			wət
Pəlci	təməni		
Hona	wuɗa		
Ngwaxi	tira		
Margi		wazəgu	
Dghwede	wùrdə		
Daba			tìm

Footnotes

*The work on this paper was supported by an NSF Grant Nr. BNS-84 18923 and by the Center for Applied Humanities, University of Colorado. I am most grateful to Ekkehard Wolff and to Hilke Meyer-Bahlburg editor of the *Afrika und Übersee*, for the close reading of a previous version of this paper and for the comments and suggestions on its form and content. Most of them are reflected in one way or another in the revised version. A few have not been incorporated. As always, however, I alone am responsible for any mistakes and infelicities in the content and form.

[1] There is considerable terminological diversity in the current literature. For motion toward the speaker the terms most often used are 'ventive' or 'venitive'. For motion away from the speaker, 'allative', 'efferential' (Newman 1983), and several other terms are used. Perhaps the term 'centrifugal' ("Moving or directed away from a center or axis" -- American Heritage Dictionary) would be most appropriate for the motion away extension. Then one could also use 'centripetal' for motion toward the speaker. Note that the two terms have been in usage in French linguistic literature for quite some time. Haller et al. 1981 use the terms 'egressive' and 'ingressive' and I have preserved their terms in word-for-word translation of their examples.

[2] Data on Pero, Bole, Mupun, Hona, Mandara, and Cibak are from my own fieldnotes sometimes supplemented with information from other sources. I am most grateful to Daniel Barreteau, Michka Sachnine, Theda Schumann, and Henry Tourneux who shared with me their expertise on Mofu, Zime, Masa, and Munjuk (Mulwi). The sources of data from other languages are listed in the references. Information on extensions in other African families I owe mainly to Heine and Reh 1984.

[3] Prepositions in turn may ultimately be derived from verbs, names for body parts, and/or from names denoting spatial orientation (cf. Frajzyngier 1987a).

[4] I reconstruct just one vowel in accordance with the hypothesis about the structure of the verb root in P.C. postulated in Frajzyngier 1982. Note that the second consonant [n] in Tangale can be explained by assimilation rules similar to the ones described for closely re-

lated Pero in Frajzyngier 1978, and the [r] in Bulli and Dghwede may be a result of independently attested rules of rothacization of /t/.

5 Newman 1983 postulates that PC had 'efferential' extension *də. The functions of this
extension were to include both motion away and the causative transitivizing function and in
the reconstruction both types of suffixes were taken into consideration. With respect to this
analysis cf. also Frajzyngier 1985 and the present volume.

6 I am grateful to the editor of *Afrika und Übersee* for drawing my attention to this correlation.

7 Most of the data in this chart and the names of languages are from Kraft 1981. Entries
for Pero are from my own fieldnotes and for Hausa are from Bargery 1951. The chart
should by no means be considered complete. Entries in Kraft presumably contain glosses
corresponding to the most general notions of the lexical items. It is very likely that a fuller
list of lexical items would exhibit many more cognates, with somewhat shifted meanings.

INTERROGATIVE SENTENCES IN CHADIC:
RECONSTRUCTION AND FUNCTIONAL EXPLANATION

1. Introduction

There are two interconnected aims of the present study. The first one is to attempt a reconstruction of the form of the interrogative sentence in Proto-Chadic (PC). The second is to provide a synchronic and diachronic explanation for several hitherto unobserved and unexplained facts concerning the form of these sentences in contemporary Chadic languages. This explanation is an example of the advantages offered by looking at language as a system whose parts have well-defined communicative functions. While any scientific work is subject to modification, rejection, or confirmation through the use of different theories or analytic techniques, a work on reconstruction of the Chadic grammatical system is additionally subject to change when new data become available. The present investigation is based on descriptions of and field notes on some thirty languages out of an estimated one hundred forty Chadic languages.[1] There is, however, a pattern emerging from the present investigation that is not likely to be affected by any new data.

The paper will deal with questions concerning truth (in English the so-called yes/no questions) and specific questions, i.e., questions relating to a certain element of a proposition (in English the wh-questions). Several issues related to interrogatives have been touched upon in Schuh 1971 and more recently in Newman and Ma Newman 1981. The scope of the present paper is much larger than the scope of either of the preceding works. It differs from Schuh 1971 in considering a much larger body of data and in providing historical reconstruction and functional explanations for the interrogative sentences. It differs from Newman and Ma Newman 1981 in proposing a different reconstruction with supporting evidence. Also it offers functional explanations totally missing from Schuh 1971 and Newman and Ma Newman 1981. The rest of the paper is divided into the following sections: a. synchronic picture; b. formal reconstruction; c. functional explanation; d. implications for the methodology of historical reconstruction and theory of language.

2. Synchronic picture

The synchronic data are presented in Charts 1-4 where the following regularities can be observed: The yes/no questions are formed through either tonal modifications of the sentence or addition of a sentence-final interrogative particle (i- particle), e.g., in Kanakuru:

> 1. gáawì à ɗəktéè-ni
>   'Is the room built?'

> cf. gáawì à ɗəktè-ní
> 'The room is built'

Although the tonal structure of affirmative and negative is the same, the last high tone in the interrogative is higher than the last high tone in the affirmative sentence

> 2. Adáamù à nà nè rú
>   'Did Adamu call me?'

> cf. Adáamù à nà né
> 'Adamu called me' (Newman 1974:70)

Note that in many languages from different families it is possible to ask a yes/no question and at the same time to narrow the scope of the question from the whole proposition to only a part of it. Consider the following example in Polish:

> 3. Czy tygrysy lubia oset?
>   'Do the tigers like thistle?'

If a heavy stress is added to any element of the proposition in 3 it will limit the scope of the question to the stressed element, e.g., the verb, the subject, or the object of the sentence. No information about devices to narrow the scope of the interrogative is available for any of the Chadic languages, although it is difficult to imagine such devices not being available. The specific questions are formed through the use of 'question words' (q-words) and in some languages addition of an i- particle at the end of a sentence. Note that the specific questions in Charts 1-4 have been labeled as 'who' and 'what'. As in English the two q-words in Chadic encode the semantic distinction between the [+human] and [-human], i.e., the rest of the nouns. The q-words in Chadic, however, never encode the grammatical role, unlike in English and most other I.E. languages (e.g., English 'who/whom' or Russian *kto/kogo*). If a language is to encode the semantic role of the arguments in a sentence, it must have some other means to do so. In most Chadic languages the semantic role of arguments in the interrogative sentences is encoded in the same way as in the affirmative sentences (cf. Frajzyngier 1983a and the present volume), i.e., by the position of the q-word in respect to the verb. Question words occupy the same position that the non-q-words occupy in the affirmative sentence, e.g.:

4. Agèlèem lɔ́tán mintí mó?
   Whom Agele hit?

   cf. (A. lɔ́tan) nəwri
   Agele hit your sister

5. A áyá n kúsúkí n á mintí mó
   To whom did she give meat?

   cf. (A áyá n kúsúkí n) á hɔ̀lgən
   (She gave the meat) to the woman.

6. A bɔ̀n dɔ̀ mintí mó
   With whom did they come?

   cf. (A bɔ̀n) dɔ̀ šeená
   They came with their brother (Kera, Ebert 1979:224 ff.)

The above examples are typical for the majority of languages. There are, however, in each branch, several exceptions to this generalization:

West Chadic: In Kanakuru q-words can be fronted for emphasis (Newman 1974). In Ngizim q-words relating to subject are in S-final position.

Biu-Mandara: In Kapsiki a q-word relating to the object is fronted and in Padoko all q-words occur in the focus position, i.e., the position after the verb. In Daba a q-word for the subject is fronted and a q-word for the object is in the S-final position. In Logone all q-words are sentence final and in Gude they are all fronted.

In Masa, all q-words except for those related to subject are in S-final position.

The questions about arguments other than subject and object, i.e., questions about benefactive, instrumental, locative, etc., differ from the questions about subject and object in the form of the q-words and in the presence of the markers of the grammatical or semantic role. These markers are again the same as in the affirmative sentence, i.e., they consist of the same prepositions and they are marked by the same position in the sentence, e.g., in Pa'anci:

> 7. a. məna   cin sona
>   we +cont. go where
>   'Where are we going?' (Skinner 1979:88)

>   cf. mi cin 'hwocu Kano suu
>   we+subj we+go go Kano tomorrow
>   'We will go to Kano tomorrow' (ibid. 42)

> 8. ú   dava kaacəna
>   you+compl came when
>   'When did you come?' (ibid. 88)

3. Yes/no questions

3.1. The structure of the yes/no question

The general form of the yes/no question in PC can be reconstructed as consisting of S+ i-particle/tone. There are no other forms of the yes/no questions in contemporary Chadic languages, and therefore there is no reason to postulate any other form as a candidate for

PC. The postulated structure, moreover, occurs in many languages from three branches of Chadic.

3.2. The yes/no i- particle

Newman and Newman 1981 postulate, without providing any evidence, that Chadic had a yes/no q marker *à, i.e., a marker consisting of the vowel a and a low tone. Although [a] is indeed a frequent component of the yes/no question markers, one has to note that it occurs with some frequency in two branches only, viz., West Chadic and Biu-Mandara. It certainly can be reconstructed as an interrogative marker (i- marker) for the yes/no questions. But a closer look at the charts will indicate that perhaps a was not the only i- marker for these questions. In particular, note that in the West Chadic language, Pero, and in two languages of the Biu-Mandara branch, the i- marker has an initial d. Note also that in two branches there is a yes/no i- marker with initial mV (Tera in Biu-Mandara, Kera and Somrai in East Chadic). Instead of the Newman and Ma Newman reconstruction of just one yes/no i- marker it appears unavoidable to reconstruct several i- markers, only one of which will be /a/. The most widespread device to distinguish between affirmative and interrogative sentences in Chadic is the use of tone. Virtually all languages on which the data are available can mark the interrogative by tonal changes only, e.g. in Kanakuru, as in example 1, repeated here for convenience, in which the last high tone of interrogative is considerably higher than the last tone of affirmative sentence:

9. gáawì à ɗɔktée-ní
   'Is the room built?'

   cf. gáawì à ɗɔktè-ní
   'The room is built'

That contradicts the claim of Newman and Ma Newman that tone was a part of the q-morpheme whose other part was [a]. Unfortunately, for languages other than Hausa, the information about the tonal differences is not very precise (with the notable exception of Leben 1989). Most authors indicate that the final tone, or sometimes the last high tone, becomes higher in the interrogative than in the affirmative sentence. The existing descriptions offer no information about the differentiation between the functions of tone and the functions of other markers. Note, however,that it is often the case in other languages that intonation is an interrogative marker that may be used alone or in conjunction with some other syntactic or morphological devices (cf. Ultan 1978).

In respect to the reconstructible marker $*\textit{d'V}$, it appears that it had a narrower meaning than /a/. In Pero it forms an incredulous question, in Margi it forms an 'urgent' question, and in Tera, negative sentence question. The information concerning the functions of the marker /mV/ is very scanty. Note, however, that in Tera and Somrai it is the principal yes/no i- particle. There is some problem concerning the widespread marker *ko* or *kwa* . The number of branches and languages in which it occurs make it an excellent candidate for a PC i- marker. It is, however, also one of the i- markers in Hausa, a vehicular language in Northern Nigeria and a second language for many speakers of other Chadic languages. That makes it entirely possible that the widespread use of *ko* or *kwa* may be due to borrowing from Hausa rather than to retention from the PC. A careful look at charts 1-4 indicates that *ko/kwa* is not used in languages whose speakers usually do not know Hausa, i.e., Chadic languages spoken in Cameroon or Chad, e.g., Padoko, Mofu-Gudur, Daba, Buduma, Mulwi, Kera and all languages of the Masa group. Even in languages in which *ko* is used it appears to be used along with other markers. Thus in Mupun it is used along with the i- particle *a* in yes/no questions.

4. Q-word question

4.1. The structure of the specific interrogative in PC

In most of the languages from three branches the q-word occupies the same position as its non-interrogative counterpart. In addition there is an i- particle occurring at the end of the sentence. Since it is unlikely that such a specific construction emerged as a result of independent innovation, it is necessary to postulate it as a construction that represents a common retention from PC. Since PC had the word order VSO (for the discussion and documentation in support of this hypothesis see Frajzyngier 1983a and this volume) I would like to postulate that the specific interrogative sentence in PC had the form: V (X NPi.Y) i-particle. Any of the NPs, or an adverb, could have been replaced by an appropriate q-word. Languages in which the q-word is at the beginning or the end of a sentence represent innovations in syntactic structures. Such innovations could have been motivated by the rules of focusing, which in Chadic languages most often involve displacement of the focused element (cf. Frajzyngier 1983a and present volume).

4.2. Reconstruction of the q-words

The evidence provided by the Charts 1-4 leaves little doubt that the PC equivalent of 'who' was *wa. A number of languages have innovated either by replacing *wa by some other morpheme or by adding to it some markers. Thus Pero has *non*, Kanakuru has *man-dai*, Ngizim has *tà-i*, Tera has *ki*. I will have more to say about some of these innovations later in the paper. There is even stronger evidence that the PC equivalent of 'what' was *mi. The evidence for the vowel is provided by the fact that the vowels of the contemporary markers are [i], [e], and shwa. The number of innovations for this q-word is much smaller than the number of innovations that replaced *wa. One of the most puzzling facts is that in a number of languages, viz., Pero, Lamang, and Logone instead of initial [m], there is [n]. I do not have any explanation to offer for this difference.

4.3. The specific i- particle

Newman and Newman 1981 postulate that the specific i- particle was *ya. They do not, however, provide any justification for this claim, and no evidence to support it. A look at charts 1-4 clearly shows that out of several possibilities for the PC specific i- marker, *ya is not a very likely candidate. The most frequent component of the specific i- particle is the alveolar nasal [n]. Thus Pa'anci in West Chadic, and Tera and Padoko in Biu-Mandara have the specific i- particle [na]; Lamang has [ne] and Margi has [rá]. Recall, however, that according to Newman and Ma 1966 and Newman 1977 the Margi [r] quite frequently corresponds to [n] in other Chadic languages. It would appear therefore that *na is a more likely candidate than *ya for the specific i- particle. Several particles that occur in other languages, such as *e/yi/ye* in the Angas group, *ka/ke* in Mofu-Gudur, *da* in Mulwi, and *mo* in Kera would have to be considered innovations. Thus in Kera the specific i- particle is identical with the yes/no i- particle. There is also a frequent interrogative particle of the form *-kV* discussed already in 3.1.2.

5. Summary of reconstruction

5.1. The yes/no questions

For the yes/no question for PC we will reconstruct the following structure: S -- i- marker.
There were at least three different i- markers:

> 1. The tonal marker, most probably raising of the last high tone or a high tone on
>   the last syllable.
> 2. The marker *a.*
> 3. The marker *dV.*

It appears that the first two were the most general markers, both indicating just a yes/no
question. It is possible, however, that there used to be a functional differentiation between
the two, which cannot be reconstructed. The third marker had a much more narrow function than the preceding markers, perhaps that of indicating an incredulous question.

5.2. The specific questions

The specific questions had the following form: *V (Argument [i]...Argument [j]) na,* and
any of the arguments in the sentence could have been replaced by an appropriate q-word.

At this point a traditional reconstruction usually ends. It is, however, quite obvious
that such a reconstruction does not contribute to the knowledge of language universals or to
the methodology of historical reconstruction and is not illuminating with respect to any
possible connections among the various elements of the language structure. Note that such
a reconstruction did not pose a single question regarding the motivation for such rather than
other markers. As the next section will show, the questions about the sources and motivations for various markers are much more interesting and reveal much more about language
structure than traditional reconstructions of phonological forms, and at the same time contribute to the knowledge of language change.

6. Functional explanation

In this section I propose to ask a few questions about the sources of interrogative particles and the reasons for their existence. In a few cases I will provide answers, some of them admittedly speculative, concerning the syntax of the interrogative in PC and contemporary Chadic languages.

6.1. Where does the specific i- particle come from?

There is always a possibility that a given grammatical morpheme will have only one function, and the question about the origin of the morpheme may not be answered. A close look at the specific i- particles reveals, however, that they are very similar to the markers that in many Chadic languages are associated with the demonstrative/definite function. Thus, many languages have *ni* or *na* as the masculine demonstrative or definite marker. Pa'anci provides excellent evidence for the proposed hypothesis because it actually has two forms of the specific i- particle, *na* and *ya*, the first corresponding to the masculine predicative particle and the second, to the feminine predicative particle. In Tera the demonstrative 'this' is *na*; in Logone, the demonstrative is *ne*. The best evidence comes from languages that innovated: In Margi one of the specific i- particles is *ri*, and there is a definite marker *ari*. In Mulwi the specific i- particle *da* is also a definite marker. Since it has been shown that the specific i- particle is etymologically connected with a demonstrative pronoun, one may ask whether the demonstrative pronoun is derived from the i- particle or the i- particle derives from the demonstrative. It is more likely that the development was from demonstrative to the i- particle rather than the other way around, since the demonstrative markers are cognate among most Chadic languages, while the interrogative words are not. It is necessary to ask why a demonstrative pronoun and not some other marker came to be used in the interrogative sentences. As an answer to this question I would like to propose that the demonstrative at the end of interrogative sentences functions as a copula, and the whole interrogative sentence has actually the form S-Be, regardless of what the language-particular equivalents of the verb 'to be' were, or how S was realized. It has been known to scholars of Semitic languages for at least sixty five years (cf. Cohen 1924) that copulas may develop from pronominal forms. Li and Thompson 1977 have shown it to be a much more widespread phenomenon. The definite marker serves as a copula in Basque (cf. Lafitte

1944 and Frajzyngier 1985e.) Schuh 1983 has demonstrated such development in one Chadic language, Kilba, and claimed it for Hausa as well.

Thus development from pronoun to a copula in Chadic is entirely possible. The marker of the interrogative is, however, not the copula by itself but, primarily, its position at the end of the sentence. If the PC had a VSO word order, then for PC and the majority of contemporary languages, the verb's occurrence in sentence-final position is a highly marked phenomenon. It is, however, very frequent for interrogative sentences to have a word order different from affirmative sentences as one of the devices to mark the interrogative function.

6.2. The yes/no i- particle

After considering where the specific i- particles come from, it may be tempting to speculate about the possible origin of the yes/no i- particle. The natural hypothesis would be that the yes/no i- particle is also a copula. For a few languages we have clear evidence that this is indeed the case. Thus in Mulwi *di* is also a definite pronoun, and in languages of the Angas group it serves as a copula, e.g., in Mupun:

```
10 a.  a      wur a    miskom mopun
        Cop 3sg Cop chief     Mupun
        'He is the chief of Mupun'


     b. səm wur   a     devid
        name 3sg  Cop
        'His name is David'
```

For other languages, however, the evidence is not so transparent. I would like to propose that the reconstructed yes/no i- particle *a derives from the copula *a, which used to exist in PC. This hypothesis may appear to be implausible if one were to believe an assertion in Schuh 1983:312 that 'In Chadic languages, copulas of any kind are rather rare'. This assertion, however, appears to be based on rather superficial analyses of the syntax of contemporary languages.

There exists in a number of Chadic languages a locative construction typically analyzed as consisting of a preposition, followed by a locative noun serving as spatial specifier, and then followed by a head noun, e.g., in Hausa:

11. ajiye shi a   kai- n   gado
    put it Prep head-Gen bed
    'Put it on the bed' (Bargery 1951:528)

12. ga ni   a ɗaki
    look 1sg house
    'Here I am in the house' (ibid. 1)

This type of locative phrase is more often than not a complement of the stative verbs, but it does occur with verbs of movement as well. I would like to propose that the contemporary preposition *a* occurring in a number of Chadic languages, is derived from a verb meaning 'to be at' in a manner very similar to the development of *zai* and other prepositions from verbs in Chinese (cf. Li and Thompson 1981) or to the similar developments in Kwa languages described in detail in Lord 1973. The development of the interrogative copula and the preposition from the locative copula **a* were two independent processes:

Loc. copula > preposition

The yes/no i- particle would be derived at the PC stage from the copula, i.e.:

Loc. copula > i- particle

This last development occurred most probably through the process of putting the copula at the end of the sentence. The occurrence of the *a* at the end of interrogative sentences in contemporary languages constitutes one piece of evidence for the proposed hypothesis. Another piece of evidence is the fact that *a* is a copula in all languages of the Angas group (cf. ex. 10 above). The third and final piece of evidence is provided by languages that have innovated in the form of the yes/no i- particle. In Tera, one of the yes/no i- particles is *yà*, and there is in this language a locative preposition *ye*.

Typologically, the proposed hypothesis fits nicely with such languages as Chinese and most of Kwa where the locative stative construction consists of a verb, a noun phrase, and a spatial specifier, most often a postposition. The verb in these constructions eventually becomes a preposition. For the crucial change from verb to preposition there is independent evidence in Chadic, where in Hausa the preposition *zuwa* 'toward' is derived from the verbal root z_'go'.

6.3. Why is there an i- particle in specific questions?

A possible justification for the presence of the i- particle would be that it is the main carrier or marker of the interrogative function. Note, however, that according to all descriptions, the interrogative function is already carried by the q-words; therefore, the presence of the i- particle is at best redundant. In addition, if it were to be the marker of the interrogative function, one would expect the i- particles in yes/no questions and in specific questions to be identical. But this is not the case. Only a few languages have identical i- particles, viz. Kera *mo*, Pero and Gude *a*. Thus the answer proposed above has to be rejected. Another possible answer is that specific questions were formed by analogy to yes/no questions. This answer has to be rejected as well, and for the same reason as the previous answer. That is, if the i- particle in specific questions were the result of analogy one would expect this i- particle to be identical with the yes/no i- particle.

In lieu of the above unsatisfactory answers, I would like to propose that the i- particle was the main, if not the only, carrier of the 'specific' interrogative function in PC. In order to provide evidence for the above hypothesis one has first to explain what the function of the q-words was, if the i- particles were to be the main carriers of the interrogative function. For the q-words I would like to propose that their only function in interrogative sentences was to indicate which argument the question was about. This hypothesis implies, of course, that q-words did not carry the interrogative function, i.e., they did not mark the sentence as interrogative. In order to prove this hypothesis about the q-words, I will show that they used to have a different function in PC.

In a number of languages from different language families there is a connection between the q-words and the indefinite words (cf. Ultan 1978). Thus in Chinese they are identical; *Sheir* 'who' and *sherme* 'what' function as indefinite words as well (Chao 1968:651). In Slavic languages the two forms are very close, e.g., Russian *kto* 'who' and *ktoto* 'someone'; *cto* 'what' and *čtoto* 'something'. There is some evidence that this is also the case in Chadic. The indefinite pronouns in Hausa, *wani* m., *wata* f. and *waɗansu* pl., all contain the marker [wa]. In Mupun, a West Chadic language, the indefinite word is *me* 'some', similar to the reconstructed PC q-word for 'what'.

More important evidence for the proposed hypothesis about the meaning of the q-words comes not from languages that retained the old marker, but rather from languages that innovated. In Pero the word for 'who' is *non*, which should be compared with *nen* 'person'. In Pa'anci, the q-words consist of a q-marker followed by a suffix *-sV*, whose vowel is identical with the vowel of the preceding morpheme. For 'what', the q-marker is *mi*, identical with the reconstructed PC marker. But for 'who', Pa'anci innovated; it has *a*. Note that *a* in Pa'anci is also the indefinite marker 'one'. The importance of the argumentation based on analysis of phonological innovations and functions of morphemes, lies in the fact that even if there is an innovation in the language, in which a new phonological form replaces the old one, the new form has the same function that has been postulated for the Proto-language, a function which is not necessarily obvious in the contemporary languages. It means that for the speakers of Pa'anci, the 'indefinite' function was very much a part of the meaning of the q-words. When the form of the q-word is replaced by another form, it is an indefinite marker that is chosen for replacement. In a number of Chadic languages the indefinite markers seem to differ from the interrogative by the addition of another marker, e.g., Logone 'who' *báke*, indef. *bake-ma*; Daba 'who' *yi*, indefinite *ko-yi*. This may lead some to claim that the indefinite markers are morphologically derived from the q-words. Although this may indeed be the case in some contemporary languages it does not indicate that it was true for PC. Note that one cannot reconstruct the alleged marker that would derive the indefinite from the q-words. Moreover, a look at charts 1-4 indicates that some of the q-words are also morphologically derived. Compare the following table which illustrates some of the morphemes used in derivation of 'question words' in a number of languages from three branches:

TABLE

Language	Prefix	Suffix
Kanakuru		-dai
Mupun	a-	
Ngizim	ta-	
Pa'anci		-sV
Bachama		-no
Buduma		-ni
Masa		-ge

I have no explanation concerning the origin of these prefixes and suffixes, but it appears that they do not derive from the same proto-form. The above data indicate that there must have been two different developments that led to the formation of the present q-words and indefinite markers. In some languages the indefinite words became q-words without any change in form. After this functional change, the indefinite word was derived through morphological means. This is the situation in languages in which the indefinite marker seems to have been derived from the q-word. In other languages the q-word was morphologically derived from the indefinite word. In some languages the original indefinite marker may have been lost; it would have to be derived from the q-word, as is the case in Ngizim, where the indefinite marker is *tiike* 'everyone' and *tànke* 'everything' (Schuh 1972:178). I would like to postulate that in PC a sentence with indefinite words but without an i- particle was affirmative, rather than interrogative. Thus a PC sentence with lexical items 'see X q-word' actually meant 'X saw someone,' rather than 'Whom did X see?'. The specific i- particle appears therefore to be the only candidate for the main marker of the interrogative function.

7. Methodological and theoretical implications

7.1 Implications for the methodology of syntactic reconstruction

The most important implication of the above study is the advantage that is provided by taking into consideration not only formal but also functional information. Thus, although the specific i- particles have different phonemic structure, they are all cognate through the functions they perform **outside** of interrogative sentences. The same was shown to be true for the general i- particles and the q-words. Even if one were not able to determine the phonological shape of a yes/no or specific i- particle one could still reconstruct the interrogative sentence in Proto-Chadic in terms of the function and place of its components. The other implication is that when one takes into consideration not the form of the morphemes but their function, the innovations become important evidence for an historical reconstruction. If one were to ignore the function of the morphemes involved, this important evidence would not be available for historical reconstruction.

7.2. Theoretical implications

There are several possible implications of the findings in this paper for the theory of language. I will concentrate for the time being on two only: The first is the implication concerning substantial universals of the interrogative sentence structure; the second is the implication for the grammaticalization processes in languages.

7.3. Implications for the universals of interrogative sentences

Two elements of the interrogative sentence structure in Chadic should help in understanding interrogative sentences in other languages: One is the connection between q-words and indefinite words, and the other is the role of the copula in interrogative sentences. Studies of Proto-Indo-European syntax and universals (e.g., Lehmann 1974; Ultan 1978) are not very explicit about the historical development of the q-words and indefinite words although they all point to a connection between the two. The evidence from Chadic points clearly to a possibility that the two may be derived from the same morpheme. Use of the copula in interrogative sentence formation is certainly a widespread phenomenon, but there are no studies concerning conditions under which copula, rather than some other device, is used in languages. However, the use of the copula in the formation of interrogative sentences was not mentioned in Ultan's study.

7.4. Implications for the study of grammaticalization

By the term grammaticalization I understand encoding of certain semantic or discourse functions in the grammatical system of the language. What is of interest in this respect in Chadic is that just a few lexical morphemes, such as demonstrative pronouns and the verb 'to be,' are used in the creation of a very wide range of constructions, such as prepositional phrases, equational sentences, and interrogative sentences, to name just a few discussed in this paper.

8.   Charts

For yes/no questions only two devices are included in the charts: tone and sentence final markers. 'Tone' indicates that the yes/no question is marked by tone alone or in conjunction with some other device. For specific questions the charts include information on 'who' and 'what' questions and sentence final markers, which often co-occur with other devices.

CHART 1

West Chadic

Language		yes/no question		Specific question	
	Tone	S-final	who	what	S-final
Hausa	H	length ko	wa	me	---
Kanakuru	H	-ru -kwa	mandai	məndai	---
Pero	H	-a dee	non	ni	-á
Angas		-a	we	me	é
Mupun		-a	wa	m	yi
Sura		-a	awe	ame	ye
Fyer		ewa(m.) iwa(f.)			kwa
Ngizim	---	tài	tàam	----	
Pa'anci	H	wa	asa	mišii	na

Comments: In Hausa the sentence final vowel is lengthened in the interrogative.

CHART 2
Biu-Mandara

Language	yes/no question			Specific question	
	Tone	S-final	who	what	S-final
Ga'anda		wa	wunə	mə	---
Tera	Tone	mú	ki	nəm	na
		yà			a
		(asking for confirmation)			kwa
Cibak		yà	wa		
Margi	H	yà	wa	mi	ra
		rà (emph.)			ri (emph.)
Kapsiki		yi	wa nde	wa	wa
		wú			
Padoko		nana	wa	tawə	na
Lamang		re	we	ne	ne
		(wa ya)	(nuwa ya)		
Mandara			ware	uwe	
Gisiga		kwa	wa	me	ka(ke)
					Emph. only
Mofu-Gudur		dà	wa	me	
Daba		vu	yi	mi	yi
Bachama		yò	weno	muno	
		à			
Gude		a	wu	mi	a
		kwa			kwa
		nii			
Buduma		ba	wo-ni	mi-ni	
		a			
Logone		ɗa	bake	xwani	ne
		ra		(only after 'why')	
Mulwi		ɗí	siya	ma	ɗa

Comments: Tera *ya* is used in questions asking for confirmation. Margi *ra* and *ri* and Gisiga *ka* are used in emphatic questions. Logone *ne* is used after questions asking 'why'.

CHART 3
East Chadic

Language	yes/no question			Specific question	
	Tone	S-final	who	what	S-final
Somrai		mo			
Kera		mo	minti	ma	mo
Dangla			we	me	

CHART 4
Masa

Language	yes/no question			Specific question	
	Tone	S-final	who	what	S-final
Masa		su	gige	mige	
Mesme		su			
Zime		su	sa/sasa		

Footnotes

[1] The published sources from which the data were taken are listed in the bibliography. Data on Pero, Hona, Cibak, and Mandara are from my own fieldnotes. I would like to thank Daniel Barreteau, Henry Tourneux, Ekkehard Wolff, Theda Schumann, and Mishka Sachnine for generously sharing with me their knowledge of Mofu-Gudur, Mulwi, Lamang, Masa, and Zime respectively. I would also like to thank the anonymous referee of the *Journal of West African Languages* for many helpful suggestions, which prompted me to reconsider several statements in the paper.

LOGOPHORIC SYSTEMS IN CHADIC

1. Introduction

1 1 The aim and scope of the paper

The term logophoric, widely accepted since its introduction by Hagège in 1974, is used here to refer to syntactic contexts of complements of the verbs of saying, the contexts most often known as 'indirect speech'. The term 'logophoric' is also often used in reference to pragmatic contexts which involve a report of someone else's speech, without necessarily being a complement of a verb of saying.

The aim of the present paper is to propose, for the first time, a comparative study of the form and function of logophoric systems in Chadic languages, and to formulate a hypothesis regarding logophoricity in Proto-Chadic. It will also offer a description of the logophoric system of Mupun, which differs in an important respect from descriptions of the related languages, Angas and Mwaghavul (Sura). The description offered here proves to be illuminating for the description of logophoric systems in other Chadic languages.

1.2. Organization of the paper

There are at least two types of logophoric systems in Chadic languages. Both types may exist in one language, as is the case in Mupun, which will be used to illustrate the form and function of the two types. The rest of this paper is organized as follows:

1. Presentation of the two systems on the basis of data from Mupun.
2. Comparative data, presented in centrifugal fashion: Starting with the smallest unit, the Angas group, I will then present data from a larger unit, i.e., the West Chadic branch, and finally data from other branches of Chadic.
3. Problems of possible reconstruction.

2. The two systems

2.1. The three sets of Mupun

The logophoric system of Mupun consists of the following sets of pronouns:[1]

TABLE 1

	A	B		C[2]
	subj./obj.	subj.	obj.	subj.
m sg	wur	ɗi	ɗin	gwar
f sg	war	ɗe	ɗe	paa
pl	mo	ɗu	ɗun	nuwa

The full set of pronouns from which set A was extracted is the following:

TABLE 2

	Subject	Object
1sg	n	an
2m	a	ha
f	yi	yi
3m	wur	wur
f	war	war
1pl	mu	mun
2	wu	wu
3	mo	mo

The first and second person pronouns used with sets B and C (i.e., logophorically) are the same as in Table 2.

For the sake of the clarity of presentation I will discuss first the functional relations between sets A and B and then the relations between sets A and C.

2.2. Relations between sets A and B: Reference to subject

In sentential complements following the verb *sat* 'say', set A indicates disjoint reference and set B indicates coreference with the speaker of the main clause, i.e., the subject of the verb *sat*. Compare (1a) and (1b):

1a. wur/war/mo sat nə wur/war/mo ta dee n jos
    he/she/they say Comp he/she/they stop stay Prep Jos
    'He₁/She₁/They₁ said that he₂/she₂/they₂ stopped over in Jos'

   b. wur/war/mo sat nə ɗi/ɗe/ɗu ta dee n jos
    'He₁/She₁/They₁ said that he₁/she₁/they₁ stopped over in Jos.'

The object pronouns of the sentential complements behave in the same way as subject pronouns:

2a. wur/war sat nə n nas wur/war
    he/she say Comp I beat him/her
    'He₁/She₁ said that I beat him₂/her₂'

   b. wur/war sat nə n nas ɗin/ɗe
    'He₁/she₁ said that I beat him₁/her₁'

The following examples provide one more piece of evidence for the logophoric only (i.e., coreference with the subject of the verb 'to speak') function of the set B:

3a. *a sat nə ta ɗi dee n denva
    2sg say Comp stop 3sg stay Prep Denver
    'You said that he stopped in Denver'

   b. *wu sat nə ta ɗu dee n denva
    2pl   3pl
    'You said that they stopped in Denver'

The above sentences are ungrammatical because the subjects of the embedded clauses, ɗi and ɗu, are set B pronouns and they cannot be coreferential with the subject of the main clause, which is second person. The requirement of coreferentiality does not apply to the set A pronouns and therefore they can occur in environments in which set B pronouns cannot.

4. a sat nə mo ta dee n denva
   2sg   3pl
   'You said that they stopped over in Denver'

The distinction between direct and indirect speech is also marked with the help of the set B pronouns:

5a. wur sat   nə   ɗi n nas an
    3m say Comp 3m Fut beat 1sg
    'He said he will beat me'

b. wur sat nə a   n nas ha
   3m   1sg Fut   2m

The system further makes explicit whether or not third person singular is a part of the set referred to by the third plural:

6a. wur/war   sat   nə n nas mo
    'He$_1$/She$_1$ said that I beat them$_2$'
    ('he/she' is not part of 'them')

b. wur/war   sat   nə n nas ɗun
   'He$_1$/She$_1$ said that I beat them$_1$'
   ('he/she' is part of 'them')

7. wur sat nə ta ɗu dee n jos

       stop 3pl stay Prep

'He said they stopped over in Jos' ('he' is part of 'them')

When the subject of the main clause is plural and the subject of the embedded clause is singular the distinction between logophoric and non-logophoric reference is neutralized:

8. mo sat nə wur ɓe yol kwat lusım

   3pl   3sg Fut go hunt leopard

'They said that he will go to hunt a leopard'

In the above sentence the subject of the embedded clause may be, but does not have to be, properly included in the subject of the main clause. A similar phenomenon has been noted in Gokana (cf. Hyman and Comrie 1981).

   In complement clauses following non-verba dicendi, instead of the three sets of pronouns only one set. A, is used in all persons. Unlike in the complement clauses following verbs of saying, such a use more often than not indicates coreference with an argument of the main clause.

9. yak sə wur man me takarda wur cin n an n tan

   then take 3sg take some book 3sg give Prep 1sg 1sg read

'Then he took a book and gave it to me to read'

10. n tal pə wur a nə ko ket wur kə la siwol nə a

    1sg ask Prep 3sg Cop Def Interr 3sg Perf receive money Def Interr

'I asked him whether he had received the money'

In (10) the third person masculine singular pronoun *wur* in the embedded clause may or may not be coreferential with the same pronoun in the main clause.

   Although it is implicitly indicated in the content of Table 1, it is nevertheless, worth stating that the second and the first person pronouns have only one set in the logophoric situation:

11a. n-sat   ha   nə   a   naa kə n kes   makaranta
     1sg-tell 2m(O) Comp 2f(S)   look Perf 1sg finish school

  b. n-sat   yi nə   yi   naa kə n kes   makaranta
     1sg-tell 2f Comp 2f   look Perf 1sg finish school

  c. n-sat   wu nə wu   naa kə n kes   makaranta
     1sg-tell 2pl Comp 2pl look Perf 1sg finish school
     'I told you (m/f/pl), look, I have finished school'

  d. n-sat   wur nə   an angu kwat
     1sg -tell 3sg Comp 1sg man hunt
     'I told him that I am a hunter'

  e. a   sat nə   mo nas mun
     2sg say Comp 3pl beat 1pl
     'You$_{1,2}$ said that they beat us$_1$'

  f. a sat   nə   ta mu dee n jos
     2sg say Comp stop 1pl stay Prep Jos
     'You$_{1,2}$ said that we$_1$ stopped at Jos'

In e. and f. the person referred to by second person singular *a* may or may not be a part of
the group referred to by first person plural *mu* (subject) or *mun* (object). Like many other
Chadic languages Mupun can make a distinction between first person plural inclusive and
exclusive through a periphrastic construction consisting of: 1sg/pl + associative particle
'with' + 2sg/pl. Quite often the first person singular or plural pronoun is omitted and the
construction consists only of the associative particle and the second person singular or plural pronoun. Despite the existence of these constructions, I have not come across their use
to disambiguate sentences such as e. and f. in the texts gathered.

    It has been shown that the function of sets A and B consists of marking the coreferen-
tiality or inclusion of the third person pronoun in the embedded clause. In the system of
marking, the use of set A pronouns indicates disjoint reference and use of set B pronouns
indicates coreference.

2.3. Relationship between sets A and C

Unlike the relatively simple functional relationship between sets A and B, the relationship between sets A and C is more complex. There are two types of structures that have to be taken into consideration: one type in which the reference to addressee[3] is grammatically encoded and the other in which it is not.

2.3.1. Reference to addressee

If the third person pronouns in the embedded clause refer to the addressee rather than to the speaker (subject) of the main clause, then the pronouns must be drawn from set C but never from set B. If the reference in the embedded clause is made to persons other than the addressee of the main clause then the pronouns must be drawn from set A. Compare the following examples:

    12a. n- sat   n- wur   nə   wur ji
        1sg say Prep- 3m Comp 3m come
        'I told him$_1$ that he$_2$ should come'

    b. n-sat   n-wur   nə   gwar ji
       1sg-say Prep- 3m Comp 3m   come
       'I told him$_1$ that he$_1$ should come'

    13a. n-sat   n wur   taji   wur dəm n-kaano
        1sg-say Prep- 3m Prohib 3m go Prep-Kano
        'I told him$_1$ that he$_2$ may not go to Kano'

    b. n sat n wur taji gwar dəm n kaano
       'I told him$_1$ that he$_1$ may not go to Kano'

Similarly to pronouns of set B, pronouns of set C cannot be used in non-logophoric contexts, i.e., in complement clauses of verbs other than the verb *sat*. In such contexts only pronouns of set A are allowed:

> 14a. n- pet war ɓe war/*paa ji
>   1sg call 3f Comp come
>   'I called her and she came'
>
> b. n-pet mo ɓe mo/*nuwa ji
>   3pl
>   'I called them and they came'

Compare also the following examples:

> 15a. n-naa   wur wur pə   dəm n   kaano
>   1sg- see 3m 3m   Prog go Prep
>   'I saw him going to Kano'
>
> b. *n naa wur gwar pə dəm n kaano
>   3sg
>   'I saw him going to Kano'

The set C pronouns, which refer to third person masculine, feminine, or plural may become forms of address, thus changing for the speaker from third to second person pronouns. Compare the following examples:

> 16a. n   sat n war   nə   paa naa kə   n kes makaranta
>   1sg say Prep 3f   Comp 3f look Perf 1sg finish school
>   'I told her, look, I have finished school'
>
> b. n sat mo nə   nuwa an nə gwar tan me mbi n an
>   3pl   3pl
>   'I told him that he should find something for me'

c. n sat   n-wur   an   nə   gwar tan me   mbi n   an
   1sg-say Prep- 3m 1sg   Comp 3m   find 1sg thing Prep 1sg
   'I told him that he should find something for me'

Note that the use of a set B pronoun in the embedded clause would produce an ungrammatical sentence:

17. *n sat   n-wur   nə   di   naa kə   n   kes makaranta
      1sg-say Prep- 3m(A) Comp 3sg(B)   look Perf 1sg finish   school
      'I told him, look, I have finished school'

This change from third person referring to addressee into the vocative use, also with reference to addressee, enables the speaker to report a conversation and at the same time to distinguish between his present addressee and the addressee of the reported conversation. This development occurred also in Pero, to be described later.

One can use set C pronouns in reference to addressees without having any third person pronoun in the main clause:

18. an nə   ko   a   iri ɗak ɗə gwar sin an   ɓe   an mbi cin nə
      1sg Comp any Cop kind work Rel   3m give 1sg Consec 1sg Fut do   it
      'I said that any kind of work which he gives me, I will do it'

This will most often be the case when the embedded clause is in the imperative or prohibitive mood, e.g.:

19. wur sat nə   taji   paa   dəm n   kano
      3m say Comp Prohib 3f   go Prep Kano
      'He said that she should not go to Kano'

2.3.2. Free variation between sets A and C

Consider now the following examples:

20a. wur sat nə gwar/wur ta dee n jos
3m say Comp 3m stop Prep-Jos
'He$_1$ said that he$_2$ stopped at Jos'

b. war sat nə paa/war ta dee n jos
3f
'She$_1$ said that she$_2$ stopped at Jos'

c. dapus sat nə n nas gwar/wur
'Dapus$_1$ said that I beat him$_2$'

cf.

d. dapus sat nə n nas ɗin
1sg Past
'Dapus$_1$ said that I beat him$_1$'

In light of what has been stated in the previous section one could expect set C pronouns to refer to the addressee who has not been overtly marked in the main clause, and set A to refer to still another person. This, however, is not the case.

According to my informants, one can use pronouns of either set A or set C in the embedded clauses of (20a, b, c) without any change in meaning of these sentences. Besides the native speaker's intuition there is much more substantial evidence for the free variation between sets A and C in certain syntactic environments:

21a. wur sat n an nə gwar/wur ta dar n jos
Prep 1sg
'He$_1$ told me that he$_2$ stopped in Jos'

cf.

b. wur sat n an ɗi ta dar n jos
'He$_1$ told me that he$_2$ stopped in Jos'

The importance of the examples in (21) lies in the fact that the addressee of the main clause is first person singular and yet in the embedded clause there is a pronoun from set C. If the function of the set C were to indicate coreferentiality (21a) would be ungrammatical with *gwar.*

2.3.3. Conclusions about sets A, B, and C

In logophoric environments, set B pronouns indicate coreferentiality with the subject, set C pronouns indicate coreferentiality with the addressee when they share with the addressee the features of gender and number. Set C pronouns may also refer to the addressee who is not overtly marked in the main clause, when the embedded clause is in either the imperative or the prohibitive mood. In other environments, set C pronouns indicate disjoint reference. Set A pronouns always indicate disjoint reference with either the subject or the addressee of the main clause.

2.4. Origin of the three sets

The question of the origin of the pronouns of the three sets involved in logophoricity in Mupun is not very important for a description of their syntax, but it is important for a comparative study of logophoric systems in Chadic languages with respect to the question of possible retention or innovation.

As has been shown, set A pronouns are identical to the set of subject or object pronouns of the main clause. For the purpose of this paper there is no need to go beyond this statement, although it does not answer the question about the origin of the subject pronouns.

Set B pronouns all have the same initial consonant *ɗ* and they differ only in the vowel that follows it. In Mupun there seems to be a cognate morpheme *ɗi* which introduces relative clauses. In Frajzyngier (1987b) it has been postulated that relative markers in Chadic derive from demonstrative pronouns. It is therefore possible that the set B pronouns also derive from some demonstrative pronouns.

There is no clear indication about the origin of set C. The word *gwar* occurs as an independent lexeme meaning 'man'. I expect that the remaining elements of the set, i.e., *paa* and *nuwa*, also derive from independent words, although I do not have evidence to support this hypothesis.

3. Comparative data

3.1. Angas group

At least two other languages of the Angas group have logophoric pronouns. The pronouns in Angas are cognate with the pronouns of Mupun (Burquest 1973:195):

    Set B: dyii (m)   ɗa (f)   ɗu (pl)

    Set C: gwa (m)   pe (f)   nywe (pl)

The description of the functions of logophoric pronouns in Angas as given by Burquest differs, however, in an important way from the description of Mupun given above. In particular, Burquest postulates that set C has a coreferential function and that it refers to the indirect object of the main clause. Therefore, both set C and set B would have an anaphoric function in Angas.

All the examples that Burquest quotes support his description of these functions. There are, however, no examples given that have set C pronouns in the embedded clause and that have no overt indirect object in the main clause. In view of the data from Mupun, only such sentences, grammatical or ungrammatical, should be considered proper evidence. If Burquest's analysis is correct, such sentences should be ungrammatical in Angas.

It appears that also in Angas set B derives from demonstrative markers. The initial ɗ is part of the demonstrative locative ɗii 'there' and the pronoun ɗa 'that'.

Jungraithmayr (1963/64:27) gives only a short description of what appears to be an equivalent of set B, i.e., of anaphoric pronouns, in Sura. The Sura logophoric pronouns wuɗi, ɗi (m), wuɗa, ɗa (f) and wuɗun, ɗun (pl) are said to indicate coreferentiality with the subject of the main clause. Since there is scanty evidence for Sura, and the language is closely related to Mupun, it is possible that Sura also has pronouns belonging to set C.

On the basis of the three languages belonging to the Angas group one can certainly postulate that logophoricity as described for Mupun was also a feature of the Proto-Angas sub-branch.

3.2. West Chadic

3.2.1. The form

The only West Chadic language outside of the Angas group for which logophoric pronouns have been observed and described is Pero (Frajzyngier 1989), belonging to the Bole-Tangale group.

In Pero there are two sets of pronouns which differ only in the form of the second person markers. In one system these pronouns are *ka* (m) and *ci* (f) and in the other, *peemu* (m) and *peeje* (f).

3.2.2. Distribution

The most important fact about the distribution of the *'peemu'* set is that it may be used only in one type of discourse, i.e., in reference to the addressee of reported conversation. In the same type of discourse the *'ka'* set may not be used. Thus the environment for the use of the two sets of pronouns is determined pragmatically rather than syntactically. In fact, it is the use of one set of pronouns rather than the other that makes it possible to determine whether what is being said is directed to the present hearer or is a quote of what was said to a hearer of the reported conversation, e.g.:

22a. ɗi-   ko   kan ka   daklani-a
     settle Comp Assoc 2m   bad Interr
     'Is it bad that he settled with you?'

b. ɗi-ko kan peemu daklani-a
              2m
   'Is it bad that he settled with you?'

Given the above conditions for the distribution of the two sets, the *'peemu'* set may, but does not have to, occur in sentential complements of the verb *ca* 'say', e.g.:

23a. ca   mu   kayu   peemu
     said Opt   drive away
     '[He1] said that he2 should be driven away'

   b. ca peemu ta kayu laa   mu mijiba
      said   Fut   man Dem stranger
      '[He1] said that he2 is going to drive the stranger away'

Note the difficulty involved in translation between two systems that do not encode the same semantic notions. While *peemu* in Pero refers specifically to the addressee of the reported conversation, the pronoun 'he' in English may refer to any third person. Contrary to what is implied by the English translation it is not any disjoint reference that is encoded in Pero but rather the distinction between a speaker and an addressee of the reported conversation.

   Similarly to the situation in Mupun, the addressee of the reported conversation may become subject of a sentence:

   24a. peeje wat-na
         2f   come Vent-Comp
         'you came'

     b. peemu ma   yi-ko   bure
        2m   if make-Comp fight
        'if you fight'

3.2.3. Classification of the '*peemu*' set

As the examples quoted above clearly indicate, the '*peemu*' set refers to the second participant, i.e., to the addressee of the reported speech. The addressee may be mentioned only once, at the beginning of the conversation, and then is referred to by one of the pronouns of the '*peemu*' set in all kinds of syntactic environments. Thus Pero has only the equivalent of set C of Mupun. In logophoric contexts its function is anaphoric only in the sense that it refers to somebody who was mentioned previously as an addressee of the reported conversation.

Although there is a clear indication that Pero shares a grammatical property with the languages of the Angas group, this does not mean that this property cannot be an independent innovation in Pero. However, there is also an indication of a historical connection between the markers of the logophoric systems. Note that the logophoric pronouns in Mupun and of Angas have, respectively, *paa* and *pee* as the markers of the third person feminine. Note also that these sets are equivalents of the Pero logophoric set. I do not think that this phonological similarity is accidental, and therefore, unless the similarity can be shown to be a result of borrowing, it must be considered a common retention from Proto-West Chadic.

Note that the second element of the logophoric pronouns in Pero also seems to be derived from a demonstrative marker; the form -*mu* is similar to the demonstrative suffix -*mo*.

3.3. Other branches of Chadic

In East Chadic a logophoric system has been reported for Kera. Ebert 1979:260 ff. states that there is a set of indirect speech third person pronouns *to* (m), *ta* (f) and *te* (pl) which indicate coreferentiality with the subject of the main clause. These pronouns are identical with the set of independent pronouns in Kera, but different from the set of independent pronouns in unmarked sentences. Interestingly, these pronouns are used in dialogues to indicate switch reference (Ebert 1979:130).

In indirect speech this set corresponds to set B of Mupun, i.e., it has an anaphoric function. The use of the logophoric system in Kera is much more widespread than in the languages of the Angas group. Apparently all of the verba dicendi and some of the verba sentiendi allow for the use of these pronouns.

4. **What can be reconstructed for Proto-Chadic**

4.1. Methodology

The choice of the method that one should follow in answering the question as to whether or not Proto-Chadic has a system of logophoric markers as exemplified in one of the present languages is not a trivial one.

I will use the following simplified principles: If markers having the same function are found to be cognates, then they are considered to be retentions from an earlier system. If elements of the same functional system are found in different languages with different markers, then there is a possibility that in each language the system emerged independently or that the functions constitute a retention of the same system, the form of the markers having changed.

Since the markers of logophoricity are found to be derived from demonstrative pronouns, showing that they are related amounts to no more than a statement that the demonstrative markers are related. Showing that languages from more than one branch of Chadic have logophoric systems cannot be considered as evidence for the presence of logophoric system in Proto-Chadic, because languages from different families in Africa have logophoric systems. The only type of evidence that one could use would be very specific non-pronominal markers that would have to be shown to be related. Unfortunately, such markers do not exist.

One should also take into consideration information about the spread of logophoric systems in Chadic languages. If such systems were to be found in many languages from all branches of Chadic, then, more likely than not, they would constitute a retention from a Proto-Chadic system. If, on the other hand, they occur only in a few languages, then the possibility that they represent a retention would be greatly diminished. In what follows I will review the evidence available for both the set referring to the speaker (corresponding to set B of Mupun) and the set referring to the addressee (corresponding to set C of Mupun).

4.2. Reference to speaker

The set referring to the speaker has been noted in two branches, West and East Chadic. In West Chadic this set was certainly present in Proto-Angas. There are no claims that any other language of this branch has the logophoric system of set B. This set cannot be reconstructed as a retention from Proto-West Chadic. Although a logophoric system has been reported in Kera, this is the only language in the East Chadic Branch that has it. There is therefore no evidence to show that Proto-Chadic had a set B logophoric system. Unless more Chadic languages are shown to have such a system one would have to assume that set B logophoric systems in Angas languages and in Kera result from borrowing of an areal feature from some non-Chadic languages.[4]

4.3. Reference to addressee

Since no evidence for the existence of set C was found outside of the West Chadic branch one cannot postulate the existence of this set of pronouns in Proto-Chadic. Within West Chadic, however, the markers of set C are cognate, mainly because of the forms involving *p* in the Pero *peemu* set and *paa* in the Angas group. The fact that outside of the Angas group only Pero has set C pronouns argues against reconstruction of set C for Proto-West Chadic. It is possible that this set developed within the West Chadic branch only as a result of borrowing of an areal feature.

Footnotes

1 Tones do not bear on the problems discussed and are not marked in the paper.

2 I have no data on whether or not the object forms of set C are identical with the subject forms or not.

3 I use the term addressee following the proposal by Stanley 1982. The system in Tikar described by her shares certain similarities with the system in Mupun.

4 Compare studies of logophoricity in the Ubangi languages (Cloarec-Heiss 1969), Tuburi (Hagège 1974), Gokana (Hyman and Comrie 1981), Ewe (Clements 1975), and Tikar (Stanley 1982).

FROM PREPOSITION TO EQUATIONAL COPULA

1. Introduction

1.1. Justification of research

If we dismiss every case of polysemy as accidental we deprive ourselves of the possibility of ever finding out whether the two functions are in fact related or not. If, in contrast, we try to discover a relationship, in the worst case we may find that none exists. But in an optimal case we may find out that a connection exists, and the explanation of this connection may shed some light on the nature of language structure and of language change.

1.2. Purpose and scope of the paper

The development of prepositions from verbs and of copulas from demonstratives has been postulated for many languages (Lord 1973, Li and Thompson 1977). There has not yet, however, been a documented case of grammaticalization from preposition to copula (cf. Lehmann 1985).

The first purpose of the present paper is to show that grammaticalization from preposition to equational copula has occurred in several Chadic languages. The second purpose is to show the possible motivation for this process. Note that although many cases of grammaticalization have been described, the motivation for the grammaticalization process is still poorly understood.

In the present paper I will be concerned mainly with two types: locative copulas, i.e. copulas in locative clauses, equivalents of 'be' in the clauses of the type 'X is at Y', and copulas in equational clauses, equivalents of 'be' in 'X is Y' as in 'John is a soldier'. I will not deal with copulas that constrain time, e.g. copulas that distinguish between temporary and permanent condition or state. It appears that there were two processes in Chadic languages. The change **Locative Copula ---> Preposition** was followed in some languages by the change **Preposition ---> Equational Copula**. In Section 2, I will discuss the possible direction of the change involving locative copulas and prepositions. In Section 3, I will discuss the possible sources for the equational copula.[1]

2. Locative copula

2.1. Existence of the locative copula

Locative copulas have been claimed to exist only in the Ron subgroup of West Chadic (Jungraithmayr 1970), represented in the chart by Fyer. In my own work I have found that the locative copula a exists also in Bole. The evidence that Bole must have had a preposition *a* comes from comparative study of marking locative in Chadic (Frajzyngier 1987a and this volume).

Whenever a claim is made about the similarity between a locative copula and a preposition, and when both occupy the same syntactic position, one has to show that the distinction between the two is a fact of language and not merely an artifact of the linguist's analysis. Since the description of the syntax of Fyer in Jungraithmayr 1970 is rather sketchy, the following discussion will be based mainly on data from Bole. The evidence that *a* is indeed a copula rather than a preposition comes from contrasting sentences of the type (I) 'X is in/at Y' with sentences of the type (II) 'X VERB Z in/at Y'. If the equivalent of 'is' in (I) is a copula rather than a preposition we would not expect it to occur in sentences of the type (II). On the other hand, if there is no distinction between preposition and copula, we would expect the same morpheme to occur in both types of sentences. Sentences of the type (I) in Bole have the form Subject *à* Prep NP, e.g.:

1 a. kòún   à gá àmá
     buffalo   in water
     'a buffalo is in the water'

   b. kòún à gá àmá sà
                     Neg
      'the buffalo is not in the water'

c. sùɓá-nò   à kò réwè
   shirt-1sg   on tree
   'my shirt is on the tree'

d. sùɓá-nò à ném-gè réwè
              near-with?
   'my shirt is near the tree'

e. kòlbá ámà à wèté réwè
   bottle Dem   under tree
   'that bottle is under the tree'

Sentences 1a-e are ungrammatical if either à or the spatial specifier following it is deleted. Although the above examples alone could be accepted intuitively as evidence for the copular status of à there may be another possibility, viz., that they in fact represent two prepositions in a sequence. The necessary evidence is provided by sentences of the type (II) in which, as stated above, we should not find à.

2 a. zéetì sùɓá gà kó réwè
     put shirt in on tree
     'put the shirt on a tree'

   b. ísín zòu sùɓá-nì   gà gà ngírkì
      3sg put shirt-3sg   in in bag
      'he put his shirt into a bag'

   c. ísìn fóɗù sùɓá-nì ká gà ngírkì
        take-out   out in bag
      'he took his shirt out of a bag'

   d. mèmú ámà gà kólbà gà gà sàrá-nì
      person Dem with bottle in in hand-3m
      'that man has a bottle in his hand'

Sentences 2a-e are ungrammatical if *à* is inserted before the prepositions or if it replaces the prepositions. These sentences are also ungrammatical if the prepositions are deleted. There is thus evidence that *à* is a locative copula in Bole.

Jungraithmayr 1970 gives the following examples as containing copula in Fyer:

3 a. ma-á-na
　　 he-is-here
　　 'he is here'

　b. ma-á-ti
　　 'he is there' (Jungraithmayr 1970:78)

4 a. yis-a-à-táá
　　 'he is there'

　b. yít-a-n táá
　　 'she is there'

　c. són-a-n-táá
　　 'they are there' (ibid.)[2]

My argument that *a* in 4 a,b,c is indeed a copula rather than a preposition runs as follows: There exist in Chadic languages, including Fyer, constructions consisting of two prepositions. In such constructions, the second preposition has a spatial specifier function, indicating spatial relationship between objects, (cf. Frajzyngier 1987a) e.g.:

5 'á ɗikín　　 ti
　 in between　 with　 (ibid.)
　 'between, under'

In 4 a,b, and c, however, the second preposition *n* or *à* does not indicate spatial relationship, but has a most general meaning 'at, in, toward'. Since two prepositions marking just the locative case do not co-occur, the first instance of *a* may be analyzed as a copula.[3]

There are thus enough arguments to postulate the existence of a locative copula in Fyer as well.

2.2. Direction of change

If we assume that there exists a connection between the locative copula and the preposition, we are faced with three possibilities. The first is that prepositions derive from the locative copulas, and the another that locative copulas derive from prepositions. I am not going to explore a third possibility, that both forms derive from some other morpheme, because I do not see what this other morpheme might have been.

Assuming that prepositions derive from copulas in Chadic would force us to accept the following scenario: Most Chadic languages had a locative copula *a*; this morpheme became a locative preposition in many languages; subsequently it ceased to function as a copula in most of the languages, and moreover, its function was not replaced by another morpheme. In effect this scenario postulates two processes: grammaticalization, viz., introduction of a new grammatical category (preposition), and degrammaticalization, i.e., elimination of a grammatical category (locative copula). The change from locative copula to preposition has been postulated for Kwa languages (Lord 1973) and for Chinese (Li and Thompson 1977), and for Chadic (Frajzyngier 1987a and the present volume). This change may cause the elimination of a copula, hence we would have an explanation for the degrammaticalization process.

The locative copulas in Bole and Fyer may be considered as retentions facilitated perhaps by the emergence of new prepositions marking locative case, *ga* in Bole and *n* in Fyer.[4] The evidence that *ga* is a locative case marker in Bole is provided by examples 2a,b,d, where *ga* precedes spatial specifiers 'on', 'in', i.e., it behaves like locative case markers in other languages. The evidence that it is an innovation comes from the comparative data on the enclosed chart.

The structure of the locative expression in Bole is thus:

6. NP a Prep NP (examples 2a-e and 4a-c)

One may ask why Bole has retained the locative copula *a*. Although I am not sure that anyone will be ever able to give a definite answer to such a question, I would like to propose that in Bole the locative copula makes possible a better differentiation between locative prepositional phrases as (examples 2a-d), locative clauses, and equational sentences that have the form $NP_{[+DEF]}$ NP/ADJ, e.g.:

7 a. mémù émè nàsárà
       person Dem European
       'this man is European'

   b. làwò yè gàdáatì
       child Def tall
       'the child is tall'

   c. ítà mòndú-nò
       3f woman-1sg
       'she is my wife'

   d. yúsúfù móy
       'Yusufu is a chief'

Note that insertion of *a* between subject and predicate in 7a-d would produce ungrammatical sentences, e.g.:

7e *làwò émè à gàdáatì

3. Equational copula

3.1. Two types of equational copulas

Equational copulas have been observed in all branches of Chadic. In most of the languages, equational copulas are related to demonstrative pronouns, and for some languages they have actually been claimed to be derived from one or another kind of demonstrative (cf. Schuh 1983), thus adding to the data presented in Li and Thompson 1977. However, in the Ron and Angas groups of West Chadic, the equational copula is similar to the reconstructed (Frajzyngier 1985) preposition marking locative case rather than to a demonstrative, e.g.:

8 a. yis-a   ma doóhò
     he-COP   father   (Fyer, Jungraithmayr 1970:76)
     'he is your father'

  b. wàr á wì
     she   who
     'who is she?' (Mupun)

3.2. Arguments for direction Preposition ---> Equational copula

Evidence that Mupun once had a preposition *a* is provided not only by comparative data but
also by archaic constructions in this language. Thus *a* has the function of preposition in the
expressions:

9 a. a yíl   'on the farm, to the farm'
   cf. n-yíl   'on the ground'

  b. ndìrít kìén   ké   sìwá ám   à   kùwór
     finch benefit chicken drinks water Prep feeder
     'The finch bird benefits when chicken drinks from a feeder'

Example 9b. is a proverb, and it has *a* in prepositional rather than copular function. The
same meaning in everyday language has a different form, e.g.:

10 ás sìwá ám kó   kùwór
   dog drink water with   feeder
   'a dog drinks from the feeder'

The question to be answered is again whether the direction of change was from equational copula to locative preposition or from preposition to equational copula. In the previous section it has been shown that the locative copula became a preposition. In the present
section I will show that preposition became the equational copula. There are two issues in-

volved in the change from preposition to equational copula: The first is the motivation for
the existence of the equational copula, and the second, once such motivation was found, is
the question why the preposition rather than some other morpheme was chosen to serve as
copula.

3.3. Motivation for the existence of equational copula

Normally a question about the reasons for the existence of a given grammatical category
does not arise. When, however, we find that within the same family, and for the same semantic function, some languages have a grammatical category that others do not, the question about the reasons for the existence or nonexistence of a category has to be posed and
ultimately resolved.

In Mupun the copula *a* is used only in two functions: one as a contrastive focus marker,
and the other in the equational function in constructions of the type '(X) is Y', where 'Y'
may be only a nominal predicate, e.g.:

11 a. mìskóom á nàat
        chief   white man
        'the chief is a white man'

   b. nàat   nì   á   mìskóom nì
        white man   Def Cop chief   Def
        'the white man is the chief'

   c. mìskóom nì   á mòpún
        'the chief is a Mupun man'

   d. mìskóom nì   á   láa
        chief   Def Cop child
        'the chief is a child'

e. mbì-sé   à lúà   ík
   thing-eat   meat goat
   'the food is goat's meat'

The presence of the copula in Mupun allows for a richer system of semantic functions involving two NPs. The structure NP NP in some dialects has a part-whole, or possessive function, e.g.:

12 a. flòk   láa
      liver boy
      'a boy's liver'

   b. pò   cìán
      blade hoe
      'a blade of the hoe'

   c. mìskóom mòpún
      'a chief of Mupun' (cf. 11c)

   d. láa mìskóom
      'a child of the chief' (cf. 11d)

   e. mbì-sé ík
      'goat's food' (cf. 11e)

Copula is the only element in Mupun that distinguishes between an equational construction, which has the copula, and a part-whole construction, which does not. Additional evidence for the functional motivation of equational copula comes from the fact that the copula cannot occur in clauses with adjectival predicates, i.e., when there is no possibility of semantic ambiguity, e.g.:

13 a. wùr *a   ɓál/kát
      3sg,m   strong/small
      'he is strong/small'

b. wàr *a rét
    3sg,f   beautiful
    'she is beautiful'

c. wàr *a bís
    'she is ugly'

In fact, the presence or absence of copula may determine whether the following potentially polysemic item is to be interpreted as a noun or an adjective, e.g.:

14 a. wùr ráp
       'he is dirty'

b. wùr à ráp
    'he is garbage' (an obvious insult)

Another piece of evidence for the functional motivation comes from the fact that copula
usually does not occur in existential clauses with prepositional predicates, i.e., once again,
when there is no possibility of any ambiguity, e.g.:

15 a. wùr kɔ́   sìwól
       3sg with   money
       'he has money'

b. dò   án n-tùl
    yesterday 1sg Prep-home
    'yesterday I was at home'

c. mùn gèt kí wàr
    1pl Past with 3f
    'we were with her'

The only case when *a* occurs with a prepositional phrase predicate is in an interrogative sentence, e.g.:

15 d. wàr á kɔ́   wí
      she   with who
      'with whom is she?'

The equational construction in Mupun may have the form of 'a NP', i.e., it may be lacking the first NP. This is the case when the first element of the equation is known or has been mentioned before, e.g.:

16 a. ɗési à mwés óñ?
      Dem   wine Interr
      'is this wine ?'

   b. í,   á mwés
      'yes, it is wine'

The form 'a NP' is typically used in response to the equivalent of the question 'What is this?' accompanied by a hand or head gesture, e.g.:

17 à   jép   fén mò
   Cop children 1sg Pl
   '[these] are my children'

The fact that the existence of a morpheme is functionally justified does not imply that it must emerge, and moreover, in our case, it does not imply that an equational copula must emerge from a preposition rather than from some other source.

3.4 Role of contrastive focus

In many languages, the same construction that is used in an equational sentence is used as well in contrastive focus marking, often in association with a relative clause as in example 18.

> 18 a. It is the cat that killed the bird, not the dog.
>
>   b. C'est le chat qui a tué l'oiseau, ce n'est pas le chien.

In Mupun, contrastive focus marking has the form 'a NP', i.e., the same form as the equational sentence without the first element of equation. Unlike in I.E. languages, the focused element does not have to be fronted, and in fact any NP in a clause can be preceded by a. Moreover, in contrast with equational sentences, the focused element can be a prepositional phrase, not only a noun phrase, e.g.:

> 19 a. à   D. amerika bà à   N. kàs
>   Neg   Neg
>   'It is D. who is in America, not N.'

>   b. n- kwat à   sii sìwól bà à   sii ik   kàs
>   1SG-pay   with money Neg à with goat Neg
>   'It is with money that I paid, not with a goat'

>   c. à   dím á n-tùlú   bà a màkàrántá kás
>   1sg,m go   Prep-home Neg school   Neg
>   'go home, not to school'

>   d. n-tàl   à tíbà   bà à šúgà kás
>   1sg-ask   tobacco Neg   sugar Neg
>   I asked for tobacco, and not for sugar'

>   e. n-tàl tíbà à pí   wúr bà á kà   kás
>   Prep 3sg   2sg,m
>   'I asked him for money, not you'

Instead we have to answer the question about how syntactic patterns are transmitted. The answer to this question has to be the same as the answer to the question about the transmission of phonological systems, i.e. the forms of the underlying structures and the phonological rules. Although we do not yet know the answer to either of these questions, that does not mean that we should not proceed with the reconstruction of syntax.

The final issue raised by Mithun and Campbell as an argument against the comparative method in syntax is our lack of knowledge of the causes of syntactic change, a lack that prevents us from predicting a change and its possible direction. 'In diachronic phonology, we can often establish directionality by explaining what could have caused the change. If we understood why grammars change, we could search for the known causes of effects observed in related languages. An understanding of causation could also yield motivation for choosing certain reconstructions over others' (Mithun and Campbell 1982:284 ff). This argument is not valid for several reasons. First, in the comparative method as applied to phonological changes, we do not know the causes of these changes beforehand either, and yet we do proceed with phonological reconstruction. If knowledge of the causes of change were to be a prerequisite rather than a product of historical studies, discoveries in evolutionary theory would be significantly delayed because the causes of change are discovered, if at all, only after the change has been described. The causes of syntactic change have to be discovered through the study of specific cases of language change. Syntactic reconstruction and the comparative method will ultimately help in finding out possible causes of syntactic change. In what follows I will try to show that it is possible to choose among several competing reconstructions without knowing beforehand the causes of syntactic change.

3. The data base

The data for syntactic reconstruction consist of two elements: a list of meanings encoded in the grammatical systems of languages compared and the description of how those meanings are encoded.

4. Syntactic patterns

Syntactic patterns are the first products of grammatical analysis. We assume the list of syntactic patterns to be quite large, but certainly much shorter than either the list of all possible sentences or the list of the lexical items in the language.

4.1. A list of grammatically encoded functions

This is the list of the semantic or pragmatic functions that have been encoded in the languages compared. This list is to be obtained through the analysis of individual languages and constitutes a verso side of the syntactic analysis. For each language a certain functions is assigned to every syntactic pattern. The list of functions should thus contain as many items as the list of syntactic patterns or fewer. The latter situation may occur because some syntactic patterns may be ambiguous. We should expect that when languages are compared the lists of grammatically encoded functions will overlap in some cases, but in other cases they will not, because one language may have encoded functions that have not been encoded in another language. In fact, we may expect to find a certain hierarchy of meanings, with some elements encoded more often and other elements encoded less often. It should be possible to construct such a hierarchy for languages from different families, a sort of universals of meanings encoded in the grammatical systems. This work still remains to be done. We should expect that such notions as truth, question, negation, imperative will occupy the top places in the hierarchy.

4.2. Procedure

The crucial problem in reconstructing syntax is to determine what constitutes cognate syntactic structures and what does not. I propose that in resolving this problem we proceed in the manner somewhat similar to the one followed in morphological and lexical comparisons: Two or more structures are cognate when their functions are similar and their forms are similar too. The meaning of a syntactic construction will be obtained through contrasting it with another syntactic construction in the language. The form of a syntactic construction may be described from several viewpoints but it must include the points listed in

1.1. The syntactic reconstruction will then proceed in the following manner. We first choose a certain semantic or pragmatic function that we would like to reconstruct, and then we examine whether or not the structures through which it is realized are cognate or not. If they are, then the possibility that similar structures emerged independently in different languages to express the same meaning is less likely than the possibility that these structures are evidence for the contemporary languages' inheriting both the form and the function from a proto-language. Let me illustrate this with three examples from Chadic: A straightforward example in which reconstruction was not problematic; one negative example, in which it was not possible to reconstruct a semantic function as being grammatically encoded in Proto-Chadic; and one example in which the reconstructed form was preserved only in a minority of the languages investigated.

4.2.1. Interrogative sentences in Chadic

Specific questions in some Chadic languages are formed through the use of the Q-words either in the position that would have been normally occupied by the questioned argument or by a displacement of the Q-words into some other position in the sentence (cf. Frajzyngier 1985b, and present volume). In other Chadic languages, in addition to the above devices there exists also a particle added at the end of the sentence, a structure quite similar to the specific interrogatives in Japanese. The first question to be answered was whether or not in Proto-Chadic the specific interrogative had a sentence-final particle. Specific interrogative sentences with final particles are found in all branches of Chadic. Thus the form of the specific interrogative sentence in Chadic is: V (NPi.....NPj) i-particle, where one of the NPs is realized by a Q-word equivalent of English 'who', 'what', etc. The Q-words indicate only which argument of the sentence the question is about. The i-particle is the main morpheme carrying the interrogative function. Some of the sentence-final particles are cognates, but others are not. This is the evidence that the forms of these particles were not borrowed. When, however, we look at the function of these particles in constructions other than interrogative, they all appear to be functionally cognates: They are all demonstrative or definite pronouns. The pronominal origin of the sentence final particle makes this construction very specific. Therefore the possibility that all languages have developed it independently is less likely than the possibility that it is a retention from some earlier stage of the language, which we may call Proto-Chadic.

With respect to Q-words it is postulated that in P.C. they occupied the position normally occupied by the non-interrogative argument. This was the only way in P.C. to indicate the grammatical relation (semantic function) of the questioned argument. And this was the only function of the Q-words in P.C. The interrogative function was completely carried by the sentence-final demonstrative pronoun. The yes/no questions in P.C. appear also to have been formed through the addition of a sentence final particle to the indicative sentence. But this particle was different from the specific interrogative particle, being derived from the locative copula rather than a demonstrative pronoun. This rather than some other way of forming interrogative sentences cannot be predicted from universal principles. Therefore the occurrence of so specific and yet similar constructions in two out of three branches of Chadic has to be explained either by borrowing or by retention from P.C. Borrowing has to be ruled out because languages are not always contiguous, and in addition, the vehicular language of the area, Hausa, does not have this construction. The sentence-final yes/no interrogative particles are not always formally cognates, (an additional argument against their being borrowed), but they are cognates functionally; i.e., they carry the same functions in contexts other than interrogative sentences.

4.2.2. Logophoricity in Chadic

In several languages from the Chadic group there exist two systems of pronouns, one referring to the speaker of the main clause (logophoric), and the other referring to the addressee of the main clause (for a full description cf. Frajzyngier 1985c and present volume). The systems referring to the addressee were found in languages of only one branch. Moreover the forms referring to the addressee are cognate with and derived from lexical items meaning 'man', and probably 'woman'. The possibility that a few languages within one branch have innovated by encoding a new semantic notion is more likely than the possibility that the majority of languages in the three groups have innovated by losing a grammatical device, i.e. the grammatical means of expressing a semantic notion. Therefore this system could not be reconstructed for Proto-Chadic.

The logophoric systems are found in languages from two branches, and are therefore an excellent candidate for reconstruction in Proto-Chadic. The structures through which the logophoricity is realized in the two branches are also similar, hence, one more argument for the reconstruction in the grammatical system of P.C. There is, however, one problem.

Although in both branches the logophoric pronouns are cognate, they are identical with the demonstrative pronouns. Showing that they are cognate amounts therefore to nothing more than saying that demonstrative pronouns are cognate, a fact we would expect from the knowledge of the genetic relationship between these languages. Additionally, the logophoric pronouns occur only in one language of the East branch and only in one group of languages from the West branch. Therefore, there is not enough evidence that the logophoric system existed in P.C. Unless more Chadic languages are found with logophoric pronouns, we would have to explain the emergence of logophoric systems in the contemporary languages as a borrowing from the surrounding non-Chadic languages in which logophoricity is a common phenomenon. What has been borrowed was a new semantic category, which came to be realized by the means already existing in the languages, viz. by the demonstrative pronouns.[3]

So far I have been following an assumption that if a certain structure is shared by the majority of the branches of a given family then it is more likely a retention than an innovation. This general assumption can and should be modified when no plausible explanation can be found for certain changes. I will illustrate just such a situation, with discussion of changes in word order in Chadic.

4.2.3. Word order in Chadic

On the basis of independent evidence it was shown in Frajzyngier 1983a that in P.C. word order was the principal device to mark the semantic role (grammatical relations) of the arguments in the sentence. There was a limited use of prepositions as well, but their use can be best explained in conjunction with the reconstructed word order. Certain languages of the Biu-Mandara branch have the word order VSO. The remaining languages of the branch and the rest of the Chadic languages in three other branches have the order SVO. If we were to apply the 'majority rule' of the comparative method we would have to assume that Proto-Chadic had SVO order that later became VSO in some languages. This obvious solution was, however, rejected in Frajzyngier 1983a because there is no synchronic rule in the Chadic SVO languages by which the order of principal elements could become VSO. There are, however, a number of processes in the VSO languages by which the order of principal elements could become SVO. This brings us to one of the most interesting issues in the recent historical studies of syntax; causes of syntactic change. In what follows I will describe some of the causes of syntactic change in Chadic and how they relate to claims about the universals of change.

5. Causes of syntactic change in Chadic

Some of the causes of syntactic change in other languages are strongly linked with various kinds of movement rules and the resulting neutralization of meaning distinctions. The main movement rules in Chadic are linked with contrastive focus. The following table presents the main types of marking of contrastive focus for subjects and objects in contemporary Chadic languages:

Focus Constructions in Chadic

Neutral	Subject focus	Object focus
VSO	SVO	OVS
(Lamang, Gude, Ga'anda, Hona)		
SVO	S Marker VO	O Marker SV
(Most Chadic languages)		
SVO	VO Marker S	O Marker SV
(Kanakuru, Pero, Ngizim)		

In the majority of Chadic SVO languages, the subject is focused through the addition of a marker, which results in a construction similar to English 'It is X that. . . '. As can be seen, in some SVO languages the focus constructions for subjects involve the movement of the subject toward the end of the clause, or at least toward the position after the object, giving VOS. The focus construction for the object in all languages involves the movement of the object toward the beginning of the clause giving the order OSV.[4] As may be seen from the above table, focusing rules in the SVO languages do not produce the VSO word order. On the other hand focus rules in the VSO languages do produce the SVO order.

However, advancement of the focused element to the beginning of the sentences alone cannot and should not produce syntactic change. In order for this process to happen there must have been another process present that affected a communicative function of language. Such a process in Chadic was the formation of the future tense and possibly of other tenses and aspects.

In most contemporary Chadic languages the future tense marker can still be recognized as cognate with the verb 'to go'. The formation of the future tense involves the preposing of the verb 'to go' before the main verb of the sentence. But at some earlier stage it was not the verb alone that was preposed, but also its subject, which, in accordance with the VSO hypothesis, followed the verb. Thus the form of the future tense structure was the following:

V   NP   V   NP
[go] 1   [main] 2

NP 1 is the subject of the verb 'to go', while NP 2 is the subject of the main verb of the sentence, both subjects being of course identical. The evidence that this indeed was the case is provided by contemporary Hausa and other languages. In these languages, the future tense forms (such as Hausa za-, 'go') have the subject pronoun **following** the tense marker, while in all other forms the subject pronoun **precedes** the tense marker.

In Mupun, a West Chadic SVO language, the perfective aspect is formed through the use of a marker kə which in some persons is preceded by the subject marker but in others is followed by the subject marker. The perfective marker appears to be of verbal origin. What happened next is that the verb 'to go' was grammaticalized, i.e., it ceased to be a lexical verb and became a grammatical morpheme. In this situation the function of the NP 1 is no longer clear, for it occupies the position of a focused NP. This structural ambiguity is resolved by reanalyzing the position before the verb as neutral. This is what I postulate happened in all languages of West and East Chadic and in a number of languages from the Biu-Mandara branch, where some languages, such as Ga'anda and Hona, have SVO structure in the future tense and VSO structure in other tenses. That is why I have chosen the VSO order as the probable order for P.C. despite the fact that it is the order of the minority of the languages.

The above explanation illustrates a 'therapeutic change' (Vennemann 1973; Mithun and Campbell 1982), whereby a language develops devices in order to preserve a certain function or to prevent a possible ambiguity. This purely functional consideration appears to be the most important motivation for syntactic change in Chadic. It does not, however, explain the direction of the word order change.[5]

6. Direction of word order change

Several studies have aimed at finding universal principles that would allow prediction of the direction of word order change. Some of the strongest claims concerning the direction of word order change were made by Vennemann in his 1973 paper. The sequence and direction of the change are illustrated by the following diagram (Vennemann 1973:40) (FWO stands for Free Word Order):

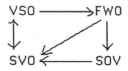

Concerning the change from a VSO language, Vennemann wrote, 'A VSO language may develop a case system and become an FWO language, or it may change back into an SVO language by making a stylistic nominal subject topicalization rule an obligatory S position rule'. The direction of the change in Chadic languages confirms the second part of Vennemann's hypothesis, but the reasons for this change are different. Topicalization alone would not bring about the change; a resulting ambiguity as illustrated earlier for Chadic, or some other disturbance of communicative function is also needed. Moreover, there is no evidence in contemporary Chadic languages that Proto-Chadic ever had the SVO order, therefore the change to SVO is not the change 'back to SVO'. For Givón (1979) the most common change is pragmatically motivated. He also made a claim about Chadic and other Afro-Asiatic languages, stating that 'the entire Afro-Asiatic group must have been SOV, as a detailed analysis of the bound morphology [of] Chadic, Berber and Old Egyptian is bound to show' (Givón 1979:275). The argument concerning bound morphology rests on the assumption that bound derivational and inflectional morphemes derive from the 'free' morphemes and that the order of the bound morphemes retains the order of free constituents in the sentence (cf. Givón 1971:409). This may be true for some languages; it is, however, also clear that not all inflectional and derivational morphemes derive from 'free' morphemes. What would be the free morpheme that gave rise to the plural stem formation in verbs in Semitic and other Afro-Asiatic languages, a formation that involves either gemination of one of the consonants or reduplication of usually the second syllable (cf. Frajzyngier 1979)? In its extreme form, the hypothesis about the role of pragmatics assumes a certain optimal position for the constituents of a sentence. Thus, the old information, or the topic, should occur first, and the new information, the comment, should occur after it. This assumption is usually associated with another assumption in which the subject is taken to represent old information. According to Givón, languages have a tendency to drift toward a certain order of constituents. Givón 1977 illustrated such a process of drift in Hebrew, which shows the change from VSO to SVO order in several constructions. Although in Chadic there was a change from VSO to SVO it occurred not because of the advancement of old information toward the beginning of the sentence, but rather because of the neutralization of two semantic functions resulting from the advancement of new information to that position. Although in Hebrew it was the topic, the old information (according to Givón, realized by the subject), that was advanced, in Chadic it is the constituent that contradicts the hearer's presupposition, hence the new information, that is advanced to the beginning of the sentence. Assuming that both the analysis for Hebrew as proposed by Givón and the analysis for Chadic as proposed in Frajzyngier 1983 are correct, it is obvious that different causes of syntactic change may lead to identical results, and that the change in the word order does not necessarily depend on the pragmatic properties of the sentence constituents. If it did, the change in Chadic should not have occurred, assuming that the pragmatic properties described by Givón are correct.

7. Conclusions

It has been shown that syntactic reconstruction is a useful and necessary device for the study of historical change in syntax. It has been also shown that this study can best be achieved through the comparison of various languages by making constant reference to the reconstructed form, hence by using the comparative method. It has been argued that the proper object of syntactic reconstruction should be syntactic patterns formulated in terms of functional categories obtained from the analysis of particular languages. A methodology of syntactic reconstruction was proposed and its application was illustrated on the data from Chadic.

With respect to the causes of syntactic change it has been shown that the most important cause is therapeutic. The main function of syntactic change is preservation of the communicative function of the language. The introduction of new communicative functions can also be a cause of syntactic change. The introduction of logophoric systems into Chadic languages through borrowing from other languages illustrates this type of change. But the borrowing of new constructions may occur also without the introduction of a new semantic category into the language. Thus the syntactic change may be triggered by a variety of causes.

Concerning the direction of the word order change it has been shown that the same direction, viz., from VSO to SVO may come about as a result of different causes for different languages. In Chadic pragmatic conditions as described by Givón appear to have had no part in either the causes or the direction of the word order change. The data in Chadic also contradict the claim about the word order in Chadic (and by implication in Afro-Asiatic) as well as Givón's claim about the evidence provided by the bound morphology.

Footnotes

[1] The work on this paper was supported by an NEH Grant for the study of the Proto-Chadic Simple Sentence and by the Center for Applied Humanities, University of Colorado. The help of both institutions is gratefully acknowledged. I would like to thank Scott DeLancey for comments on parts of an earlier version of this paper.

[2] Both papers by these authors are but are representative of their other works on the theory and methodology of historical syntax.

[3] Syntactic borrowing does not have to occur only when a new semantic category is introduced into the language. In Frajzyngier 1984b I described an instance in which a construction involved a complementizer has been borrowed from a number of West African languages into the English-based Creoles. Unless one assumes that at the time of borrowing this construction the speakers of Creoles did not yet learn the English complementizer

'that', one has to consider the possibility that a construction may be borrowed even if there is a native construction with the same function. There are not enough well documented cases of this nature.

4 The above data contradict the Harries-Delisle 1978 claims that the focus position for all constituents is the position of the object in the neutral sentence, 'focus' in her terminology being the same as in the present paper, viz., the marking of contrastive emphasis. Only a few languages, specifically those that served as the source for Chadic in Harries-Delisle's data, support her hypothesis, and then only partially; the position for object emphasis is obviously different from that of the object in the neutral sentence. The data from a larger number of Chadic languages clearly indicate that the focus position for a constituent is very much dependent on its neutral position, and will usually be different from the neutral position.

5 In the above discussion I did not take into consideration claims that languages tend to conform to the types as postulated in Greenberg 1966. There is an implied principle behind such claims, according to which a certain word order of construction X will cause the emergence of a certain word order of construction Y. Examples of such studies are Li and Thompson 1974, Lehmann 1975, 1980. This approach has been criticized by Watkins 1976, Mithun and Campbell 1982, and Lightfoot 1983. But even if such an explanation were to be correct, it could not have been a factor in the syntactic change in the Chadic languages, because for both of the existing word orders, SVO and VSO, the order of other constituents, i.c., prepositions, constituents of the noun phrase, etc., appears to be the same (cf. Greenberg 1966, Harries-Delisle 1978).

REFERENCES

Abraham, R. C. 1959. *Hausa Literature and the Hausa Sound System.* London: University Press.

Bargery, G. P. 1951 (1934). *A Hausa-English Dictionary and English-Hausa Vocabulary.* London: Oxford University Press.

Burquest, Donald A. 1973. A Grammar of Angas. Ph.D. Dissertation, UCLA.

Bybee, Joan L., and William Pagliuca. 1985. Cross-linguistic comparison and the development of grammatical meaning. *Historical semantics and historical word formation,* ed. by Jacek Fisiak, 59-83. Berlin: Mouton.

Caprile, Jean-Pierre, and Herrmann Jungraithmayr. 1978. *Préalables à la reconstruction du proto-tchadique.* LACITO-Documents. Afrique 2. Paris: SELAF.

Caprile, Jean-Pierre. 1978. Notes linguistiques sur le tobanga à partir d'un conte en cette langue. Jungraithmayr and Caprile 1978, 121-175.

Carnochan, Jack. 1970. Categories of the verbal piece in Bachama. *African Language Studies* 11.81-112.

Chao, Yun Ren. 1968. *A Grammar of Spoken Chinese.* Berkeley: Univ. of California Press.

Clements, George N. 1975. The logophoric pronoun in Ewe: Its role in discourse. *Journal of West African Languages* 10.141-77.

Cloarec-Heiss, F. 1969. *Les modalités personelles dans quelques langues oubanguiennes (Discours direct-Discours indirect).* Liège: SELAF.

Cohen, Marcel. 1924. *Le système verbal sèmitique et l'expression du temps.* Paris: Imprimérie Nationale.

Comrie, Bernard. 1981. *Language universals and linguistic typology.* Chicago: University of Chicago Press.

Diakonoff, Igor M. 1965. *Semito-Hamitic Language.* Moscow: Nauka.

Dixon, R. M. W. 1971. *The Dyirbal Language of North Queensland.* Cambridge: University Press.

Downing, Bruce. 1978. Some universals of relative clause structure. *Universals of Human Language*, ed. by Joseph Greenberg, 375-418. Stanford: Stanford University Press.

Ebert, Karen H. 1976. *Sprache und Tradition der Kera (Tschad). Teil II. Lexikon.* Berlin: Reimer.

Ebert, Karen H. 1979. *Sprache und Tradition der Kera (Tschad). Teil III. Grammatik.* (Marburger Studien zur Afrika und Asienkunde, Serie A. Afrika, 15.) Berlin: Reimer.

Ebobissé , Carl. 1979. *Die Morphologie des Verbs im Ost-Dangaleat.* Berlin: Reimer.

Eguchi, Paul Kazuhisa. 1969. Notes on the Mandara language of Mora. *Kyoto University African Studies* 3.133-41.

Fédry, Jacques. 1971. Masculin, féminin et collectif en dangaléat. *Journal of West African Languages* 6.5-19.

Fédry, Jacques. 1971. *Dictionnaire dangaleat.* Lyon: Afrique et Langage.

Fischer, P. R. 1980. *Untersuchungen zur Sprache der Mesme.* M.A. Dissertation, Philipps University, Marburg.

Frajzyngier, Zygmunt. 1965. An analysis of intensive forms in Hausa verbs. *Rocznik Orientalistyczny* 29.2.31-51.

Frajzyngier, Zygmunt. 1974. Postpositions in Awutu. *Journal Of West African Languages* 9.2.61-70.

Frajzyngier, Zygmunt. 1976. Rule inversion in Chadic. An explanation. *Studies in African Linguistics* 7.2.195-210.

Frajzyngier, Zygmunt. 1977a. On the Intransitive Copy Pronouns in Chadic. *Studies in African Linguistics*, Supplement 7, ed. by Martin Mould and Thomas J. Hinnebusch, 73-84.

Frajzyngier, Zygmunt. 1977b. The plural in Chadic. *Papers in Chadic Linguistics*, ed. by Paul Newman and Roxana Ma Newman 37-56. Leiden: Afrika-Studiecentrum.

Frajzyngier, Zygmunt. 1978. Neutralization in the consonantal system of Pero. *Hamburger Phonetische Beitraege* 25.97-119.

Frajzyngier, Zygmunt. 1979. Notes on the $R_1R_2R_2$ stems in Semitic. *Journal of Semitic Studies* 24.1.1-12.

Frajzyngier, Zygmunt. 1980. The vowel system of Pero. *Studies in African Linguistics* 11.1.39-74.

Frajzyngier, Zygmunt. 1981. Some rules concerning vowels in Chadic. *Bulletin of the School of Oriental and African Studies* 44.2.334-348.

Frajzyngier, Zygmunt. 1982a. On the form and function of pre-pronominal markers in Chadic. *Bulletin of the School of Oriental and African Studies* 45.2.323-342.

Frajzyngier, Zygmunt. 1982b. Another look at West-Chadic verb classes. *Africana Marburgensia* 15.1.25-43.

Frajzyngier, Zygmunt. 1983a. Marking Syntactic Relations in Proto-Chadic. *Studies in Chadic and Afroasiatic Linguistics,* ed. by Ekkehard Wolff and Hilke Meyer-Bahlburg, 115-138. Hamburg: Buske.

Frajzyngier, Zygmunt. 1983b. The underlying form of the verb in Proto-Chadic. *The Chad Languages in the Hamitosemitic Nigritic Border Area,* ed. by Herrmann Jungraithmayr, 123-143. Berlin: Reimer.

Frajzyngier, Zygmunt. 1984. On the Proto-Chadic Syntactic Pattern. *Current Progress in Afro-Asiatic Linguistics. Papers of the International Hamito-Semitic Congress,* ed. by John Bynon, 139-160. Amsterdam. Benjamins.

Frajzyngier, Zygmunt. 1984b. On the origin of *say* and *se* as complementizers in Black English and English-based Creoles. *American Speech* 59.3.207-210.

Frajzyngier, Zygmunt. 1985a. Causative and benefactive in Chadic. *Afrika und Übersee* 68.1.23-42.

Frajzyngier, Zygmunt. 1985b. Interrogative sentences in Chadic. Reconstruction and functional explanation. *Journal of West African Languages* 15.1.57-72.

Frajzyngier, Zygmunt. 1985c. Logophoric systems in Chadic. *Journal of African Languages and Linguistics* 7.23-37.

Frajzyngier, Zygmunt. 1985d. Truth and the indicative sentence. *Studies in Language* 9.2.243-254.

Frajzyngier, Zygmunt. 1985e. On two problems regarding stativity. *Relational Typology,* ed. by Frans Plank, 61-88. Berlin: Mouton.

Frajzyngier, Zygmunt. 1986. From preposition to copula. *Proceedings of the 12th Annual Meeting of the Berkeley Linguistics Society,* ed. by Vassiliki Nikiforidou, Mary VanClay, Mary Niepokuj, and Deborah Feder, 371-386.

Frajzyngier, Zygmunt. 1987a. Encoding locative in Chadic. *Journal of West African Languages* 17.1.81-97.

Frajzyngier, Zygmunt. 1987b. Relative clause in Proto-Chadic. *Proceedings of the 4th International Hamito-Semitic Congress*, ed. by Herrmann Jungraithmayr and Walter W. Müller, 425-450. Amsterdam: Benjamins.

Frajzyngier, Zygmunt. 1987c. From verb to anaphora. *Lingua* 72.15-28.

Frajzyngier, Zygmunt. 1987d. Ventive and centrifugal in Chadic. *Afrika und Übersee* 70.1.81-97.

Frajzyngier, Zygmunt. 1987e. Theory and method of syntactic reconstruction. Implications of Chadic for diachronic syntax. *Linguistische Berichte* 109.184-202.

Frajzyngier, Zygmunt. 1989. *A Grammar of Pero*. Berlin: Reimer.

Frajzyngier, Zygmunt and Wendy Ross. in press. The structure of the Migaama verbal stem. *Studies on Near Eastern Languages and Literatures*, ed. by Petr Vavroušek and Petr Zemanek. Prague.

Frick, Esther. 1978. The verbal system of Dghwede. *Linguistics* 212.5-43.

Givón, Talmy. 1971. Historical syntax and synchronic morphology. An archeologist's field trip. *Papers from the Seventh Regional Meeting, Chicago Linguistic Society*, 394-416. Chicago.

Givón, Talmy. 1977. The drift from VSO to SVO in Biblical Hebrew. The pragmatics of tense aspect. *Mechanisms of Syntactic Change,* ed. by Charles N. Li, 181-254. Austin: University of Texas Press.

Givón, Talmy. 1979. *On Understanding Grammar*. New York: Academic Press.

Gouffé, Claude. 1962. Observations sur le degre causatif dans un parler haoussa du Niger. *Journal of African Languages* 1.2.182-200.

Gouffé, Claude. 1978. *Extrait des rapports sur les conférences. Linguistique tchadique*. Paris: Ecole pratique des hautes études.

Greenberg, Joseph H. 1955. Internal a-plurals in Afro-Asiatic (Hamito-Semitic). *Afrikanistische Studien*, ed. by Johannes Lukas, 198-204. Berlin.

Greenberg, Joseph H. 1966. *The Languages of Africa*. Bloomington: Indiana University.

Greenberg, Joseph H. 1966. Some universals of grammar with particular reference to the order of meaningful elements. *Universals of Language*, ed. by Joseph Greenberg, 73-113. Cambridge. MIT Press.

Greenberg, Joseph H. 1978. *Universals of Human Language, vol. 4.* Syntax. Stanford: Stanford University Press.

Guthrie, Malcolm. 1971. *Comparative Bantu*. Part 1, vol. 2. Bantu Prehistory. Farnborough, Hants: Gregg International Publishers.

Hagège, Claude. 1974. Les pronoms logophoriques. *Bulletin de la Société de Linguistique de Paris* 69.287-310.

Haller, Beat, Sylvia Hedinger, and Ursula Wiesemann. 1981. The verbal complex in Zulgo. *Africana Marburgensia*, Special Issue 5, *Chadic Language Studies in Northern Cameroon*. 17-54.

Harries-Delisle, Helga. 1978. Contrastive Emphasis and Cleft Sentences. *Universal of Human Language*, Vol. 4. *Syntax*, ed. by Joseph Greenberg, 419-486.

Heine, Bernd, and Mechthild Reh. 1984. *Grammaticalization and reanalysis in African languages*. Hamburg. Buske.

Hodge, Carleton T., and Ibrahim Umaru. 1963. *Hausa. Basic Course*. Washington, D.C.: Foreign Service Institute.

Hoffmann, Carl. 1963. *A Grammar of the Margi Language*. London: Oxford University Press.

Hoffmann, Carl. 1955. Zur Sprache der Cibak. *Afrikanistische Studien* ed. by Johannes Lukas, 146-178. Berlin.

Hoskison, James T. 1983. A grammar and dictionary of the Gude language. Ph.D. Dissertation. Ohio State University.

Hyman, Larry M. and Bernard Comrie. 1981. Logophoric reference in Gokana. *Journal of African Languages and Linguistics* 3.19-37.

Jarvis, Elizabeth. 1983. Podoko Verbal Directionals. *Studies in Chadic and Afroasiatic Linguistics*, ed. by Ekkehard Wolff and Hilke Meyer-Bahlburg, 317-328. Hamburg: Buske.

Jeffers, Robert. 1976. Syntactic change and syntactic reconstruction. *Current progress in historical linguistics*, ed. by W. Christie, 1-10. Amsterdam: North Holland.

Jungraithmayr, Herrmann. 1961/62. Beobachtungen zur tschadohamitischen Sprache der Jegu (und Jonkor) von Abu Telfan (Republique du Tchad). *Afrika und Übersee* 45.95-123.

Jungraithmayr, Herrmann. 1963. On the ambiguous position of Angas. *Journal of African Languages* 2.272-78.

Jungraithmayr, Herrmann. 1963-64. Die Sprache der Sura (Maghavul) in Nordnigerien. *Afrika und Übersee* 47.8-89, 204-220.

Jungraithmayr, Herrmann. 1964/65. Materialen zur Kenntnis des Chip, Montol, Gerka, und Burrum (Südplateau Nordnigerien). *Afrika und Übersee* 48.161-82.

Jungraithmayr, Herrmann. 1965. Internal A in Ron plurals. *Journal of African Languages* 4.102-107.

Jungraithmayr, Herrmann. 1970. *Die Ron-Sprachen. Tschadohamitische Studien in Nordnigerien.* Afrikanistische Forschungen 3. Glückstadt: Augustin.

Jungraithmayr, Herrmann. 1975. Der Imperfektivstamm im Migama. *Folia Orientalia* 16.85-100.

Jungraithmayr, Herrmann. 1978. Les langues tchadique et le proto-tchadique: documentation, analyse et problèmes. in Caprile and Jungraithmayr, 17-30.

Jungraithmayr, Herrmann. 1978. Ablaut und Ton im Verbalsystem des Mubi. *Afrika und Übersee* 61.312-320.

Jungraithmayr, Herrmann, ed. 1982. *The Chad languages in the Hamitosemitic-Nigritic border area.* Berlin: Reimer.

Jungraithmayr, Herrmann, and Jean-Pierre Caprile, ed. 1978. *Cinq textes tchadiques.* Berlin: Reimer.

Jungraithmayr, Herrmann, and Kiyoshi Shimizu. 1981. *Chadic lexical roots.* Vol. II. Berlin: Reimer.

Keenan, Edward. 1976. Towards a Universal Definition of "Subject". *Subject and Topic.* ed. by Charles N. Li. 305-333. New York: Academic Press.

Koehler, Oswin. 1981. La langue Kxoe. *Les langues dans le monde ancien et moderne.* 1ère partie. *Les langues de l'Afrique subsaharienne,* ed. by Jean Perrot, 483-555. Paris: Editions du CNRS.

Kolver, Ulrike. 1984. *Local prepositions and serial verb constructions in Thai.* Arbeiten des Kolner Universalien-Projekts Nr. 56.

Kraft, Charles H. 1981. *Chadic Wordlists.* Vol.1-3. Berlin. Reimer.

Kuryłowicz, Jerzy. 1964. *The inflectional categories of Indo-European.* Heidelberg: Winter.

Kuryłowicz, Jerzy. 1972. *Studies in Semitic Grammar and Metrics.* Wrocław: Zakład Narodowy Imienia Ossolińskich.

Lafitte, P. 1944. *Grammaire basque.* Bayonne: Amis du Musée Basque.

Leben, William R. Intonation in Chadic languages. *Précis from the 15th Conference on African Linguistics,* ed. by R. Schuh.

Lehmann, Christian. 1985. *Thoughts on grammaticalization.* AKUP Nr. 48.

Lehmann, Winfred P. 1974. *Proto-Indo-European Syntax.* Austin: University of Texas Press.

Lehmann, Winfred P. 1980. The reconstruction of non-simple sentences in Proto-Indo-European. *Linguistic reconstruction and Indo-European Syntax*, ed. by Paolo Ramat, 113-144. Amsterdam: Benjamins.

Leslau, Wolf. 1968. *Amharic Textbook*. Los Angeles: Univ. of California Press.

Li, Charles N., and Sandra Annear Thompson. 1974. An explanation of word order change SVO ---> SOV. *Foundations of Language 12*. 201-214.

Li, Charles N., and Sandra Annear Thompson. 1981. *Mandarin Chinese*. Berkeley: Univ. of California Press.

Li, Charles N., and Sandra Annear Thompson. 1977. A mechanism for the development of copula morphemes. *Mechanisms of Syntactic Change*, ed. by Charles N. Li, 419-444. Austin: Univ. of Texas Press.

Lightfoot, David. 1983. On reconstructing a proto-syntax. *Language Change, vol. 1*. ed. by I. Rauch, and G. F. Carr, 129-142. Bloomington: Indiana Univ. Press.

Lord, Carol. 1973. Serial verbs in transition. *Studies in African Linguistics* 4.3.269-296.

Lord, Carol. 1975. Igbo verb compounds and the lexicon. *Studies in African Linguistics* 6.1.23-48.

Lukas, Johannes. 1936. *Die Logone-Sprache im Zentralen Sudan*. Leipzig: DMG

Lukas, Johannes. 1941. *Deutsche Quellen zur Sprache der Musgu in Kamerun*. Berlin.

Lukas, Johannes. 1970. *Studien zur Sprache der Gisiga (Nordkamerun)*. Afrikanistische Forschungen 4. Glückstadt: Augustin.

Lukas, Johannes. 1970-72. Die Personalia und das primäre Verb im Bolanci (Nordnigerien). Mit Beiträgen über das Karekare. *Afrika und Übersee* 54.1-86, 55.114-39.

Lukas, Johannes. 1971. Über das erweiterte Verb im Bolanci (Nordnigerien). *Journal of African Languages* 10.1. *Special Chadic Issue*, ed. by P. Newman, 1-14.

Lukas, Johannes. 1974/75. Ein Text in der Sprache der Djonkor des Gera-Massivs (République du Tchad). *Afrika und Übersee* 58.212-26.

Lukas, Johannes. 1977. Beiträge zur Kenntnis des Mukulu. *Afrika und Übersee* 61.1-2. 1-58 and 192-229.

Lukas, Renate. 1967/68. Das Nomen im Bade (Nordnigerien). *Afrika und Übersee* 51.91-116, 198-224.

Meillet, Antoine. 1925. *La méthode comparative en linguistique historique*. Oslo.

Meillet, Antoine. 1937. *Introduction à l'étude comparative des langues indo-européennes*. Paris: Hachette.

Meillet, Antoine. 1967. *The Comparative Method in Historical Linguistics.* trans. by G. B. Ford. Paris: Champion.

Melcuk, Igor. 1977. *The Predicative Construction in the Dyirbal Language.* Bloomington: Indiana University Linguistics Club.

Meyer-Bahlburg, H. 1972. *Studien zur Morphologie und Syntax des Musgu.* Hamburg: Buske.

Mirt, Heide. 1969. Einige Bemerkungen zum Vokalsystem des Mandara. *Zeitschrift der Deutschen Morgenländischen Gesellschaft,* Supplementa I. XVII Deutscher Orientalistentag vom 21 bis 27 Juli in Würzburg, Vorträge, ed. by W. Voigt, 1096-1103.

Mirt, Heide. 1969/1970. Zur Morphologie des Verbalcomplexes im Mandara. *Afrika und Übersee* 54.1-76.

Mithun, Marianne, and Lyle Campbell. 1982. On comparative syntax. *Papers from the 3rd International Conference on Historical Linguistics,* ed. by J. Peter Maher, Allan R. Bombard, and E. F. Konrad Koerner. Amsterdam: Benjamins.

Mouchét, Jean. 1967. *Le parler daba.*

Newman, Paul, and Roxana Ma. 1966. Comparative Chadic: phonology and lexicon. *Journal of African Languages* 5.218-251.

Newman, Paul, and Russell G. Schuh. 1974. The Hausa aspect system. *Afroasiatic Linguistics* 1.1.1-39.

Newman, Paul. 1970. *A Grammar of Tera. Transformational Syntax and Texts.* University of California Publications in Linguistics 75. Berkeley and Los Angeles: University of California Press.

Newman, Paul. 1971. Transitive and Intransitive in Chadic Languages in *Afrikanische Sprachen and Kulturen.* Ein Querschnitt (Festschrift J. Lukas) ed. Veronika Six et al. Hamburg. 188-200.

Newman, Paul. 1974. *The Kanakuru Language.* West African Language Monographs 9. Leeds: Institute of Modern English Language Studies of the University of Leeds.

Newman, Paul. 1975. Proto-Chadic Verb Classes. *Folia Orientalia* 16.65-84.

Newman, Paul. 1977a. Chadic extensions and pre-datives verb forms in Hausa. *Studies in African Linguistics* 8.275-297.

Newman, Paul. 1977b. Chadic classification and reconstructions. *Afro-Asiatic Linguistics* 5.1.1-42.

Newman, Paul. 1977c. The Formation of the Imperfective Verb Stem in Chadic. *Afrika und Übersee* 3.178-192.

Newman, Paul. 1983. The efferential (alias causative) in Hausa. in Wolff and Meyer-Bahlburg, 397-418.

Newman, Roxana Ma. 1971. A Case Grammar of Ga'anda, Ph.D. Dissertation, University of California at Los Angeles.

Parsons, F.W. 1960/61. The verbal system in Hausa. *Afrika und Übersee* 44.1-36

Parsons, F.W. 1961. The operation of gender in Hausa: the personal pronouns and genitive copula. *African Language Studies* 2.100-24.

Parsons, F.W. 1962. Further observations on the 'causative' grade of the verb in Hausa. *Journal of African Languages* 1.3.253-272.

Parsons, F.W. 1971/72. Suppletion and neutralization in the verbal system of Hausa. *Afrika und Übersee* 55.49-97, 188-208.

Platiel, Suzanne. 1972. *Esquisse dune étude du Musey*. Informations. Bulletin de la SELAF, 6.

Rufai, A. 1983. Defining and Non-defining Relative clauses in Hausa. in Wolff and Meyer-Bahlburg 1983, 419-427.

Schuh, Russell G. 1972. Aspects of Ngizim Syntax. Ph.D. Dissertation, University of California at Los Angeles.

Schuh, Russell G. 1975. Nunation and Gender in Bade. *Afrika und Übersee* 58.106-19.

Schuh, Russell G. 1981. Types of genitive constructions in Chadic. *Studies in African Linguistics*, Supplement 8.117-121.

Schuh, Russell G. 1982. Questioned and focussed subject and objects. in Jungraithmayr 1982

Schuh, Russell G. 1983. Kilba equational sentences. *Studies in African Linguistics* 14.3.311-328.

Schuh, Russell.G. 1977. West Chadic verb classes. *Papers in Chadic Linguistics*, ed. by Paul Newman and Roxana Maa Newman, 143-166. Leiden: Afrika Studiecentrum.

Schuh, Russell.G. 1978. *Bole-Tangale Languages of the Bauchi Area (Northern Nigeria)*. Berlin: Reimer.

Schumann, Theda. 1983. Gender markers in Masa. Wolff and Meyer-Bahlburg, 1983, 429-439.

Semur, Serge, avec la collaboration de Nossor Doungouss et Oumar Hamit et de Damin Abdoullay, Bichara Abras, Amir Allamin, Jacques Fédry, Harine Ottman, Issa Tom. 1983. *Essai de classification des verbes migaama (Baro-Guera, Tchad).* Sarh (Tchad): Centre d'Etudes Linguistiques.

Skinner, Margaret G. 1979. Aspects of Paanci grammar. Ph.D. Dissertation. University of Wisconsin.

Smith, David M. 1969. The Kapsiki language. Ph.D. Dissertation. Michigan State University.

Stanley, C. 1982. Direct and reported speech in Tikar narrative texts. *Studies in African Linguistics* 13.31-52.

Tourneux, Henry. 1978a. *Le mulwi ou vulum de Mogroum.* (Tchad). Paris: SELAF.

Tourneux, Henry. 1978b. Racine verbale en Mulwi. in Caprile and Jungraithmayr 1978.

Ultan, Russell. 1978. Some general characteristics of interrogative systems. *Universals of Human Language*, ed. by J. Greenberg, vol. 4, *Syntax.* 11-50.

Vaillant, André. 1966. *Grammaire comparée des langues slaves.* Vol. 3. *Le verbe.* Paris: Klincksieck.

Vennemann, Theo genannt Nierfeld. 1973. Explanation in syntax. *Syntax and Semantics* vol. 2. ed. by John P. Kimball, 1-50. New York: Seminar Press.

Voeltz, Erhard F. K. 1977. Proto-Niger-Congo verb extensions. Preliminary version. UCLA. (MS)

Watkins, Calvert. 1976. Toward Proto-Indo-European Syntax. Problems and pseudo-problems. *Diachronic Syntax*, ed. by S. Steever, C. Walker, and S. Mufwene, 305-326. Chicago: Chicago Linguistic Society.

Welmers, William. 1973. *African Language Structures.* Berkeley and Los Angeles.

Westermann, Diedrich, and Margaret A. Bryan. *The Languages of West Africa.* London.

Whaley, Annie, and Cheryl Fluckiger. 1980. *Mandara Pedagogical Grammar Notes* 1, 3, and 7. Mora.

Williams, Charles Kinston. 1989. Chadic historical syntax: Reconstructing word order in Proto-Chadic. Ph. D. Dissertation. Indiana University.

Wolff, Ekkehard, and Hilke Meyer-Bahlburg, ed. 1983. *Studies in Chadic and Afroasiatic Linguistics.* Hamburg: Buske.

Wolff, Ekkehard. 1977. Patterns in Chadic (and Afroasiatic?) verb base formations. *Papers in Chadic Linguistics*, ed. by Paul Newman and Roxana Ma Newman, 199-233. Leiden: Afrika-Studiecentrum.

Wolff, Ekkehard. 1977. Verb Bases and Stems in Migama. *Afrika und Übersee* 60.3.163-177.

Wolff, Ekkehard. 1979. Grammatical categories of verb stems and the marking of mood, aktionsart, and aspect in Chadic. *Afroasiatic Linguistics* 6/5.

Wolff, Ekkehard. 1983. *A grammar of the Lamang language.* Glückstadt: Augustin.

Zima, Petr. 1972. *Problems of Categories and Word Classes in Hausa.* Prague: Oriental Institute.

INDEX OF TOPICS AND GEOGRAPHICAL NAMES

INDEX OF NAMES

Does not include self references

CONTENTS